SHOOK

JENNIFER HULL

AN EARTHQUAKE,
A LEGENDARY
MOUNTAIN GUIDE,
AND EVEREST'S
DEADLIEST DAY

University of New Mexico Press Albuquerque

ISBN 978-0-8263-6194-3 (paper)

ISBN 978-0-8263-6195-0 (electronic)

Library of Congress Cataloging-in-Publication data is on file
with the Library of Congress.

Cover illustration: Rescue helicopter. Courtesy of Robert Massie.

Designed by Mindy Basinger Hill

Composed in 10/15 pt Minion Pro

To Jack and Liam

Benedicto: May your trails be crooked, winding, lonesome, dangerous, leading to the most amazing view. May your mountains rise into and above the clouds. May your rivers flow without end, meandering through pastoral valleys tinkling with bells, past temples and castles and poets towers into a dark primeval forest where tigers belch and monkeys howl, through miasmal and mysterious swamps and down into a desert of red rock, blue mesas, domes and pinnacles and grottos of endless stone, and down again into a deep vast ancient unknown chasm where bars of sunlight blaze on profiled cliffs, where deer walk across the white sand beaches, where storms come and go as lightning clangs upon the high crags, where something strange and more beautiful and more full of wonder than your deepest dreams waits for you—beyond that next turning of the canyon walls.

EDWARD ABBEY

CONTENTS

CAST OF CHARACTERS

Guides

DAVE HAHN The lead guide of the expedition, his childhood was
fractured by loss and he struggled to find his way in life until he
began guiding others in the mountains. He eventually summited
Everest fifteen times.

CHHERING DORJEE SHERPA A professional mountain guide born
in the Khumbu and sherpa sirdar of the expedition, he was forced
to abandon his childhood aspirations of becoming a doctor or software engineer when his older brother was killed in an avalanche.

JEFFREY JAMES JUSTMAN "JJ" A burly mountain guide with a
fondness for motorcycling and the Argentinian tango, he called
upon his eighteen years of experience on the world's highest mountains as the assistant guide of the expedition.

Base Camp Manager

MARK TUCKER Having summited Everest as a member of the 1990
Peace Climb, he served as the base camp manager of the expedition
and was at Everest Base Camp when disaster struck.

Clients

HANS HILSCHER The kind and affable CEO of a German technology company longed to climb each of the "Seven Summits."

ERIN MACHINCHICK An elite rock climber from the Midwest,
she contended with the physiological challenges of stage-three
polycystic kidney disease during the high-altitude trek to Everest
Base Camp.

ROBBIE MASSIE The strong and fit thirty-one-year-old Minnetonka, Minnesota, native had trained at the YMCA and saved up for five years to bankroll his trip to the highest mountain in the world.

HEMANSHU PARWANI "HP" Born in India, the forty-six-year-old CEO from Dallas, Texas, viewed the Everest expedition as an opportunity to pursue his boyhood dream while raising money for cancer research.

BONNY ROGERS An acupuncturist and experienced trekker from the Washington, DC, area, Bonny reluctantly accepted her husband Peter's desire to climb Everest and later decided to join him for the trek to Everest Base Camp.

PETER ROGERS Having already summited Aconcagua, Denali, Elbrus, and Vinson, he celebrated his sixty-second birthday on the first night of the Everest Expedition.

LARRY SEATON The sixty-four-year-old founder of a construction firm in Napa Valley, California, had previously scaled the highest peaks of five continents but was stymied by illness and injury during the Everest Expedition.

HAO WU After his 2014 Everest attempt was thwarted when an avalanche in the Icefall brought the season to an aborted end, the tenacious venture capitalist was attempting to summit Everest, the final peak in his quest for the Seven Summits, for the second time in two consecutive years.

Everest figures

MISS ELIZABETH HAWLEY An American journalist who moved to Kathmandu in 1960 and never left, she chronicled Everest expeditions for over fifty years, conducting dogged and exacting interviews with elite mountaineers and compiling her records in the authoritative Himalayan Database.

LAMA GESHE The beloved and revered Tibetan Buddhist Lama
blessed trekkers and climbers en route to Chomolungma.

BILLI BIERLING A journalist and mountaineer from the Bavarian
Alps, she worked as an assistant to Elizabeth Hawley at the Himalayan Database.

2015 MOUNT EVEREST EXPEDITION

This latest disaster comes a year after an avalanche killed sixteen guides in what was then the deadliest disaster to hit the world's highest peak.

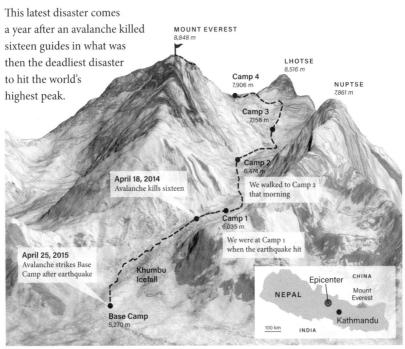

MOUNT EVEREST
8,848 m

LHOTSE
8,516 m

NUPTSE
7,861 m

Camp 4
7,906 m

Camp 3
7,158 m

Camp 2
6,474 m

We walked to Camp 2 that morning

April 18, 2014
Avalanche kills sixteen

Camp 1
6,035 m

We were at Camp 1 when the earthquake hit

April 25, 2015
Avalanche strikes Base Camp after earthquake

Khumbu Icefall

Base Camp
5,270 m

Epicenter

CHINA

Mount Everest

NEPAL

Kathmandu

100 km   INDIA

Everest image: Dreamstime.com | Reference map: Hao Wu

MOUNT EVEREST SCHEDULE

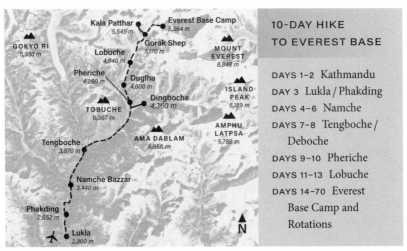

Kala Patthar
5,545 m

Everest Base Camp
5,364 m

Gorak Shep
5,170 m

GOKYO RI
5,330 m

Lobuche
4,940 m

MOUNT EVEREST
8,848 m

Pheriche
4,280 m

Duglha
4,600 m

Dingboche
4,360 m

ISLAND PEAK
6,189 m

TOBUCHE
6,367 m

AMPHU LATPSA
5,780 m

Tengboche
3,870 m

AMA DABLAM
6,856 m

Namche Bazzar
3,440 m

Phakding
2,652 m

Lukla
2,800 m

N

10-DAY HIKE TO EVEREST BASE

DAYS 1–2 Kathmandu

DAY 3 Lukla / Phakding

DAYS 4–6 Namche

DAYS 7–8 Tengboche / Deboche

DAYS 9–10 Pheriche

DAYS 11–13 Lobuche

DAYS 14–70 Everest Base Camp and Rotations

Reference map: Hao Wu

SHOOK

1 ⛰ CAMP ONE, EVEREST

More than 25 million years ago, India, once a separate island on a quickly sliding piece of the Earth's crust, crashed into Asia. The two land masses are still colliding, pushed together at a speed of 1.5 to 2 inches a year. The forces have pushed up the highest mountains in the world, in the Himalayas.

New York Times, April 4, 2019

In the vast bowl of the Valley of Silence, four canary-yellow tents sat in a row, perched on a narrow fin of glacier, like birds on a wire. Dave Hahn, the lead guide of the 2015 RMI Everest Expedition and his assistant guide JJ Justman were in the second tent. Beside them, clients Robbie Massie and Peter Rogers shared the first tent. On their other side, sherpa sirdar Chhering Dorjee and client Hemanshu Parwani, HP as he liked to be called, listened to tinny Nepali music playing from an iPhone in the third tent. Clients Hao Wu and Hans Hilscher occupied the tent on the end. They had just crawled wearily inside of their nylon shelters, their heads throbbing from the oxygen-deprivation hangovers of their first night at 19,689-foot Camp One, and thirsty and exhausted from their successful morning rotation to 21,000-foot Camp Two. Moments earlier, they had crossed quivering metal ladders over deep crevasses, scraping their crampons on the frozen metal as their gloved hands clutched thin ropes on either side. It was 11:56 a.m. on April 25, 2015. Dave was wiggling out of his climbing harness and JJ was bent over a camp stove melting snow to make tea when they felt the ground move in waves below them. Dave froze. At nearly 20,000 feet on Everest, he suddenly felt like he was in a boat on the ocean. He and JJ glanced at each other and at the same time said, "Earthquake!"

All eight of the climbers instinctively shot their heads out of their four tents, but, socked in by the weather, they could see nothing but snow falling and a dense grey fog as the ground below them rocked.

"What is this? Dave, what's going on? Is this normal?" shouted HP from his tent. Then, above them, they heard a roar of cracking ice. Avalanches began to rumble downward, echoing in the bowl between the mountains that amplified sound like an amphitheater. The ground jolted and dropped. In the first tent, Robbie Massie remembered what he had said to his family when they expressed concern about the 2014 Icefall avalanche. "Lightning doesn't strike twice," he had told them.

"Oh my god!" JJ blurted.

Dave took a mental inventory of the situation. Mount Everest was shaking like jello. He and his team were camped between two crevasses and below 3,000-foot-high towers of ice. Avalanches thundered down every mountainside around them. He found himself considering whether it would feel better to die from an avalanche off of the peak of Nuptse, or from one off of Everest's west shoulder. During those brief seconds of assessment, which stretched out in slow motion, he also took stock of the possibilities that the ice shelf on which they were camped could collapse out from under them or could break loose and slide 3,000 feet down into the Icefall.

"It's an earthquake," he heard himself shout. "But we're alright!"

"Zip up your tents and stay inside them," Chhering instructed. "Get your helmets and transceivers on."

The bewildered team obeyed, sliding on their helmets and strapping on their transceivers as they stared wide-eyed at their tentmates. HP's hands trembled while he set his beacon to transmit mode. The roar of snow and ice grew louder and closer. Robbie and Peter grappled with tent zippers flapping wildly in the wind, as they contemplated their own deaths. Chhering thought of his wife, pregnant with their first child. The ground below them shook violently, swaying and popping. Before they could manage to zip all their tent flaps and vents shut, they were hit.

2 ⛰ KATHMANDU

March 24, 2015
Posted by: Dave Hahn
Categories: Expedition Dispatches; Everest
Elevation: 4,383 feet

RMI EXPEDITIONS BLOG

We had climbers circling the thunderclouds, climbers flying
back and forth to Delhi, planes delayed back on the Great Plains
... but ultimately, we had the entire RMI Mount Everest 2015
climbing team assembled on time and with all gear at the Yak
and Yeti Hotel in Kathmandu. Six climbers, two base camp
trekkers, two guides, one base camp manager and one sherpa
sirdar enjoyed a fine dinner together—without so much as one
person falling asleep at the table. Quite a feat considering all the
time zones and datelines crossed.

By the time of the expedition in 2015, Dave had already summited Everest fifteen times, more than any other non-Nepali. He had summited
North America's Denali twenty-one times, Antarctica's Vinson Massif
thirty-five times, Africa's Kilimanjaro three times, South America's
Aconcagua once, and Cho Oyu, Everest's near neighbor to the west, two
times. At last count, he had guided clients to the summit of Washington's
Mount Rainier 275 times. Elite members of the climbing community
likened him to the Michael Jordan, Cal Ripken, or Michael Phelps of the
climbing world, while emphasizing the distinction that Dave had not
only shattered world records but had done it while climbing as a working
guide, with nonprofessional climber clients safely in tow.

Still, Dave felt a wave of nerves when he let himself into his hotel
room at the Yak and Yeti, turned on the lights, and saw a message from

Miss Elizabeth Hawley waiting for him on the nightstand. Somehow, she always seemed to know just when he had landed in Kathmandu.

He slid his backpack off of his shoulders and stretched his long legs out on the bed. He was jet-lagged, and his stomach felt full from the dinner he, JJ, Chhering, their base-camp manager Tucker, and their 2015 RMI Everest Expedition clients had devoured downstairs in the restaurant. He closed his eyes just for a moment. All in all, it had been a happy evening. They hadn't discussed any of the intricacies of Everest yet. They had spent it simply getting acquainted and reacquainted with each other and celebrating their arrival in Nepal, as well as client Peter Roger's birthday.

In spite of the pleasantries, Dave couldn't get the Icefall off his mind. The chunk of glacier that calved off of Everest the previous season, in 2014, crashing down below the west shoulder and then detonating like a bomb blast above the Khumbu Icefall, had been the size of a ten-story building. He trusted that the Icefall Doctors, a team of Nepalese mountaineers hired by the government and charged with the formidable task of building and maintaining a rope-and-ladder passage through the glacial labyrinth of the Icefall, would find the best possible route through the constantly moving crevasses of the Khumbu. And he knew that ultimately, Mother Nature was in charge. What he feared was that the explosive avalanche of ice, and the death and grief it had caused, may have revealed equally significant fractures in the relationships between the Western guides and the Sherpas, two groups who shared so much and who routinely put their lives on the line for each other.

By the time Dave opened his eyes again, sunlight streamed through the windows. He stood up and pulled the gauzy curtains back. The hotel, built as an elegant theater and palace residence over a century earlier during the Rana Dynasty, still emanated the nostalgic glamour of a bygone era with its neoclassical architecture, salmon-colored walls, ornately carved windows, emerald-green gardens, and winged Garuda statues guarding pagoda shrines. Dave jolted when he spotted out the window Miss Elizabeth Hawley's driver, Suban, and her 1963 royal-blue Volkswagen Beetle already waiting for him in the parking lot below. He hurried downstairs.

Dave ducked his head and squeezed his six-foot two-inch frame into the Beetle's passenger seat, pulling his knees up to his scruffy, square chin as they left the confines of the hotel and barreled through the streets choked with smoke-spewing trucks, rattling old school buses, and buzzing motorcycles. Horns bleated and yelped like the goats that shared the streets. The familiar smell of exhaust fumes, wet earth, laundry soap, cumin, coriander, turmeric, rotting fruit, sewage, and milk tea wafted through his window. Stray dogs and monkeys scampered across ancient, gilded stupas, the dome-shaped Buddhist shrines dotting the city.

They wove through throngs of people: Western tourists with cameras dangling from their necks, wandering Hindu Sadhus in saffron-colored robes, sari-clad women, uniformed schoolchildren, and marigold vendors. They drove past impossibly stacked office buildings, vegetable stands, apartment complexes, and finally into a quiet residential neighborhood and up a driveway ringed by manicured footpaths and lilac bushes to Miss Hawley's home. Dave unfolded himself from his seat, thanked Suban, and passed through a black iron gate. He let himself inside the house and walked up the stairs to her office. A string of bells on the screen door jingled behind him.

Ninety-two-year-old Miss Elizabeth Hawley greeted him matter-of-factly from behind her desk, peering over her glasses at Dave.

He thought she actually looked glad to see him, though he was pretty sure she was trying not to show it. Miss Hawley slid her glasses, through which her eyes appeared even larger and more piercing, back up the bridge of her nose and stood up. She wore her typical uniform on her slender, birdlike frame: a floral, short-sleeved blouse with a Peter Pan collar, a crisp khaki skirt, and sandals.

"Hello, Elizabeth," he said. He smiled and hunched his shoulders, as if to tower over her less.

"On time, as usual. I couldn't swear that I'd see you back here after what happened last year," she said.

Dave nodded. "I told you I'd be back."

"Please, sit down. I would have met you at the hotel but you know I'm not getting any younger, and my balance isn't getting any better. Would you like a cool drink?"

Miss Elizabeth Hawley had served as Everest's unofficial yet legendary gatekeeper and recordkeeper for the last fifty years. Born in Chicago and raised in Scarsdale, New York, she quit her research job at *Fortune* magazine in New York City when she grew bored of sitting behind a desk to go travel the world and figure out what she wanted to do next. She ended up in Kathmandu in the Himalayan Kingdom of Nepal in September of 1960, soon after the country's curtain had been lifted to foreigners and after Westerners had begun attempting to conquer the world's highest peaks. The opening of virgin Nepal to the outside world and the subsequent influx of climbers fascinated her. In a letter to her mother, she wrote, "The mountains hereabouts are infested with men mad enough to want to slog to the tops." She found work as a reporter with the Reuters news agency covering the high-altitude dramas unfolding in what had previously been known as The Forbidden Kingdom and never left. Her extensive expedition records, which she collected over time as journalistic research, had since been archived in her authoritative Himalayan Database.

Dave first met Elizabeth Hawley, universally known in the climbing community as Miss Hawley, during the 1990s while leading trips on Cho Oyu before his first Everest trip as an expedition lead guide in 1998. She made a point of interviewing every lead guide both before and after their expeditions to gather pertinent information for her records. Some referred to her meticulous interrogations as Everest's "second summit." Dave thought back to one of his first post-trip interviews, when she had asked him at what point he had turned on his supplemental oxygen on the way up Everest. He had answered 24,000 feet, which was about 1,000 feet lower than he normally would turn on oxygen on the North Face route, and he had done it because he was aiding a sick client. He still winced when he recalled the way Miss Hawley had then squinted at him and said, "Huh, bringing Everest down to your own size?"

Dave, offended by the implication that he had somehow cheated, had responded by asking her what mountains she had climbed.

"Oh, I've never climbed," she had replied coolly. "I wouldn't think of it. . . . I want to sleep in a bed, eat at a table, and be driven around in my Beetle."

Their relationship had warmed into one of genuine affection and mutual respect over the years, particularly after a historic expedition in 1999 when Dave helped find the body of British explorer George Mallory, lost on the North Face of Everest in 1924. Since then, Dave had received the American Alpine Club's David A. Sowles Memorial Award for unselfish valor in 2001 for his rescues on Mount Everest, and he was recognized in the same year by the National Park Service for rescues he performed on Mount McKinley. He had been honored by the Nepal Mountaineering Association for his rescue of a climber in distress above 27,000 feet on Everest's South Side in 2007, and he had been presented a Citizen's Award for Bravery from the US Department of the Interior in 2009 for a rescue on Mount Rainier. In spite of this, Miss Hawley remained hard to impress, and Dave remained more than a little intimidated by her. She began to fill out the forms on her desk.

"How many members at beginning?" she asked.

"Six clients, two base-camp trekkers, two guides, one sherpa sirdar, and one base-camp manager."

"Names?"

"Clients are Robbie Massie, Hemanshu Parwani, Larry Seaton, Peter Rogers, Hao Wu, and Hans Hilscher. Our base-camp trekkers are Erin Machinchik and Bonnie Rogers. Base-camp manager is Mark Tucker. Assistant guide is JJ Justman. Chhering Dorjee is our sherpa sirdar . . ."

After the long days he had just spent traveling halfway around the globe from his home in Taos, New Mexico, to the typical circus of the Yak and Yeti Hotel lobby, Dave realized he was enjoying having a moment to just sit and talk with Miss Hawley in the respite of her quiet house. Through the window, blue mimosa trees blossomed in the courtyard, filling the room with their honey-almond and cucumber scent. He had been too uneasy to sleep on the flights. Having spent the eight previous months guiding the highest peaks of Antarctica, North America, and Africa in relative anonymity, he knew Everest would be, as always, in the spotlight. In terms of public perception, at least, it remained the gold standard, the Olympic arena of mountain climbing; the world had a way of noticing what happened on Everest. With the 2014 season upended, and without having succeeded in getting any of his three clients to the summit in 2013, he felt the pressure, more than ever, to perform. He felt the need to prove himself.

Once they completed the requisite paperwork, Miss Hawley handed Dave another stack of forms for his team, with questions ranging from the details of each 8,000-meter peak previously climbed to current relationship status. They smelled like the mothballs she kept in her filing cabinet.

"Make sure they fill them out and fill them out correctly," she directed.

Then Miss Hawley, ever businesslike, thanked Dave and sent him on his way. It was official. The only rituals left for him to perform were to secure the expedition permit from the Ministry of Tourism over handshakes and cups of sweet tea and to stop in for a haircut and straight-razor shave at his favorite barbershop in Kathmandu. He was going back to Everest.

3 ⛰ OKINAWA

> And the three men I admire most
> The Father, Son, and the Holy Ghost
> They caught the last train for the coast
> The day the music died
>
> *Bye Bye Miss American Pie*, Don McLean, 1971

The Everest Expedition, in its entirety, would take two months. Everest's 29,029-foot (8,848-meter) summit was infamous for being roughly the cruising altitude of a jetliner and for having approximately the same surface area as a dining-room table. From the first summit attempt on Everest in 1923 to Dave's first summit in 1994, the ratio of deaths to summits on Everest hovered at around one death for every five successful summits. According to Miss Hawley's Himalayan Database, the most common causes of deaths on Everest included avalanches, falls, and Icefall collapses. Dave seemed to have made a lifelong habit of surviving harrowing and often lonely journeys, beginning with his childhood.

The third child of Ronald (Ron) and Isabel Hahn, Dave was born in Okinawa, Japan, a chain of two dozen green islands lying in crystal-clear, turquoise, tropical waters. Okinawa translates from Japanese as "Rope in the Open Sea." Ringed by white-sand beaches and coral reefs, and carpeted by fields of sugarcane, the islands of Okinawa comprise Japan's southernmost prefecture, in the East China Sea, between Taiwan and mainland Japan. In spite of its tranquil beauty, Okinawa was notorious for having been the site of a bloody, 82-day battle during World War II; 95,000 Imperial Japanese Army Troops and 12,510 Americans were killed there (with 50,000 more Americans wounded). Its fields and caves were still steeped in sadness.

Ron and Isabel met at Fort Bliss in El Paso, Texas, while both were serving in the army, Isabel as an occupational therapist and Ron on a path that eventually led to lieutenant colonel. Isabel was also a classically trained pianist and a painter. Ron had grown up rock climbing in Yosemite. They found they shared a love of music, art, and the outdoors. They married, and shortly afterward moved to Okinawa when Ron was stationed there. All three of their children were born in Okinawa: David in 1961, two years after his sister Carolyn, and a year after his brother Harold.

Shortly after Dave's birth, Isabel was diagnosed with Hodgkin's Lymphoma, a cancer of the lymphatic system that limits the body's ability to fight infection. At the time Isabel was diagnosed, the five-year survival rates of Hodgkin's Disease were still below 10 percent. When Dave was six weeks old, the family moved from Okinawa to the Bay Area of Northern California, settling in Mountain View, where Ron worked for IBM. While Isabel was treated in San Francisco for several months at a military hospital at the Presidio, Dave, still an infant, lived with his aunt. Isabel painted watercolors of her view, through tall cypress and eucalyptus trees, of the Golden Gate Bridge from her hospital bed, for her children.

Dave was vaguely aware, during his childhood, of his mother's illness. The scar at her throat, where doctors had removed tissue for testing, was one of the only outward indications that there was something wrong. At home, Dave loved to listen to his mother play Beethoven on the piano in the living room. While he and his father often butted heads, Dave felt safe and content in his mother's presence. On family camping trips, his eyes lit up when she read to him and Harold and Caroline outside in the sunshine, pushing her dark hair behind her ears as she delighted them with *Charlotte's Web* and *James and the Giant Peach* and *Black Beauty*.

For Dave, Mountain View was home. Even at a very young age, he recognized that Mountain View, named for its serene view of the Santa Cruz Mountains, was quickly becoming the center of many worlds. Shockley Semiconductor Laboratory, the first company to develop silicon semiconductor devices, had opened for business in Mountain View in 1956, giving rise to what would come to be known as Silicon Valley. As Mountain View's aerospace and electronics industries boomed, its population did as well, and its agricultural past faded into history.

Dave relished the adventure of his family's occasional road trips from California to visit his Grandma Cella and the rest of his mother's family in Albuquerque, New Mexico, where they lived between the Sandia Mountains and the Rio Grande. Along the way, his parents strapped harnesses on him and Carolyn and Harold so they could keep track of their young children while they roamed through museums and national parks, and snapped photos of them standing in the foreground of the sheer, massive walls of Yosemite's El Capitan. It was during these journeys that Dave saw his first snow, while on a side trip to the Sierras, and his first desert, the Mojave, as the highway from California stretched into Arizona. He was captivated by the sight of scorpions, snakes, and roadrunners—and the crack in the pavement where the San Andreas fault had caused the road to split. At gas stations, his parents bought postcards and maps, arrowheads and polished rocks for the kids. Dave pocketed the trinkets but was most interested in the maps. He spread them out over his small lap and tried to understand where the highways went, tracing the state lines with his fingers. It was on these road trips, while he and his brother and sister laughed and argued in the back seat, that his parents seemed happy together.

In the summer of 1969, when Dave was seven years old, the Hahn family moved to Kingston, New York, in the Hudson Valley, home to another IBM plant. As their furniture was being moved into their new house on President's Place on a humid July day, Dave watched the Apollo moon landing on the TV in the quiet coolness of their motel room at the Holiday Inn. He was mesmerized by the sight of Neil Armstrong and Buzz Aldrin raising the American flag on the moon's barren surface in what Aldrin called the "magnificent desolation" of the lunar landscape.

For Dave, the transition to Kingston was startling. While Mountain View had felt exciting to him, like a place on the verge of becoming,

Kingston felt to Dave like a place whose time had passed. While Mountain View's economy thrived, Kingston remained largely depressed; it was the victim of a failed, federally funded urban renewal project in the 1960s that replaced old neighborhoods with housing projects segregated from the rest of the city. As a result, many of its downtown buildings remained boarded up and vacant. Mountain View had become a melting pot of cultures, but most of the families in Kingston had lived there for generations. Many of the kids at Dave's new school, Sophie Finn Elementary, had Dutch last names in a direct link to the Hudson River Valley's Dutch colonization in the 1600s. It was the first time in Dave's young life that he felt very much like an outsider.

In spite of his homesickness, Dave found delight in simple pleasures. He learned to ski one night beneath floodlights on a rope tow at nearby Mohonk Mountain. When he became separated from his ski-lesson group in the lodge, he plunged back out into the snow anyway and had fun figuring it out on his own. He learned how to skate at the Block Park Rink downtown, requiring stitches when his next-door neighbor accidentally ran over his thumb with his skates. He grew into an avid reader and developed a fascination with tall ships, Apollo lunar modules, and airplanes. He made gluey messes while constructing models of ships, planes, and rockets.

It was in Kingston, when Dave was ten years old, that Isabel, who had already outlived her prognosis, succumbed to complications of her disease on a cold January evening at home. She was just thirty-nine years old. Her death was incomprehensible to Dave; he felt terrified and vulnerable.

His childhood cracked along a fault line. On one side of the divide, just a few days before her death when he had come home cold and soaking wet after sledding at the golf course, his mother had helped him pull off his snow pants while he sang "Bye Bye Miss American Pie," a song he had picked up from his playmate. Holding his wet socks in her hands, she had looked at him and asked him gently, "What are you singing?"

On the other side of the divide, he would encounter the sight of his mother lying in an open casket during her wake at the funeral home in Kingston. He would be struck by the novelty of an airplane flight when he, eleven-year-old Harold, and twelve-year-old Carolyn traveled with their father to their mother's funeral in Albuquerque. He would listen to the pilot announce the score of the game as they flew through frozen Chicago during the Super Bowl. He would recognize the faces of vaguely familiar relatives sitting in the pews of the chapel. He would hear "Bye Bye Miss American Pie" coming on the radio in the car while traveling back home from the funeral, during the dreary drive back to Kingston from the airport.

Just three years after moving to what felt like a million miles away from his home community, Dave's family life, as he knew it, had irrevocably fractured. The sudden displacement of energy caused by the two sides of the fault rapidly slipping past each other put into motion seismic waves that caused his whole world to shake.

RMI ITINERARY

March 25, 2015
Kathmandu (4,383') to Lukla (9,350') to Phakding (8,700')
Trekking time is approximately 2 ½ to 3 hours.

Today we fly to Lukla, the village where our trek to Everest Base Camp begins. The airport in Lukla is the Tenzing Norgay Airport, and landing on the STOL (Short Takeoff and Landing) runway is an experience in itself. It is usually very busy in Lukla as different expeditions are getting everything organized for the trek. From here on out, there are no more vehicles or roads, just a network of villages connected by footpaths. We start trekking along the Dudh Kosi River as we travel to Phakding. We spend the night at a small teahouse on the bank of the milky-blue Dudh Kosi. Overnight in lodge.

Dave hoped that Lukla would not live up to its notorious reputation as the world's most dangerous airport on this particular Wednesday. It appeared to be a fine morning for flying the eighty-five miles from Kathmandu to Everest's gateway, but Dave knew that Lukla's weather was mercurial and often foggy, even when the sun was shining brightly in Kat. He and his RMI team briefly huddled around a hotel breakfast cart at 4:15 a.m., trying to digest more than coffee at such an early hour, along with a team of Everest Base Camp doctors who would also be flying to Lukla that morning. Piles of backpacks and gear encircled them on the floor, tagged with bits of blue ribbon on which RMI had been written with a marker. German client Hans Hilscher slipped a letter to his family into the hotel's outgoing mailbox. "I have the best guide, the best equipment, hard training, and the experience of other mountains.

I think the risk is manageable," he had penned in his best handwriting. They left the Yak and Yeti in the dark, at 4:30 a.m., crammed tightly together in a van while a golden Buddha figurine stared at them, contentedly, from the dashboard.

As they pulled up to the domestic flight terminal of Kathmandu's Tribhuvan International Airport, pigeons flew out from the rafters inside of it. With its hoards of trekkers, the dilapidated airport felt more like a bus terminal and was, as usual, a madhouse. After making their way through the metal detectors, Dave led his team to a calmer waiting area and told them they could expect to wait anywhere between one and two hours for their flight. "It's hard to say, exactly," he added. Thirty-year-old base-camp trekker Erin Machinchik, strategic and proactive by both nature and job training, went to the end of a line at the small cafeteria to buy a bottle of water so she could swallow the anxiety medication she had brought in anticipation of the flight.

Base-camp manager Mark Tucker—"Tuck," as Dave liked to call him—had flown out of Kathmandu to Lukla a day ahead of the rest of them to begin his eight-day, thirty-eight-mile trek from there to Everest Base Camp, where he would join a ten-man Sherpa climbing team in making preparations for the rest of them. Before he left, shielding his light-colored eyes and fair skin with an RMI baseball cap and mirrored sunglasses secured by a neoprene croakie, fifty-seven-year-old Tuck had explained to the clients that he never minded his "long commute to work," since Everest Base Camp sits at an altitude of around 17,300 feet, and the gradual trek upward would allow his body time to acclimate. There were no roads to be found in the Khumbu region of Nepal, and he had told them that being flown directly to such an altitude would be too much of a physiological jump for "99.9% of humans." "You would be in a world of hurt," he had said, in a matter-of-fact tone that added to the general impression that Tuck felt as comfortable managing an Everest expedition as he would surfing or coaching a little league team in Southern California. Gradual acclimatization accomplished via trekking would allow the body time to develop an increase in the number of red blood cells. This would increase the oxygen carrying capacity of the blood in order to compensate for the lower levels of oxygen in the air, and thereby reduce the chance of a wide range of high-altitude-induced ills.

Lukla's airport was perched at 9,100 feet, significantly lower than Everest Base Camp but higher than most pilots would want to take off or land. Recently renamed the Tenzing-Hillary Airport, in honor of Sir Edmund Hillary and Tenzing Norgay who in 1953 became the first people to reach the summit of Mount Everest, the airport was accessible only to helicopters and small, fixed-wing aircraft. The approach to Lukla was hazardous not only because of its mountainous topography and the decreased horsepower of planes at high altitude, but also because it was prone to low visibility, wind shear, and turbulence. Its infamous runway was only 1,600 feet long. On the southern end of the runway was a 2,000-foot drop into a deep valley, and at its northern end was a hairpin turn and a stone wall cut into the mountainside. The runway itself sat on a significant slope with a gradient of 12 percent, the equivalent of a ten-story building. While the uphill runway helped airplanes to stop in such a short distance, if a pilot were to overshoot it, the plane would crash into the side of a mountain.

Erin had done her research and was more terrified about the twenty-five-minute flight to Lukla than almost any other aspect of the expedition. Her palms were sweaty and her heart raced. Her wilting fear, and her unassuming and humble Midwestern manner, belied the fact that she was a highly accomplished technical rock climber, regularly sending 5.12 pitches (a grade of difficulty that separates expert climbers from intermediate ones) on vertical rock-face walls, hundreds of feet above the ground or sea, with names like Phantom Crack and Vomit Launch. While she was still waiting on the slow-moving line to buy a water bottle, their fourteen-seat STOL (short takeoff and landing) twin otter plane, white with blue waves painted across its belly, arrived on the tarmac. Dave called Erin back over and they were all quickly herded out to a shuttle bus that delivered them to the plane, where their Nepalese pilot, dressed in a leather bomber jacket and wearing aviator sunglasses, strolled the tarmac with a swagger. Erin, who had no qualms about rappelling off a 350-foot spire and dangling midair on a rope, began to cry as they boarded. Within minutes, the plane was pulling off onto the runway when, suddenly, the pilot stopped the plane and jumped out of his seat.

"No one move!" he said, in English, as he exited the plane.

A team of groundskeepers joined him on the runway, wielding brooms that they used to frighten away a flock of birds that had landed on it. During the commotion, Erin found a nearly empty water bottle in her backpack, swallowed the Xanax pill and chased it with one sip, then tied her long, blonde hair up in a bun behind her pink headband. Once the runway had been cleared of birds, the pilot returned and they soon took off. Erin took a deep breath and gripped her boyfriend Robbie's hand.

No stranger to physical trials, Erin had been diagnosed with polycystic kidney disease when she was eighteen years old, a genetic inheritance she shared with her brother and father. When she was eight, her father had received a kidney transplant from her mother. Though exceptionally athletic, strong, and lithe, Erin was now at stage three of the disease, which left her with 40 to 50 percent kidney function. She had decided to take three weeks off from her MBA program and her job in health insurance to join Robbie for the trek to Everest Base Camp. Robbie would continue on to attempt the summit. While Erin was eager for the endurance challenge of a high-altitude trek, as well as the opportunity to immerse herself in Nepal's culture, what she wanted most from the trip was to know and trust the guides who would be looking after Robbie on Everest. She knew from her experiences rock climbing that his life would ultimately be in his climbing partners' hands.

Erin had a good feeling about Dave from the moment they met at the Yak and Yeti, after she and Robbie had shared a cab there from the airport with Peter and Bonny. It was JJ who caught her eye first, with his big cowboy hat, muscular build, and similarly oversized personality. JJ looked and behaved so much like Robbie's best friend from home that Erin laughed, believing for a second it was him and that he and Robbie were playing a practical joke on her. She laughed again when she realized her mistake. She then noticed Dave considering them quietly.

Dave was older and taller than JJ. His face was tan, except for the faint goggle marks left around his eyes from his winter of ski patrolling, and his brown hair was speckled with grey. Her first impressions were that he had a rugged, confident, self-assured sense about him. She noticed he was measured and concise in his words and in what he chose to share, calculated in a paternal manner. His brown eyes lit up when he spoke, almost boyishly, yet his square jaw and thoughtful speech conveyed a sense of deliberateness. He shrugged his shoulders humbly, even a bit awkwardly at times, in response to some of their questions, but he commanded everyone's attention. He moved with a slow and purposeful stride. He listened and observed attentively. She felt reassured right away. Her instincts told her that Dave was everything anyone would want in a guide.

The loud buzzing of the airplane engines drowned out the sound of the team's collective gasp as they descended below the clouds and as a green mountainside appeared directly ahead of them. Erin felt her stomach drop as the plane pitched sharply right, only to face a different verdant mountainside crowned by taller, snow-covered peaks. Below them, an impossibly tiny strip of paved asphalt materialized in a deep pocket of the Himalayas. The sun was shining on it.

"Lukla," Dave announced.

As they dove downward, it felt as though they could reach out and touch the mountains on either side of them. Instead, they clutched the seatbacks in front of them and held their breath as both the ground and the facing mountainside rushed toward them through the windshield. When Erin unclenched her eyes, a blur of colorful rooftops and then a rusty chain link fence came into focus. The plane's wheels skimmed the ground with a high-pitched squeal. They bounced along the runway, hurtling forward toward the stone wall embedded in the mountain, then careened sharply right before the engines stopped. They all burst into spontaneous applause, out of both gratitude for the pilot and an irrepressible surge of relief.

5 ⛰ ANGEL FIRE

"Every man, every woman, carries in heart and mind the image of the ideal place, the right place, the one true home, known or unknown, actual or visionary."

Edward Abbey, *Desert Solitaire*

The adrenaline rush of their landing in Lukla wore off gradually as the team trekked three hours through small villages and past golden fields of buckwheat and barley, sharing the trail with uniformed schoolchildren who gazed curiously at JJ's tattooed arms and white-rimmed sunglasses. JJ, who adored kids, photography, road cycling, motorcycles, and the Argentinian tango with unabashed enthusiasm, high-fived them playfully and snapped a few photos.

The team followed the path as it wound through the forest up into Phakding, a small village composed of a collection of over a dozen trekker lodges and teahouses. They crossed a long, serpentine suspension bridge over the Dudh Kosi to their night's lodging at Jo's Garden. The tidy, camp-like compound of stone cottages capped by cerulean-blue metal roofs was nestled along the riverbank. Navy and yellow tents dotted its sprawling grounds. That night, Dave slept deeply, lulled by the sound of churning white water from the wide, ice-blue Dudh Kosi. He found that the roar of the river's rushing water, the meltwater of the Khumbu glacier beginning its thousand-mile journey from the highest points on Earth to the Bay of Bengal, masked everything.

In Kingston, the years following his mother's death were a stressful and lonely time for Dave. The loss shook his foundation and overrode his sense of childhood. As his father and siblings also grieved, home no longer felt to him like the refuge it had once been.

During middle school, Dave felt he did not fit in. He read voraciously and continued to perform well academically, but he viewed himself as weak and uncoordinated. He gravitated toward a group of boys from the neighborhood who were a grade or two older than him. He didn't skip school or smoke cigarettes like they did, but he began to hang out in the cold with them for hours and hours after school. He didn't own the same denim Timberland boots they all wore so he begged his father for a pair.

Dave figured he was the biggest chicken of all the kids in Kingston, but he worked up the courage to cross the West Shore Railroad trestle that spanned Roundout Creek and to explore the dank and musty abandoned mining caves beneath Hasbrouck Park. He wanted to belong. When he showed up after school one day wearing the same denim work boots as the other kids, his friends brought him to his buddy Louie Salvino's attic and blew pot smoke in his face in what felt like an initiation.

There was a brief glint of light for Dave, at thirteen years old, when he spent a summer in Albuquerque with his grandma Cella. That July, he hiked Sandia Peak with his Uncle Bill, his mother's younger brother. The rugged Sandia Mountains had captivated him ever since watching the Western drama *Lonely Are the Brave* starring Kirk Douglas on TV with his mother. He would later devour *The Lonely Cowboy*, the Edward Abbey novel on which the movie was based, as well as Abbey's *Desert Solitaire*. As he and his uncle climbed the rocky switchbacks of the strenuous, high-desert La Luz trail, Dave tilted his head back to take in the massive granite towers they passed between. He was equally enchanted by a ride up the Sandia Peak Tramway, climbing 4,000 feet into New Mexico's ceilingless sky, gaping at the panoramic views of granite spires, jagged cliffs, and pinnacles, the ancient cinder cones of Albuquerque's Three Sisters Volcanoes and soul-mending vistas of hundreds of miles of New Mexico, bathed in raging light.

After the summer, back in Kingston, Dave continued to earn high grades, but he found that being smart was not exactly a social asset in his middle school or his high school. He still felt scrawny and clumsy, academically advanced yet emotionally and physically immature. While Dave was in high school, his father remarried, but the marriage never took root and lasted only a year. Ron, who had been a Yosemite rock climber in the 1940s and '50s, took Dave and Harold and Carolyn on winter camping and hiking trips in the Catskills and Adirondacks, pastimes that were considered unusual, even strange, in 1970s Kingston. By the second half of high school, Dave could still not shake the feeling that he didn't belong. By then, he was 6 feet tall, 150 pounds, and still growing.

Dave had dreamed of learning to fly navy jets, ever since he had become obsessed with planes and ships as a young boy, and he had grown attached to the idea of attending college at the Naval Academy in Annapolis, Maryland. Now that he was getting closer to the prospect of applying, Dave began to have second thoughts. His meticulous father had remained in the Army Reserve while working for IBM. At home, he had imposed regimented systems to keep a sense of order and structure in their family life, insisting on regular haircuts and keeping a detailed schedule of chores on the refrigerator door. Part of Dave longed for more freedom than he suspected he would find at the Naval Academy, but he decided to go for the requisite medical exam and preliminary interview anyway.

Although not entirely surprised, Dave felt deeply disappointed when he failed the eye exam portion of the Naval Academy's physical. At an early age, he found he couldn't match socks when they came out of the dryer and had soon afterward been diagnosed by his pediatrician as colorblind. After his initial Naval Academy medical exam, he was given a second, more definitive vision test, which revealed a red-green deficiency, confirming his childhood diagnosis. Dave knew that ships and aircraft used red and green lights to denote port and starboard, and that red and green were the predominant colors in navigational aids and in warning and caution lights in cockpit displays. While he contended with the reality posed by his disqualifying condition, he also felt discouraged by the way he had struggled during his interview with two naval officers. He had shrugged his shoulders in response to some of their questions and had felt, throughout it, like a little kid. Dave was convinced that he possessed neither the self-confidence nor the emotional maturity they were seeking.

With his Naval Academy hopes dashed, Dave's father encouraged him to apply to the State University of New York (SUNY) at Buffalo instead. His sister Carolyn was already at school there, Ron reasoned, and Dave had received an in-state scholarship. Dave felt an urge to go back West, a place of happier memories, but he was not yet sure how to make that happen. Ultimately, he followed his father's advice and soon began college at SUNY Buffalo where he tried out for the swim team. Dave had never swum competitively before, but he had become certified as a lifeguard while working as a counselor in the summers at a camp for kids with developmental and intellectual disabilities. He didn't win any swim races during college, but he began to rely on the endorphin high of the workouts, and he realized he enjoyed the camaraderie of being part of a team. If someone had told him then that he would one day be inducted into the University of Buffalo (UB) Athletics Hall of Fame, he would have laughed incredulously.

Having always excelled in math and science, Dave decided to major in aerospace engineering at UB. However, while high school academics had come easily to him, Dave found he had not cultivated the study skills and academic discipline demanded by the rigorous aerospace program. His grades suffered. During his junior year, when an advisor in the department suggested to him that he ought to consider switching majors, Dave grew dispirited and considered dropping out of college altogether. Ultimately, he persisted so he could stay in the pool with the swim team. The grueling training and racing seemed to calm his brain and boost his mood. He couldn't give it up.

While still feeling the sting of rejection from the engineering department, Dave was surprised when his history professor, impressed with a paper he had written for his class, asked Dave to meet with him. "I can't promise that it'll guarantee you a well-paying job right out of college, but you should be a history major," he told Dave in the cramped office, its shelves teeming with dusty books. It was enough to convince Dave to stay in school.

When Dave's grandmother Cella passed away during January of his junior year, he flew to Albuquerque for her funeral. The sight of the watermelon hue of the Sandia Mountains at sunset solidified a notion that had resided deep inside of Dave for some time: he knew he would one day live in New Mexico. New York felt cold and mean in comparison. A few months later, Dave returned to Albuquerque, riding across the country by bus with a dorm buddy during their spring break. They drove back to grey and snowy Buffalo in the butternut-yellow '68 Chevelle Dave had inherited from his grandmother.

Dave knew exactly where he was headed when he graduated from college, as a history major, in 1984. He felt the need to reinvent himself and reignite his life. Driving the Chevelle, a sun streaking across the ashen sky, he returned to his mother's home state.

In Albuquerque, Dave scribbled down the phone number from a rental posting tacked on a bulletin board at the University of New Mexico student union building. After submitting to an interview by his potential housemates, all students at UNM, he moved into a room in the off-campus house on Hyder Avenue they called *Hyder House* for $96 per month. Dave enjoyed leisurely Sunday mornings playing Frisbee golf with his new housemates in the shade of the elm trees at Roosevelt Park. One of his new Hyder House friends, a law student named David Benavides, noticed there was something "a little bit different about Dave" when Dave would race up the grueling 13-mile La Luz hiking trail, located way out on the west face of the Sandias, every day. During a camping trip the group took together that summer, David chuckled, both knowingly and bemused, when Dave, who was wearing black jeans and hiking boots and suffering from a nasty head cold, happily offered to run 5 miles back to move their car, which they had inadvertently parked in the wrong lot. He managed to move the car and easily race back to their campsite before the rest of them woke up from naps.

In November, Dave continued northward and found seasonal work teaching skiing in Angel Fire, New Mexico, in the Sangre de Cristo Mountains, the southernmost range of the Rocky Mountains. The Sangres blushed rosily during sunrise and sunset, and they glowed even more luminously when covered with snow, giving rise to Angel Fire's name. Dave's job as a ski instructor at the small Angel Fire Ski Resort soon evolved into a job as a ski patroller. When Dave's father, Ron, came to visit him that spring, they spent a sunny afternoon together skiing dry, crystalline powder.

"I want to go to Alaska to climb Denali during my off season," Dave announced. Ron had been to Denali. He had also climbed Washington's Mount Rainier, the most glaciated peak in the contiguous United States, in 1980 while watching Rainier's sister volcano, Mount Saint Helen, erupt 30 miles south; his photos of the trip had piqued Dave's interest. During his rock-climbing days in the 1950s, Ron had participated in rescues at Shiprock and in Las Cruces, New Mexico. He was well acquainted with climbing's many dangers.

"I'll climb it with you," Ron replied, "so long as you go to Rainier first, to learn the ropes."

Rainier, Ron argued, would help Dave prepare for the glaciated peak of Denali, North America's tallest peak. He knew that on Rainier, Dave would learn how to build effective winter-storm camps and how to navigate crevasses. He would hone crevasse rescue techniques, fixed-rope ascension, and climbing strategies. He would acquire and refine skills necessary for snow and ice climbing, such as ice axe positioning and moving in balance, crampon use, belaying, rappelling, and rope management. He would become proficient in using maps, compasses, and altimeters in navigation. Such training, Ron insisted, would be essential to safely meet the demands of a Denali expedition.

"OK, deal," Dave agreed, as a smile crept across his face.

Dave went to Rainier that summer to train. When Dave discovered the guide service there, the realization dawned on him that it was possible to make a career as a professional mountain guide. The Rainier guides weren't much older than him and had already traveled all around the globe, climbing mountains. Dave knew immediately, clear to his core and with a sudden urgency, that this was what he wanted to do with his life.

When Dave told Rainier guide George Dunn, the lead guide on the five-day training course Dave took that summer, that he wanted to become a mountain guide, George explained to him that the guiding companies had already done their hiring for that season. "But I have an idea, " he said. "Why don't you try to get a job working in the dining room at the Paradise Inn, so you can climb every day and be ready for the next year's hiring season?"

Dave took George's advice. While bussing tables in the wood-beamed dining room of the historic lodge during the summer of 1985, Dave would run the 5 miles up to Camp Muir at 10,000 feet every time he had a break. Several prominent Rainier guides noticed, including Peter Whittaker, an RMI guide and the nephew of Jim Whittaker who in 1963 became the first American to summit Everest. Whenever he saw Dave on the trail, Peter would shout, "Hey, you should be a mountain guide!"

Dave's determination was not about a checklist of mountains to summit. He wanted to carve out a life in them. It wasn't until years later that Dave realized his dad had given him the mountains.

6 ⛰ NAMCHE BAZAAR

March 26, 2015
Posted by: Dave Hahn
Categories: Expedition Dispatches; Everest
Elevation: 11,300 feet

RMI EXPEDITIONS BLOG

We crossed the ultra-high cable bridges near the start of
Namche Hill and then plugged away in the heat for several
thousand feet of vertical gain through the pine forests. At one
point we heard the thunderous crashing of tons of ice cascading
down the steep gullies on the opposite wall of the canyon.
Finally we eased into the magical village of Namche Bazaar. The
town is built as a series of concentric half circles, facing the giant
peak of Kwangde, across the valley.

The team woke in Phakding to a crisp, clear morning glistening with
light frost in sunshine. They set off on their six-hour trek to Namche—
"Sherpa Capital" of the world—at 8:30 in the morning. Sparkling-pink
rhododendrons, wild poppy, magnolia, primrose, and apple and cherry
trees bloomed in the river valley, saturating the springtime air with their
sweet scents as the day began to warm. Colorful square prayer flags
strung across the hillsides fluttered in the breeze. Soon, the sharp ridges
of the giant peak of Thamserku appeared in the distance, like jagged
whitecaps, puncturing wisps of cloud in an ocean of blue sky.

The team shared the well-worn, steep, zigzagging trails with domes-
ticated yaks wearing bright-red, embroidered saddle blankets, the brass
bells around their thick necks tinkling as they transported goods up
and down. They brushed shoulders with local porters, the spine of the
roadless Khumbu's commercial transport system. The porters bore the

brunt of heavy loads of hand-hewn lumber, metal roofs, and overstuffed boxes of food on their backs, balancing their burdens with straps pressed across their sweating foreheads as they scaled the dusty switchbacks up the canyon walls.

Larry Seaton noted each one of the man-made structures he saw around him while they walked through the Khumbu Valley: every stone step, bridge, and building. As a contractor in Napa Valley, California, Larry was accustomed to the aid of engineers and technology in all of his construction projects. He was awestruck by the amount of labor and time that had been involved in building everything in the Khumbu without those benefits, and by the fact that all the materials required had been carried on the back of a man or yak. While they rounded a rocky bend of the trail, they passed a porter carrying an immense stack of framing lumber. All Larry could see of the man from behind were his feet sticking out below the long, tilted planks.

When they reached the porter's partner, resting farther ahead on the trail, Larry asked him, with Chhering's help translating, "How much is your friend carrying?"

"80 kilograms," he replied.

"That's close to 200 pounds," Larry said to no one in particular, stunned, as he did the math in his head.

Within a few hours the team reached the Sagarmatha National Park entrance at Jorsalle. A hand-painted sign, hanging over an awning, greeted them in English: "WEL COM to Sagarmatha National Park, World Heritage Natural Site, Estd. in 1976." Robbie snapped a photo of Erin standing in front of it while Dave and Chhering ducked inside the park entrance headquarters—a two-story stone building with a red metal roof, cheerful lemon yellow awnings, and square window shutters—to submit the group's permits.

Like a diamond formed by extreme pressures, landlocked Nepal is the ancient cultural jewel forged between India and China. For many centuries cut off from the outside world by its fearsome Himalayas, home to eight of ten of the highest peaks on Earth, Nepal was essentially a constellation of separate mountain kingdoms. In 1768, King Prithvi Narayan Shah began his campaign to create a unified Nepal from its fifty smaller principalities of diverse religious, ethnic, and cultural groups in order to better defend against the threat of British colonization. (Shah was convinced the British were trying to exploit feuds between Nepal's separate states and to extend their trading footholds throughout them with thinly veiled ambition to achieve their growing imperial aims in central Asia.)

Due to its dramatic changes in elevation, Nepal contains several biomes, from grasslands spanning its tropical savannah to subtropical broadleaf forests in its hills, to coniferous forests on the slopes of the Himalaya to high alpine grass and shrublands, to rock and ice at its highest elevations. Three of the world's major rivers—the Indus, the Ganges, and the Brahmaputra—rise in the snow-capped Himalayas. Nepal's three biggest river systems—the Khosi, the Gandaki, and the Karnali—originate in high-mountain glaciers and eventually flow into the Ganges river system. With a latitude not much higher than that of the tropics, some of Nepal's lower elevations, like the Chitwan National Park of south-central Nepal, are home to elephants and rhinos bathing in its rivers. Bengal tigers and sloth bears roam its grasses and jungles.

Nepal also straddles the divide between two massive tectonic plates: the Indo-Australian and Asian plates. It was the collision between these plates that had formed the Himalayan Mountains over the last fifty million years, as India slowly squeezed up from below and forced up the lip of Asia, like a piecrust rising off the plate, and it is that same tectonic friction that makes the country prone to earthquakes. In spite of the seemingly immutable nature of the mighty Himalayas, the region is one of the most seismically active on the planet. As the tectonic plates of the Earth's lithosphere grind together below the Himalayas, pressure and tension build in the Earth's crust. When the stress overcomes the friction, with a sudden slip on a fault, the seismic waves of an earthquake are released, causing the ground to shake. The epicenter of Nepal's last major quake, in 1934, was 6 miles south of Everest. With a magnitude of 8.0, it killed over 16,000 people. In spite of the devastation it caused, the 1934 quake did not release all the strain. Instead, geophysicists warned that the 1934 rupture transferred strain westward along the fault, toward Kathmandu. All of that pent-up seismic pressure would eventually, inevitably, need to be released.

Once their paperwork was processed, Dave, JJ, and Chhering led the group a short distance to the last teahouse along the trail in Jorsalle, where they stopped for lunch. Along the way they passed through a traditional *kani* or gate (essentially a doorway made of stone and wood), marking their entrance into the Khumbu Valley, the sacred valley of the Sherpa people. A metal sign at the kani inscribed with blue letters reminded visitors that the Khumbu was also a "world-renowned National Park and World Heritage site."

The sign reads that visitors are encouraged to:

1. Refrain from taking life.
2. Refrain from anger.
3. Refrain from jealousy.
4. Refrain from offending others.
5. Refrain from taking excessive intoxicants.

One after the other, they spun the cylindrical Buddhist prayer wheels, inscribed with mantras, clockwise as they passed through it, out of respect for the Buddhist belief that spinning the prayer wheels would help one to accumulate wisdom and merit, otherwise known as karma, and would alleviate and purify negative energy or bad karma.

"We need all the karma we can get," Dave said dryly.

At the teahouse they sat at a picnic table in the sunshine, encircled by their backpacks on the ground, and were reinvigorated by milk tea and *dal bhat*, a traditional Nepalese meal of lentil soup, steamed rice, and vegetable curry. Afterward they strapped on their packs and crossed the loudly churning, bouldered, icy Dudh Kosi, or "Milk River," on a sky-scraping cable suspension bridge that hung like a necklace across the gorge. It clapped and squeaked loudly as they walked across it. The hundreds of blessing scarves, called *khadas*, tied to its railings lifted like wings in the breeze. Strings of prayer flags quivered above them. The long, lofty bridge, swarming with people and pack animals, delivered them to the base of Namche Hill, a dusty, 2,000-foot vertical climb through pine forest into Namche Bazaar. They stripped off their outer layers and tucked them away in their packs before beginning the strenuous, steep hike into thinner air in the heat of the blazing afternoon sun.

As they climbed toward Namche, with Dave setting the pace, thirty-one-year-old Robbie Massie began to feel the effects of altitude: headache, shortness of breath, a lesser appetite, and burning lungs. Back home in Minnesota, he had trained for the expedition for thirty-two weeks, mostly at the gym. He had climbed on the stairmaster for hours at a time, six days a week, wearing a 40-pound backpack. While Robbie relished the preparation and the planning for the expedition, earlier stints living in Colorado and Montana during his twenties had made him aware that there was no way to simulate or prepare for the effects of high altitude while living at sea level. He knew his pulse rate and blood pressure would spike up sharply at altitude, as his heart, starved for oxygen, pumped harder to get more oxygen to his cells. His countless laps on Buck Hill, a ski hill near his home with an altitude of 1,200 feet, would hardly make a dent. A slow and steady process of acclimatization to the lower atmospheric air pressure and subsequent lower oxygen saturation of hemoglobin in the blood would be the only way for his body, for all of their bodies, to adjust. He ran the back of his hand across his forehead, wiping sweat from the edge of his mop of curly brown hair.

Dave was carefully observing all of them. He was already well acquainted with fifty-nine-year-old Hans, forty-nine-year-old Hao, sixty-three-year-old Larry, and sixty-two-year-old Peter, having guided each of them, on four different RMI trips, to the 16,067-foot summit of

Vinson Massif, Antarctica's highest peak. He remembered how Larry had donned a Santa hat and sunglasses, his beard frozen with ice, atop Vinson on that glorious, windless December day when they summited in 2013. JJ had guided alongside him in early December of 2014 when Peter—the deep-voiced, Harvard-educated founder of a home security system company—had reached Vinson's white crown. Later that same month, Dave marked his thirty-fifth summit of the mountain when he guided Hans-Jurgen Hilscher, the German CEO of a microtechnology company who sported a grey mustache and kind smile to Vinson's peak. "Is Everest harder than this?" Hans had asked Dave after a particularly exhausting, fifteen-hour day of climbing.

"Every day on Everest is harder than this," Dave had replied.

Chinese American Hao Wu—an unassuming, bespectacled venture capitalist with a PhD in electrical engineering and offices in New York, Shanghai, and Beijing—had climbed to the top of Vinson as part of a larger team guided by Dave in December of 2012. Hao had also been a capable member of Dave and JJ's RMI Everest team the previous spring, during the aborted 2014 season. HP—a forty-six-year-old CEO from Dallas, Texas—was a new client for Dave, but he had already stood atop Aconcagua and Rainier.

These five men, all fathers, were on a quest to reach the peak of the highest mountain on each of the seven continents, a mountaineering challenge referred to as the Seven Summits, first achieved in 1985 by a climber named Richard (Dick) Bass. Dave had shared a rope with Bass in Antarctica in the late 1990s. "Dick was all the over-the-top things people have said about him but I discovered he was also a thoughtful guy and I liked him," Dave told Hans. Bass—a curious, hyperactive, and poetry-spouting Texas oilman—was known for his bear hugs and for dreaming up the idea of the Seven Summits with his climbing partner Frank Wells, a former president of Walt Disney. Bass and Wells were credited, by some, with popularizing mountain adventure travel and were accused, by others, of inspiring ego-driven pursuits by inexperienced climbers.

"I know a lot of executives who wake up and say, 'My God there's got to be more,'" Bass had explained. "That's why they want to climb mountains. They want to win the self-respect that comes from doing something that really lays it on the line."

Hao, Hans, Larry, Peter, and HP were now in different stages of trying to accomplish the feat, one that took years to complete and included climbing Alaska's Denali, Argentina's Aconcagua, Russia's Mount Elbrus, Tanzania's Kilimanjaro, the Carstensz Pyramid of Western New Guinea, Antarctica's Vinson Massif, and, straddling the border of China and Nepal, Everest.

Before he left Dallas for Everest, HP slipped off his wedding ring and handed it his wife, Nomita. "Just in case I die," he told her. He had dreamed of climbing Everest ever since he was a child, but he struggled with the idea of leaving behind Nomita and their two young sons. After sitting at his withered father's bedside in India and watching him die of cancer, a disease HP called a scourge, he found himself again thinking of his boyhood dream. His father had always encouraged him to find his passion and to work hard.

"Then," his father had instructed him, "you must channel your passion into compassion."

When HP shared his dream with the CEO of the company where he then worked, she asked him, "Well, what are you waiting for?" HP began training immediately.

He decided he wanted Dave to be his guide because of his reputation and because of something Dave had told him over the phone, before they met, in what amounted to a job interview for both of them, "My job is not to get you to the summit, but to ensure that you are safely climbing. . . . It's not just about the summit. You have to enjoy the climb."

When HP, with a hint of fandom, ticked off a list of Dave's accomplishments, Dave demured, "If I'm unable to help a specific client with a specific challenge on any given day of a climb, those numbers don't make a whole lot of difference. As a guide, I'm only as good as how I do the next time." HP decided he would honor his father's life by raising money for cancer research with each foot he climbed. He confided in Nomita before he left that the Icefall was his biggest fear.

When Peter had first voiced his desire to climb Everest to his wife Bonny, her response had been, "Absolutely not ever!" The seventy-four-day door-to-door expedition seemed too long and too dangerous. Eventually, however, after Peter's successful summit of Denali, Bonny came to the conclusion that Peter's training, preparation, and previous ascents had earned him the right to attempt Everest. With Bonny's blessing, Peter committed to Everest almost a year in advance of the trip. Bonny, an athletic fifty-five-year-old and an experienced trekker herself, later decided to join him for the trek to Base Camp.

According to data from Miss Hawley's Himalayan database, men and women climbers have very similar odds of summiting and of dying on Everest. However, climbers older than forty years old have reduced odds of summiting. The data also revealed that climbers older than sixty not only achieve the summit far less frequently than climbers in their thirties (at 13.3 percent versus 35.7 percent), but they also have a death rate three times higher than that of younger climbers, most often occurring during the descent, when physical and mental exhaustion increase the peril. While Everest appeared blind to gender, she was certainly not blind to age.

Perhaps more than anyone, Dave recognized that Everest demanded a blend of climbing experience on 8,000-meter peaks, acquired skill, immense strength, and stamina. When asked by potential clients how they should prepare for Everest, he told them, "Come in the best shape of your lives." When pressed, he added, "It's a gunfight. Don't bring a knife. Fitness is not something you get extra credit for when you go to Everest. It just gets you in the door." He encouraged climbers to grow familiar with the experience of a twelve- to fifteen-hour workout with a heavy pack at high altitude in cold, rain, and snow. "Be miserable now and then," he advised. Everest also required a hard-to-quantify amount of life experience and mental maturity. "For me, it helps to come to this mountain with humility and with a little bit of fear," he explained. Youth was not necessarily an advantage. Historically, climbers in their mid-thirties tended to be the most successful.

Dave was already trying to suss out if his clients were strong enough. He dreaded the prospect of having to guide a client to a decision point, when he would essentially have to wait for the client to recognize that age, illness, injury, or insufficient fitness would prevent them from going any farther on an expedition that may have been a lifelong dream. And looming in the back of his mind, far worse than the prospect of angry or disappointed clients, was the constant fear he harbored of being responsible for an accident, in an environment where even a minor misstep could mean death. For Dave, an ideal client would have done their homework; would arrive extremely fit and strong; would be familiar with the history, features, and dangers of the mountain; and would be ready for a true adventure with an uncertain outcome — or as some guides preferred to call it, a sufferfest.

Climbing Everest with a reputable guiding company was a costly and time-consuming endeavor. A guided group climb with RMI cost upward of $70,000, with $11,000 of that going directly toward government permits. As a result, most of Dave's clients were middle-aged or older, and they were often very successful in their fields, which had enabled them to afford the expense and the time that such a trip entailed, as well as the preceding trips to climb 8,000-meter peaks that helped them prepare for such an extreme expedition. The irony was that along with the benefits conferred by middle age that allowed many of his clients to afford such a trip also came physiological differences that made climbing at such an extreme altitude even more treacherous. "They might be a long shot," he had said to Tuck, of the group, when he considered some of their ages, but he knew that none of them had come to Everest for him to simply shape their climbing potential. This climb would be the natural culmination of everything they'd ever accomplished on mountains, and they had invested a significant sum of money for him to guide them. At fifty-three years old, Dave was acutely aware that his clients weren't the only ones in a race against time.

They were all breathing heavily when, midway up the long, steep hill, the booming thunder of an avalanche startled them. Tons of ice crashed down the far wall of the canyon across from them. It was a sound to which they would grow more accustomed in the days and nights to come. Two hours above the river, Namche Bazaar, a crescent-shaped village carved into an impossibly high funnel of mountainside, appeared like a dream. Green-, blue-, and red-roofed buildings were lined in terraced half circles, perched loftily in cottony puffs of clouds. Peering above Namche to the west was the white peak Kongde Ri rising to 20,299 feet, and to the east soared Thamserku at 21,729 feet.

A little Sherpa girl who appeared to be around five years old, her head shaved and wearing a fleece jacket, approached them on the trail and gazed up at them with her expressive brown eyes. JJ snapped a photo and reached his tattooed arm out to high-five her. She leaped up, tapped his hand, and then hurried away, giggling. The team wandered into and throughout the narrow alleys of the bustling village, the Khumbu's trading post and tourist hub, where Dave ran into Sherpa friends and bid a friendly "Namaste," a traditional Nepali greeting meaning "I bow to the divine in you," to every shopkeeper they passed.

Soon Dave pointed toward a sign hanging outside a modest trekkers lodge built against a terraced mountainside, reading "Hotel Camp De Base, for quiet & comfort!" A black-and-tan dog wearing a collar embroidered with roses peered down at them from the stone terrace above, tail wagging. The square windows on the door were plastered with climbing-company stickers.

"Home sweet home, for the next three nights anyway, "Dave said as they celebrated their arrival with cups of hot lemon tea in the comfortable and clean wood-paneled dining room. They gazed up at posters of famed mountaineers Hans Kammerlander, Edmund Hillary, and

Tenzing Norgay that hung beside posters of the Dalai Lama, the revered spiritual head of Tibetan Buddhism. Then they slowly paraded down a narrow, green-carpeted hallway, squeezing past a couple of small sinks and a mirror on the wall, to the dorm-like rooms where they would stay while they gave their bodies time to acclimate to the 11,300-foot altitude.

7 ⛰ THE DEATH ZONE

> Some people climb mountains to test themselves. You're pushing
> your body to the utmost limits. . . . Another reason: there is a
> very simple goal. There's nothing complicated about it. The goal
> is to get to the top of the mountain. . . . It simplifies your life.
>
> Elizabeth Hawley in *Keeper of the Mountains:*
> *The Elizabeth Hawley Story* by Bernadette McDonald

Dave was twenty-nine years old when he made his first expedition to
Everest in 1991 with a group of friends, all of them mountain guides.
They had sold t-shirts to help pay for their trip. Dave had been on Denali
seven times as an expedition leader and guide, but Everest was different. Decades later, he would still be able to distinctly recall the feeling
of trying to sort out which fears to heed and which to dismiss during
his first time climbing the highest mountain on Earth. Hammered by
storms, Dave did not reach the summit. Afterward he fell into a de-
pression, "for longer," he later recalled while being interviewed for a
documentary, "than I would have expected." In spite of his searing and
lingering disappointment, however, that first trip had also made it clear
to Dave that he could one day stand on top of Everest, that it was indeed
possible for him. "I knew clear to my core that I wanted to *try* climbing
that thing again."

When he was on the biggest mountains on the planet, Dave found his
mind was fully engaged and his eyes were wide open. Whether getting
himself or a client out of a fix, climbing and guiding in these challenging environments involved plenty of problem solving, which seemed
to elevate his mood and buffer his brain from anxiety. With no room
for a misstep in such extreme terrain and no way to know until the last
moment of a trip whether he would be able to safely guide his clients to
a summit, he was forced to stay in the present moment. Dave knew he

had found exactly what he was looking for. He was amazed by how much life he could experience in how little time.

Dave had turned back within 1,000 feet of the summit of Everest in 1991. (He would do so three more times, in 1998, 2001, and 2002.) The first time he reached the top was in 1994 in Tibet, on Everest's North Ridge. Stymied by high winds, the first two waves of guides and climbers from his team had returned unsuccessfully from their attempts at a summit. When the winds finally quit, Dave led the next wave of five guides and three clients on a summit push from Camp 4, departing at around 4:00 a.m. By the time Dave pulled into Camp 5 with a lagging client who was going to have to turn around, it was 5:00 p.m. Within minutes he was informed over the radio that their sherpa team, after stocking Camp 6 (their highest camp) in preparation for their summit bid, had mistakenly returned with an Italian team's oxygen bottles and sleeping bags, assuming they had been left behind. Dave decided that instead of climbing into the tent with the others at Camp 5 to rest, he would try to repair the damage of his own team's mistake by continuing up to Camp 6 with oxygen regulators and tanks for the two Italian climbers attempting their own summit bid.

It was snowing, and having been to Camp 6 only once before, three years earlier, Dave struggled to find his way. Partway there, his job was made easier when he ran into one of the two Italian guides and a sherpa descending. Due to the language barrier between them, Dave and the Italians relied on their base-camp teams to communicate for them over the radio. It was decided that Dave would continue up to Camp 6 where he would join the sole remaining Italian climber for a summit bid. By the time Dave finally found Camp 6, it was 1:00 a.m. He crawled into the tent where the Italian climber, Guiliano, handed Dave a pot of warm liquid. Exhausted and thirsty, Dave gratefully guzzled it down. They pantomimed to communicate with each other. Dave helped set up Guiliano with the oxygen apparatus he had carried up with him. Then they worked together to sort out a tangle of rope, spiraling it into a coil they could use for fixing the route, and left the tent by 3:30 a.m., bound for the summit.

For much of the next ten hours, as Dave navigated hairy vertical climbing sections with ratty, old fixed rope and traversed terrifyingly narrow fins of ridges, with 9,000-foot drops, that allowed room for just one foot at a time, he repeated a single instruction to himself: "Don't fall!" When he finally reached the top of the second step in the early afternoon, after becoming totally mentally and physically absorbed in the task of propelling himself from the top of a rocking ladder up to a chest-high ledge, he realized that he and Giuliano had been separated.

When his team informed him via radio that the Italian climber had made the decision to turn around, Dave reassessed. He suspected that Giuliano had felt a bit off and therefore had made the right call by heading back down. It was late in the day, but Dave was still feeling good, and he suspected the rest of the climb would get easier. He made the decision to go on.

It did not get easier. Dave struggled to find the rock with his crampons in the knee-deep snow and felt like he had to virtually swim up the steep, exposed slopes of the final pyramid. When he stood on the roof of the world for the very first time, it was 4:50 p.m. Dave did not feel elated. He was alone, exhausted, and out of oxygen in the Death Zone, and he was entirely focused on how he would make his way back down.

The Death Zone is the name used by climbers for the region of Everest that stands above 8,000 meters, or 26,000 feet, at the very edge of Earth's troposphere. Dave knew well that the air in the Death Zone does not contain enough oxygen to sustain human life. At such extreme altitude, digestion starts to shut down and the adrenal glands, which control vital bodily functions such as heart rate and blood pressure, begin to fail. Starved of oxygen, the brain swells and the lungs collect fluid. The body begins to die. The regulators on the tanks used by climbers typically release oxygen at approximately a 2-liter flow rate mixed with ambient air; it is not pure oxygen and does not come close to bringing climbers' oxygen saturation to sea-level concentrations, but it is enough to offset some of the effects of exertion and to help prevent frostbite in the extremities.

As he hurried to descend, Dave tried to follow his own footprints, but the falling snow had already hidden them. He knew he needed to make his way back down through the most technical sections before he lost all daylight, but by the time he stood at the top rung of the ladder at the top of the Second Step, it was already dark. He turned on his headlamp and persisted, rappelling down the lower part of the Second Step. Disoriented in the weather, he grew frustrated when he found himself on dead-end ledges. At 1:00 a.m., at the top of the First Step, he reached the half-bottle of oxygen he had stashed on his way up, but he soon realized he must have put the regulator on incorrectly when the oxygen in it lasted only long enough for him to get down the First Step. At the bottom of the First Step, having finally reached what should have been easier terrain, he was without oxygen and his vision was still limited to the 6-foot circle of light provided by his headlamp in the snowstorm. By 3:00 a.m. he felt so mentally and physically exhausted, he was certain he would fall off the face of the mountain if he continued. He radioed his team at Base Camp and told them he was going to try to wait where he was until daylight.

Dave found a spot out of the wind and sat down on his backpack. He tore open a packet of hand warmers and replaced the climbing gloves he was wearing with mittens. Dave knew if he fell asleep he would die, so instead he maniacally stomped his feet and shook his hands, to try to ward off frostbite, and screamed, "Ayeayeayeayeayeayeaye!" at the top of his lungs for hours, until he noticed the light beginning to return at 4:30 a.m.

Soon after, while talking on the radio with his worried friend, Curtis Fawley, who was 15 miles away at Base Camp, Dave saw another teammate, Bob Sloezen, who had been sent to help Dave, pop his head out of a gulley. Dave, not wanting to be in need of rescue, jumped up and deliriously attempted to make small talk. Bob slipped his oxygen mask on Dave right away and helped him descend to a tent at Camp 5, where another guide, Heather Macdonald, placed mugs of water in both of Dave's hands. Dave found it a challenge to drink the water before he passed out. He had been awake for sixty hours. The last thoughts that drifted through his mind before being overcome by sleep were amazement that his feet were unharmed and that he had survived, followed by a dim realization that he had also made it to the summit.

A couple of days later, while tromping down the remaining 12 miles to Base Camp, Dave began to grasp just how beaten up he was by the experience. Every muscle in his body ached, and he was surprised to find he was peeing blood, from the toll the Death Zone had taken on his kidneys. Still, as he trudged wearily into Base Camp, he felt replenished by the welcome from both his team and the Italians and by the knowledge that he had reached the top.

Out of the nine expeditions so far that season, Dave was the only who had both made it to the summit and managed to come back down. He realized that if he had ever harbored a death wish, surviving a night alone outside in the Death Zone on Everest had squelched it. He did not want to know what it would take to kill him.

Dave's perception of his first Everest summit was radically altered just a few days later when two of his teammates made their own summit push, and only one of them returned alive. Fifty-three-year-old Mike Rheinberger—a thoughtful, humorous, and soft-spoken Australian— was attempting to make his first Everest summit in what had become a devotion verging on obsession after six previous attempts. New Zealander guide Mark Whetu wanted to help Mike achieve the dream that had remained so frustratingly out of reach. Dave watched through a telescope from Base Camp, in horror, as Mike and Mark made sickeningly slow progress up the summit ridge, in spite of good weather. He was shocked that they did not turn back, as he had watched others on the route do earlier, with the quickly closing window of daylight.

Mike and Mark reached the summit ridge at dusk, virtually guaranteeing a night outside in the Death Zone. In the pink luminescence of the setting sun, Mike ecstatically embraced the summit with his full body in an exhausted forward plunge, as if he were hugging a long lost child. Unable to descend in the dark, Mike and Mark dug a snow hole 20 meters below the summit. There, they spent the longest night of their lives, without shelter in the Death Zone, clinging to each other for warmth. By daylight, Mike was blind, could barely walk, and was speaking incoherently. In the inconceivable cold of the highest point on Earth, with their bodies starved of oxygen, Mike's brain had swelled and the skin and underlying tissue in Mark's extremities had frozen.

When they were able to finally make radio contact with Mark, the team at North Base Camp convinced him to unclip himself from Mike and temporarily leave Mike tethered to a piton in the rock in order to retrieve an oxygen bottle the team had left for them at the base of the First Step, a steep, slippery rock feature located on the route at an altitude of 27,890 feet. They reassured Mark that he could then bring the oxygen back up to Mike. By the time Mark reached the O2 bottle, however, it was already nearly dark. The team leader at Base Camp, Eric Simonson, made a triage decision. Convinced that Mark would die in the attempt to return to Mike, he decided it would be better to lose one climber than two and demanded that Mark descend. Mark resisted, insisting on returning to Mike, until he was assured that another climber had been sent to aid Mark. In the end, Mike perished on Everest and Mark lost much of both of his feet to frostbite. Mark was haunted by the searing memory of leaving his friend behind.

The tragedy impressed upon Dave just how lucky he had been. He also viewed it as a parable about the dangers of wanting something too badly and of trying something one too many times. He made a decision then and there, at thirty-two years old, in the shadow of his first Everest summit, that he would not allow himself to grow old on Everest.

As he cultivated his career as a high-altitude mountain guide over the years, Dave reached a point when he could no longer consider himself young, but he knew he was still strong, and he set out to use the wealth of experience he had accumulated on Everest to become the best Everest guide in the world. Now, at fifty-three years old, he was willing to admit that he had solidified his reputation as a guide. His fifteen summits of Everest were lauded as the world record for a non-Sherpa climber. While he appreciated the recognition, he was uncomfortable with the idea of an ethnically qualified record. He knew that Apa Sherpa, a Nepalese Sherpa mountaineer born in the same village as Tenzing Norgay, had made his twenty-first summit in May of 2011 before retiring. Phurba Tashi Sherpa and Kami Rita Sherpa tied Apa's record in 2013. "Besides," Dave liked to explain, "I figure Everest doesn't care much about my resume." He found he still needed the mental challenge and the meditative freedom that climbing high peaks gave him. Being allowed the privilege of reaching a summit now and again on a clear day brought him overwhelming joy and helped give him a way to quantify his work as a mountain guide, but ultimately it was the accomplishment of safely guiding others on mountains, the satisfaction of seeing his clients' faces melt in wonder when a fiery sunrise from 20,000 feet reminded them what they were capable of accomplishing, and the "day-to-day doing" of climbing that were most important to him. "For whatever you're trying to do," he often told to his clients, "it's the *trying* that's important."

Dave was nevertheless forced to contend with the fact that he was not immune to aging. It was difficult for him to believe he was now the same age Mike Rheinberger had been on the expedition that marked the first Everest summit for both of them, and the last for Rheinberger. Sometimes the velocity of life astounded him. Dave did not want to discover he had grown too old to climb Everest while guiding clients on Everest. He hoped he would have the wisdom to know just when to bow out.

8 ⛰ CHOMOLUNGMA

March 28, 2015
Posted by: Dave Hahn
Categories: Expedition Dispatches; Everest
Elevation: 11,300 feet

RMI EXPEDITIONS BLOG

Our last day in Namche dawned surprisingly clear and sunny. That was a little unexpected given how persistent the rain was yesterday afternoon and evening. We took full advantage after breakfast, trooping up to the Hilltop National Park Headquarters to see if the mountains were out. Indeed they were, and those of the team that hadn't yet gotten a look at the world's highest mountain were predictably in awe. Those of us that had seen it a few times were also in awe. New snow made the peaks radiant and sparkling in the strong sunshine. . . . The sunshine turned summit after summit into golden monuments around us, but our eyes kept returning to Everest . . . still about thirty miles away but regal nonetheless. Conditions were so calm and pleasant where we stood that we were tempted to gaze for hours . . .

"Food is fuel," Dave reminded his team as he sat down at a long dining table comprised of three smaller card tables pushed up against each other, draped by a blue woven tablecloth, in the wood-paneled common room of the trekker's lodge.

"Our mother hen," Larry teased Dave, playfully. It quickly became evident that Dave's eating encouragement would not be necessary tonight. By this, their third night of acclimatization in Namche, their appetites, which had been lagging due to the effects of altitude, had returned to near-sea-level intensity, and they devoured a mouth-watering meal of chapattis—a traditional unleavened flat bread, *thak tok* soup, vegetable chow mein, fried rice, boiled eggs, and yellow chicken curry.

Dave kept careful watch of what each climber consumed and was glad to see everyone eat heartily, since the altitude and exertion on Everest would make eating a chore and would subsequently make it difficult to maintain one's weight. Losing ten to twenty pounds during the course of an Everest expedition was considered typical. Every bit of fat and energy they consumed now would provide the strength and sustenance they would require to work as reliable team members higher on the mountain. A weak climber would pose a threat both to themselves and to others. Just the night before, on their second night in Namche, Dave noticed that Bonny's plate was still full by the end of dinner. He glanced at Bonny and gently urged her to eat, half-joking, "This isn't the time to lose weight."

"I can't eat another thing," Bonny replied, running her fingers through her blonde bob and resting her forehead in her hand, and then, with a sudden wide-eyed look of surprise, "I think I'm going to be sick!" She leapt up from the table and hurried back to her room. Chhering followed a moment behind her. He knocked on her door.

"Do you need any help?"

"It's OK. I think I just need to throw up!" she called back, appreciative of Chhering's concern and kindness. "Thanks for checking on me!" she managed to shout before she vomited into the toilet. Afterward, she tried to nap, but the altitude sickness that had caused her nausea kept waking her up, making her feel like she was gasping for air. Today she felt tired, but better. Dave and Chhering were relieved to see her smiling again.

During his first trips to Everest, Dave had attributed his own chronic gastrointestinal distress, including persistent diarrhea and abdominal pain, to the viral and bacterial infections common to travelers. He joked about the conveniences of drop-seat long underwear that matched up with the horseshoe-shaped zipper across the backside of his down suit.

It wasn't until his second summit of Everest in 1999 when he became so inexplicably weak and anemic near the top that he felt, as he would later explain to his doctor, "like a carp flopping around on the kitchen floor." He recognized that his loss of strength was due to something other than run-of-the-mill traveler's intestinal distress or the typical agony of 29,000 feet; this felt more like being at 29,000 feet with a plastic bag tied over his head. He was forced to rely on his climbing partner, Conrad Anker, to help get him down, and the shame he felt about having potentially put Conrad's life in danger due to his own physical incapacity motivated him to return to the doctor he had seen once before, eight years earlier. After running a panel of blood tests, she sent him to a specialist for an endoscopy.

Dave was diagnosed with celiac disease, a genetic autoimmune disorder affecting the small intestine, caused by eating the gluten protein in wheat and other grains. Celiac disease robbed his blood of essential nutrients, like iron, causing anemia. He would have never guessed that the foods he was eating to fuel himself were the cause of his debilitating symptoms, but once he eliminated grains from his diet, he felt better and stronger than he had in years. He gave up pasta, cereal, beer, and bread. "Had I not been diagnosed, I could not have continued climbing," he later told his doctor, gratefully.

Dave was glad to observe there was no shortage of dinner conversation this evening, and plenty of evidence of bonding. He knew a sense of cohesiveness and camaraderie would enable the group to function well as a team and would foster a sense of obligation to look out for one another. They had spent the previous couple of days exploring the local attractions of Namche, and they were eager to share their stories. They had ducked out of rainstorms into Namche's popular bakeries to enjoy chocolate cake and cappuccino, made use of Wi-Fi at the cybercafes to contact their families and to friend each other on Facebook, trooped up to the top of town in order to speed up the acclimatization process, and visited the Sherpa Culture Museum. They had posed for photos alongside new bronze statues of Edmund Hillary and Tenzing Norgay at the National Park Headquarters. There, when the last high white tendrils of clouds had lifted, they had been awestruck by their first glimpses of the earth's highest mountain, the mountain the Sherpa people call Chomolungma, Mother Goddess of the Earth.

"I'm still fascinated by this mountain," Dave had said longingly. "After all these years, I can't stop looking . . . or stop wondering how her ridges and faces and couloirs connect."

The name Everest didn't arrive until 1865 when the British Geographical Society renamed the mountain they had previously referred to as Peak XV after the British surveyor general of India, Sir George Everest, in spite of the Nepali and Sherpa names for the mountain and in spite of George Everest's own objections. The Sherpas, roughly translating to "people from the East," were an ethnic group who migrated from Eastern Tibet into Nepal, specifically into the valleys near Chomolungma, or Mount Everest, five hundred years earlier, before the two regions became separate countries. Before the ancient ethnic community (of some 154,000 members) became synonymous with mountaineering, they were known mainly as nomadic cattle herders, high-altitude farmers, and salt traders. It wasn't until European climbers began arriving in the Khumbu in the early twentieth century to attempt to summit the world's highest peaks, ushering in an era of tourism, that Sherpas began working as high-altitude porters and eventually as renowned mountain guides. The first Sherpa porters on the British expeditions to the Tibet side of Everest did not even have a word in their language for "summit." They surmised that perhaps the British climbers were treasure hunters seeking gold. The Sherpas revered the highest mountain peaks as homes of the gods, not as goals to be conquered. The drive to scale these peaks was, in its essence, not a Sherpa concept but very much a Western one.

As Everest grew increasingly more commercialized, the term *sherpa* came to be associated with a job description, one usually but not necessarily filled by ethnic Sherpas: a logistical professional of a trekking group whose wide responsibilities might include supporting clients along the route, ferrying supplies, setting up camp, providing meals at camp, and ensuring client safety. On a spectrum, the job referred to as sherpa now ranges from high-altitude porter to expert technical mountain guide. The highest-altitude sherpa jobs, those on Everest itself, are considered to be the most elite, highly specialized, and dangerous, and as a result they earned higher pay: approximately four to five thousand US dollars per expedition, a fraction of what Western guides earn yet approximately eight times the annual per capita income in Nepal. Many ethnic Sherpas capitalize on the demands of tourism by running hotels, teahouses, and trekking companies; however, high-altitude agriculture remains the historical mainstay for the majority of the Sherpa population.

In 1953, Tenzing Norgay became the most famous Sherpa in the world when he and New Zealander Edmund Hillary became the first two people to summit Everest. The two men claimed the summit as a team and were part of a much larger, supported expedition that involved 362 porters, 20 Sherpa guides, and 10,000 pounds of baggage. The expedition had been commissioned and funded by the British government and led by British Army officer John Hunt. Much like the race to become the first country to put a man on the moon, there had erupted a fierce competition between Western nations to summit Everest first—particularly between the British, Swiss, and French—and news of the staggering accomplishment quickly traveled around the globe.

Twenty-five-year-old Chhering Dorjee had a sparse goatee and warm brown eyes rimmed by rectangular-framed glasses. He flashed a handsome, bright, easy smile and wore a Nepal flag pin in his baseball cap; its united crimson triangles, the color of Nepal's rhododendrons, were outlined by a blue border signifying peace. His calm and personable nature made it easy to forget that his work as the team's sherpa sirdar, or leader, was highly demanding and stressful. Chhering was tasked with hiring and managing the team of ten climbing sherpas who had gone up to Base Camp ahead of the team to prepare for their arrival. He was responsible for ensuring that this team of sherpas had the knowledge and training required for working in the infamously treacherous Icefall, making certain they were outfitted with the proper gear, monitoring their health, checking route conditions ahead of them, communicating with Dave, and helping to guide the clients on both the trek and through the technical climb of Everest.

Chhering was highly trained in route setting, climbing instruction, and deep-crevasse rescue. When he was twenty-three years old, he had become the youngest Nepalese to be certified by the International Federation of Mountain Guide Associations. His fluent English, Hindi, Tibetan, and Sherpa Nepali, as well as his conversational Spanish, French, and Japanese, enabled him to act as the sole liaison between the sherpas and Mark Tucker, Dave, JJ, and the clients. Chhering did not take his job lightly. Before he left Kathmandu, he confided in his wife, Yanzee, who was pregnant with their first child: "I have to make all the right decisions. They are all in my hands."

Chhering knew well from his seven years of experience on Everest that most mountaineers would not have a chance of reaching Everest's summit without the considerable aid of sherpas. Many Sherpas in the profoundly isolated villages of the Khumbu took on the strenuous and hazardous work as high-altitude "sherpas" so they could afford to give their children the education that would allow them opportunities to work outside of the mountain valleys. Some fell in love with climbing. Others did not. Regardless, the villages' historical ties to Everest were strong, and mountaineering had become a multigenerational line of work.

Chhering had been born in such a village. Every single one of the seventy-one families in the village of Bedhing, located near the Tibet border in the valley of Rolwaling, had at least one member, and in some families up to six or seven brothers, working as climbing sherpas. There were no schools in the remote village, and in the generation before Chhering's there were no opportunities for the village children to attend school in Kathmandu in order to be educated in other fields. Mountaineering work, however, was plentiful and readily available and allowed the villagers to earn enough money to send their children to school so they wouldn't have to work in the mountains.

Chhering was just two years old when his father, Nawan Chhiri Sherpa, died as a result of complications of food poisoning. After the death of his father, Chhering's older brother, Pemba Nurbu Sherpa, a Buddhist monk living in India, returned to Nepal and found work as a climbing sherpa in order to support his family: his mother, his four sisters, and his little brother, Chhering. Chhering spent his early childhood fetching water, collecting firewood, grazing cattle, carrying loads, and helping his grandmother with housework. With his earnings as a sherpa, Pemba paid for Chhering to attend school in Kathmandu beginning when Chhering was nine years old. Chhering adored and cherished Pemba.

In 2005, when Chhering was sixteen years old, Pemba went to work as a climbing sherpa for a French team on a 22,900-foot peak called Mount Kusum Kanguru, meaning "Three Snow White Gods" in reference to the mountain's distinctive triple summit. When a wall of snow hissed and roared into their base camp, Pemba and seventeen other climbers (including seven French climbers and ten other Nepalese Sherpas) were swept away. They disappeared into a deep gorge. The only four survivors of the expedition had been in the kitchen tent preparing tea for the others when they heard the thunder of the avalanche. Their tent had been blown to the side as a sea of white swallowed the rest of the tents. At the time that Pemba died, his wife was seven months pregnant with their first child.

Young Chhering had dreamed of becoming either a doctor or a software engineer, but after his brother's death he could no longer afford to attend Golden Peak High School in Kathmandu, much less to attend a university. Following his brother's example and honoring the sacrifices that Pemba had made on his family's behalf, Chhering left school and entered the same profession that had just killed his brother. According to Sherpa tradition, as the sole remaining male he would now be responsible for supporting his family. With no climbing experience and no formal mountaineering training, he found work as a climbing sherpa, one of the most dangerous jobs in the world.

By the time he was seventeen, Chhering began working as a "kitchen boy" on a Japanese expedition to 26,289-foot Shishapangma in Tibet. The following year he went to work on Everest for the first time. By the time he was nineteen, with shockingly little preparation and without any technical instruction, Chhering had summited Everest.

9 ⛰ TENGBOCHE MONASTERY

March 29, 2015
Posted by: Mark Tucker
Categories: Expedition Dispatches; Everest
Elevation: 13,000 feet

RMI EXPEDITIONS BLOG

Here I sit in a nice tea house at 13,000', half way through my eight day trek to Base Camp. Kind of a long commute to work. But the traffic has not been too bad. Yep another season of life on the glacier for this Himalayan Veteran. Excited for the RMI 2015 Everest Expedition? I sure am. . . . I wish you could be here. I know the challenges you face in everyday life may not be as unusual as ours but in their own way, they are just as impressive. Climb your own Everest! Get out when you can! Special Shout out to—MOM. HAPPY BIRTHDAY! Love, Mark

On March 29, 2015, the team set out from Namche at 8:30 in the morning beneath a powder-blue sky. They trekked the five hours across the hillside, down to the river, across a long, rickety suspension bridge, back across the bigger hill at Tengboche, and down its other side to Deboche, where they spent the night in a cozy teahouse located next to a modest Buddhist nunnery, the oldest convent in Nepal. The convent was in the midst of a much-needed renovation that would provide running water to the ten nuns, young and old, who lived there year-round, studying and practicing the teachings of the Buddha. The nuns, their heads shaved in a display of humility and monastic devotion to their holy life, began each day with a prayer that all sentient beings might find happiness through compassion and loving kindness. Since the convent's inception, they had grown their own food and collected fresh water from nearby streams, labor that became especially difficult and sometimes treacherous during the Khumbu's frigid winters.

In the morning, Dave found it was not easy to leave the comfort of sipping milk tea near the wood-burning stove in the common room of their lodge to step out into the cold at an altitude of 12,325 feet. Soon enough, however, he became enchanted by the shadowy fir, paper birch, and rhododendron forests of Deboche as they made the short, fifteen-minute walk from their teahouse to Tengboche. Mark Tucker was a couple of days ahead of them on the trail to Base Camp, in the village of Pheriche.

While they climbed the last of the trail up toward the Tengboche Monastery, 22,349-foot, elegant Ama Dablam welcomed the team with the outstretched arms of her lower extending ridges in what felt like a warm embrace. In the hollow of her throat hung a jewel of ice, gleaming in the sunlight. It was reminiscent of the traditional pendants containing pictures of the gods worn by the elder Sherpa women. "Ama Dablam translates to 'mother's necklace' or 'mother's charm box' in the Sherpa language," Chhering explained.

Dave couldn't help but notice that the mountain's glimmering gem, an improbable hanging glacier, appeared less than half the size it had been when he first visited the Khumbu fifteen years earlier. Global warming had been causing a visible and hasty glacial retreat. Ama's "dablam" had been melting and deteriorating, causing instability. It seemed inevitable that should global temperatures remain warm, the ice that was effectively gluing the dablam to the mountain would eventually disappear. The hanging glacier would peel off and crash down. Dave wondered how long the jewel would remain—and how long there would be glaciers on Earth left to climb. There was no way to know if Ama Dablam, like his own mother, would be left with a scar at her throat.

They stepped through an ornate pagoda and climbed up a set of steep stone steps. Then Dave opened the doors of the monastery. The low buzzing hum of chanting monks resonated through the building and their bodies. Butter lamps flickered in copper chalices. Shafts of muted daylight filtered through the white-curtained, square windows, illuminating the ornately decorated room. Its intricate carvings, paintings, and hanging silk tapestries were composed in a visual feast of rich colors that, like those of the prayer flags, signified the elements: yellow, earth; red, fire; green, wood; white, iron; blue, sky and water. A golden statue of Buddha sat serenely on the altar, surrounded by a sculpted garden of carved wooden leaves and flowers. The smell of juniper incense permeated the air as curls of smoke floated toward the ceiling. The monks—clad in burgundy robes, their heads shaved—sat crossed-legged on cushions and faced the Buddha as they chanted their rhythmic prayers.

Chhering thought of his older brother. Pemba had been taken by their uncle to Golden Temple, India, when he was just two years old to begin his training to become a monk. Their uncle was believed to be a reincarnated monk himself and was therefore of high ranking in the Buddhist religion. In Tibetan Buddhism, a lama was considered to be one of a lineage of reincarnated spiritual leaders, the most famous of which was the Dalai Lama. Rebirth or reincarnation was believed to be determined by the karmas, or the actions of body, speech, and mind during previous lives. Good deeds in this life would result in positive karma and a better reincarnation in one's next life. As Tengboche's resident Reincarnate Lama liked to teach visitors, the Buddhist ways aimed to generate spiritual energy to benefit all beings by evolving consciousness of the heart and mind.

In Buddhism, the spirits of protective gods were embodied in nature. Sherpas belonged to the ancient school of Tibetan Buddhism, called Nyingmapa, which also incorporated local deities of the pre-Buddhist Bon religion. The founder of Nyignmapa, Padmasambhava, was believed to have been reincarnated as an eight-year-old boy who appeared sitting in a lotus blossom on a lake. The serene and smiling Padmasambhava, also known as Guru Rinpoche, later escaped the palace life he rejected and fled to the forests and mountains where he spent time meditating in a cave high above the nearby village of Khumjung. The handprints on the cave walls were said to be his.

Khumjung was also home to the largest school in the Khumbu, with over 350 students. Founded by Edmund Hillary in 1961, children from around the Khumbu streamed to the school, many walking for hours through the valley to attend classes there. Tourists were drawn to Khumjung for another reason. Inside its small village monastery was a padlocked, glass box containing a hairy, half-football-shaped object that had once been purported to be the scalp of Yeti.

The shaggy, ape-human creature of the Yeti, a rich part of Himalayan folklore, had its origins in Sherpa stories that had likely been told to warn children about the dangers of wild animals and to keep them from wandering too far from their village. When an early British Everest explorer spotted some large footprints in the snow, which he attributed to "an abominable snowman," the more modern version of the Yeti legend was born, sparking a fierce cryptozoological hunt. Western expeditions, including Sir Edmund Hilary's 1960 expedition, were launched to find the mythical creature. Animal skulls, bones, scat, and hair found near Everest, including the purported Yeti "scalp" now kept in the box in Khumjung, were carried across the globe for laboratory analysis. When DNA testing was later developed, it confirmed earlier findings that most of the samples, some of which were collected as early as the 1930s, came from the endangered Himalayan brown bear and the Himalayan black bear. The rest of the samples, including the Khumjung "scalp," were revealed to have come from other animals native to the area such as goats and antelopes. In spite of this debunking, the lure of the mythical Yeti persisted.

The teahouses in the Khumbu lining the route to Everest had historically been Sherpa homes, and long before climbers trekked to Everest, the Sherpa families living in these homes had welcomed and hosted visitors on religious pilgrimages to the Tengboche Monastery. Much as it had for Guru Rinpoche, the isolated Khumbu Valley for centuries had provided safe refuge for those seeking sanctuary. The Khumbu's most famous peak continued to attract pilgrims from all over the world, whether climbers and trekkers captivated by the highest place on Earth or those coming to pay homage to the goddess embodied in its Tibetan name, Chomolungma or Jomolungma, meaning "Goddess Mother." The name was derived from Jomo Miyo Lang Sangma, the protective, beautiful, golden mother goddess believed to be the resident deity of Everest. One of the five sisters of long life, Jomo Miyo Ling Sangma rode a red tiger and wore brightly colored robes and a garland of orange flowers on her head. In light of her virtuous generosity, she was also known as The Goddess of Inexhaustible Giving. She carried a bowl of fruit in her left hand and a jewel-spitting mongoose in her right one.

As he prayed for his brother in the monastery, Chhering wondered momentarily whether or not Pemba had experienced *kan runu*, or "crying ear," before the avalanche that killed him had struck. The older generation of Sherpas, more than his generation, believed that danger was sometimes preceded by the premonitory phenomenon of a buzzing, high-pitched sound in one's ear. Chhering's prayers for his brother reached upward with the wreathes of incense smoke.

Tonight the team would spend another night acclimatizing in Deboche. Tomorrow they would visit the revered Lama Geshi at his home in nearby Pangboche to seek both his permission to climb and his blessing for safety as they headed higher into the mountains. Chomolungma, the mountain home of the Goddess Mother of the World riding her tiger sidesaddle across the sky, felt near now.

10 ⛰ PANGBOCHE

March 30, 2015
Posted by: Dave Hahn
Categories: Expedition Dispatches; Everest
Elevation: 12,325 feet
Satellite phone transcript

RMI EXPEDITIONS BLOG

Hey this is Dave Hahn, phoning in from the RMI Everest Climb.
We are in Deboche still. Last night, I couldn't get a call through.
It was snowing fairly hard and I couldn't get a phone signal.
This morning, it looks a little better—a little sunshine coming
through. There are still some high clouds. But right now we're
at a green light to go up to Pheriche. Our intention is to go up
through Pangboche, see Lama Geshe, and head up to Pheriche
this evening. Yesterday was a nice, quiet day for us. We went up
to the Tengboche Monastery in the morning and then kind of
hunkered down in our tea house here in Deboche to wait out the
snowstorm. It was a nice afternoon of taking it easy. Bye now.

Dave led the pack through four inches of freshly fallen snow, from the
shadowy cedar and fir forest of Deboche toward Lama Geshe's home in
the nearby village of Pangboche. The snow muffled the sounds of their
footsteps and their voices. Dave hiked like a mountain goat, strong-
legged and sure-footed, his broad shoulders and backpack angled
forward. The movement of his long body was so deliberate it almost
appeared slow. Lifting his chin up toward the sky, he noticed the wind-
sculpted lenticulars and the cat's paw clouds hovering over Everest and
Lhotse. Views of the hundred or so other astonishing mountains in their
panorama were free of obstruction.

"Lama Geshe's very friendly," he explained to the team. "He's welcoming us into his place, his people, and he always gives us such a warm welcome. His prayers are basically asking for help in keeping us from, well, killing ourselves." Dave smiled. "His joy is pretty infectious. He'll put us in the perfect state of mind for climbing higher."

The trail led them to a home nestled in pine trees. They walked down the steps into a courtyard surrounded by a fence made of stone and earth. Prayer flags fluttered above them. Copper bells chimed in the breeze. They entered the home through a short wooden door and found themselves in a narrow, dark hallway that smelled of juniper incense, warm milk, and musty wax candles. The kitchen to their right was separated from the hallway by a cotton curtain, and around the corner appeared another curtain. Chhering pulled it aside, and there sat the adored Lama Geshe, wearing garnet robes and a gold silk sash, sitting cross-legged on a bench near the bright window, smiling.

Lama Geshe's tiny, round-faced wife shuffled into the room right behind them, holding a kettle of hot milk tea. The eleven-member team quickly consumed the space of the small room and eventually each of them found a seat on the padded wooden benches lining the walls. They all fidgeted a bit like nervous schoolchildren in the presence of the most revered Lama in the Khumbu, one who was widely believed to commune with the mountains, but eighty-four-year-old Lama Geshe's quick laugh soon put them at ease. Behind them, plastered on the wall, were at least a hundred summit photos of climbers who had been blessed by Lama Geshe and who had made it safely back down. Lama Geshe had escaped Tibet in 1947 and had migrated to Nepal, settling in Pangboche near the monastery, beneath the protective gaze of Ama Dablam.

Dave did not consider himself religious, although his mother was Lutheran and his father was Jewish. Dave had been raised Lutheran growing up, even after his mother's death, which he assumed his father had continued out of respect for his mother, but Dave had drifted away from organized religion during college. Still, the verse he had always known as the Golden Rule ("Do unto others as you would have others do unto you") remained a touchstone for him, and he felt a tide of goodwill rise up in him as Lama Geshe ever cheerful, began the prayer ceremony.

One by one, Lama Geshe called them up to him. As each climber walked toward him and sat in the plastic chair in front of him, Lama Geshe wrote a letter to the mountain as a prayer beseeching that climber's safety. On his simple table altar sat a brass-handled bell and a *bumpa*, a teapot-shaped ceremonial vase filled with peacock feathers. Since peacocks were able to safely consume venomous snakes and poisonous plants, their feathers symbolized purification, transformation, and the ability to thrive in the face of suffering.

Lama Geshe handed Robbie his prayer card. Then he draped a white, silk khata scarf over Robbie's broad shoulders. He picked up a saffron-red string from the table and tied it around Robbie's neck with a loose knot, which represented his prayer to the goddess for his safety. For the duration of the blessing, he looked Robbie straight in the eyes, then ducked his head and giggled as he gave him a gentle head-butt. He repeated the same ritual for each of them. Chhering later explained to Robbie and the rest of the team that tradition dictated that they should wear the string until it fell off. "Lama Geshe said, 'Don't take it off until it falls off, unless you need to remove it for dental work or surgery,'" he translated.

After he had blessed each of the climbers in the same fashion, Lama Geshe gave Dave a pouch of rice he had blessed for him to carry through the Khumbu Icefall, or whenever he otherwise felt danger to be near, for the protection of the team. He completed the ceremony by chanting prayers and ringing the bell. The bell represented wisdom, which when paired with compassion, symbolized by a nearby *dorje*—a small brass club with a sphere on each end—would lead to enlightenment. According to Buddhist teachings, wisdom and compassion should always exist together, never apart. While smiling and laughing, he reminded them, as Chhering later translated, to keep their thoughts positive, to forgive mistakes, and to be good to other people.

HP cradled his folded prayer card in his hands. On its exterior were three small illustrations of Everest. The top-left image depicted Everest as the head of a mountain resting in a sea of sky below the moon and sun. On the top right was a picture of Everest and two smaller mountaintops emerging from a swirling ocean, below the moon, sun, stars, and clouds. Below these, the third illustration portrayed Everest in it its entirety, surrounded by lesser peaks, with rivers running from the mountains through the verdant green valleys below it. These visual connections of Everest to water resonated deeply for HP. The three most commonly used names for the mountain—the British name Everest, the Tibetan name Chomolungma, and the Nepali name Sagarmatha—had each sprung from different cultures. Born in India, HP had been raised in the Hindu faith. In the Hindi language, Sagarmatha literally meant the forehead or head of the sea or ocean. Seeing images capturing this on his prayer card validated a personal connection HP felt between his Indian heritage and the mountain he had set out to climb.

After Lama Geshe finished his blessing, they wished him goodbye and "namaste" and set out for Shomare, where they would have lunch at a teahouse before making their final push for Pheriche. On the trail, HP shared with Dave how the depiction of the sea on the prayer card had moved him.

As Dave and HP chatted, HP found it humbling to imagine that 470 million years earlier, the sea floor of the Tethys Ocean had been carried north, had become caught up in the tectonic collision zone between India and Eurasia, and eventually had been lifted up to form the highest mountain on Earth. The fossils of tiny marine invertebrate animals had been found in the limestone near the summit of Everest ever since the very first expeditions up the mountain. In the spring of 1924, British geologist Noel Odell had climbed to the North Col where he collected samples from the banded layers of rock he found. Odell published a report a year later, exclaiming his discovery: "At about 25,000 feet I came upon a limestone band which to my joy contained fossils—the first definite forms found on Everest!" At every turn, Everest reminded HP of his insignificance in the grand scheme of things. Coming to the Khumbu from his job as a global executive in Dallas, and from a world where he felt social media seemed to amplify and exaggerate everyone's individual importance, including his own, HP found this sense of perspective to be an enormous relief.

From Shomare they proceeded to Pheriche, sharing the trail with yak trains carrying loads to and from Everest Base Camp. The bells around their burly necks clanging, these yaks were notably brawnier and more stubborn about sharing the trails than the yaks they had seen below Namche, most of which Dave had clarified were actually Dzokials, or crosses between these imposing high-altitude yaks and lowland cows. The topography, too, changed as they climbed higher. No longer were they in the sheltering forests of Deboche. As they ascended above the tree line, they moved through open tundra with low-lying juniper to a barren, windswept rocky plateau that more closely resembled the surface of Mars.

Having gained 1,500 feet in altitude since they first set out from Deboche that morning, they finally rounded the big sweeping corner around the jagged mountain Tawatse and headed north into the remote settlement of Pheriche, which consisted of a collection of eight or so teahouses, a few farms, some yak pasturing land, and the Himalayan Rescue Association clinic. Soon enough they spotted the Himalayan Hotel, a stark yet spacious teahouse and lodge built from grey stones and green corrugated tin. Their understanding of the word *hotel* had broadened while in the Khumbu to incorporate these hostel-like accommodations, and they were unanimously glad to see the place that would be their home for the next couple of nights waiting for them. They knew tent life would begin soon enough.

Harold, Ron, Dave, and Carolyn Hahn in Yosemite, 1975.
Courtesy of Dave Hahn.

Dave Hahn. Courtesy of
International Mountain Guides.

Elizabeth Hawley.
Courtesy of Stock.

A porter carries a heavy load
of lumber on the trail.
Courtesy of Larry Seaton.

Lukla. Courtesy of Larry Seaton.

Dave Hahn and the RMI team cross a suspension bridge.
Courtesy of Robert Massie.

Erin Machinchik, Robbie Massie, Hemanshu Parwarni, and Hao Wu take a break at a teahouse. Courtesy of Dave Hahn.

Namche Bazaar. Courtesy of Robert Massie.

Geshe blesses Robbie Massie with Chhering Dorjee Sherpa looking on. Courtesy of Erin Machinchik.

Everest prayer card. Courtesy of Bonny Rogers.

Ama Dablam. Courtesy of Robert Massie.

Dave Hahn with Ang Phinjo, on the summit of Cho Oyu
in 1995. Courtesy of Dave Hahn.

The Dudh Kosi. Courtesy of Robert Massie.

Dave Hahn, Larry Seaton, Peter Rogers, Hans Hilscher, Hao Wu, Hemanshu Parwani, JJ Justman, and Robbie Massie. Courtesy of Dave Hahn.

Erin Machinchik, Robbie Massie, Bonny Rogers, Peter Rogers, Hao Wu, Larry Seaton, Hemanshu Parwani, Hans Hilscher, and porter. Courtesy of Dave Hahn.

Trekking. Courtesy of Robert Massie.

Yak train. Courtesy of Robert Massie.

Larry Seaton arrives at Base Camp. Courtesy of Robert Massie.

Sherpa team; *top row*: Nima Wangchu Sherpa, Pasang Temba Sherpa, Chhering Dorjee Sherpa, Chetan Bhote, Rinjin Bhote; *bottom row*: Yuba Raj Rai, Lapka Gyaljen Sherpa, Densa Bhote, Fura Sonam Sherpa, Pasang Bhote (Pemba Norbu Sherpa not pictured). Courtesy of Dave Hahn.

Gorak Shep. Courtesy of Robert Massie

RMI Sherpa team photos posted at
Base Camp. Courtesy of Dave Hahn.

Hans, HP, and Hao.
Courtesy of Dave Hahn.

Puja. Courtesy of
Robert Massie.

Chhering Dorjee Sherpa.
Courtesy of Robert Massie.

11 ⛰ PHERICHE

April 1, 2015
Posted by: Dave Hahn
Categories: Expedition Dispatches; Everest
Elevation: 15,500 feet
Satellite phone transcript

RMI EXPEDITIONS BLOG

Dave Hahn calling in from Pheriche on our Everest climb.
Hey, we're still in blackout zone—a temporary blackout for all
internet and cell phones, so I'm calling from the satellite phone.
It's our last night in Pheriche tonight. We had a great easy day
here in Pheriche. The team went hiking this morning about
1,500 feet above Pheriche, about 15,500' or so. It was a nice hike
and nice views of Makalu the 5th highest mountain. We had
views of Lhotse, Cho Oyu the 6th highest mountain, great views
all around. . . .We attended a high altitude medicine lecture that
was given by the Himalayan Rescue Association next door in
the afternoon. We then had a pretty easy afternoon of resting,
playing games, reading and nice dinner. A treat for us: Casey
Grom's Base Camp and Island Peak Trekking Group fresh from
Base Camp shared the . . . dining room with us for the evening
It was nice to visit with some friends. We're looking forward to
moving up to Lobuche. [The weather] is currently nice, but we
will see what we get this evening. All things being equal we'll be
in Lobuche tomorrow. We will keep you informed.

In remote, barren, and windswept Pheriche, where short, hardy grasses and mosses clinging to dirt and rock were the only vegetation to be found, altitude announced its presence more loudly than it had yet. While it was technically a rest day for the team, their bodies were hard at work. Headaches set in as their brains grew hungry for more oxygen. Sleeping became more challenging and their appetites all but evaporated. The very pH of their blood was altering as their hearts and lungs struggled to compensate for the increasing loss of atmospheric pressure. Their mantra of "climb high, sleep low" resonated deeply now, as it was one of the few strategies at their disposal to give their bodies a fighting chance to adjust to the thin air.

Physiologically speaking, climbing a couple of thousand feet higher than their sleeping altitude and then recuperating at a lower altitude would allow their bodies to acclimate more efficiently. The climb to the higher altitude would spur their bodies to produce more red blood cells, and the sleep at the lower altitude would allow their bodies to accomplish this more rapidly and with fewer complications.

Assessing that most of the team was feeling relatively well at breakfast, considering their recent gain in elevation and how much worse they had looked the previous day, Dave hiked them later that morning to about 1,500 feet above Pheriche under the partial pretense of enjoying the epic views. And while the giant white peaks of Lhotse, Makalu, and Cho Oyu—the fourth-, fifth-, and sixth-highest mountains in the world—never failed to impress and astound, his team remained quite aware that Dave's ulterior motive was, as always, acclimatization.

In addition to contending with the 15,500-foot altitude, Peter had also been experiencing diarrhea, abdominal cramps, and fatigue—symptoms of the type of bacterial gastrointestinal infections commonly picked up in the crowded teahouses and lodges during the trek. Peter had grown worried, recognizing that illness and dehydration would only serve to decrease the resources his body could use to acclimatize. When they arrived in Pheriche, he decided to pay a visit to the nearby Himalayan

Rescue Association (HRA) clinic, a nonprofit health clinic staffed by volunteer doctors from around the globe, housed in a humble, two-room, stacked-stone structure with a blue metal roof. The doctor on call gave Peter antibiotics from the clinic pharmacy to fight his infection. "Gastrointestinal infections account for the majority of the visits to our clinic," she mentioned, "followed by upper respiratory ailments."

Larry's dry and persistent cough was one such respiratory ailment common in the Khumbu. Often referred to as the "Khumbu cough," it was caused by the lower humidity and cold temperatures at such high altitudes and could be triggered by overexertion. The cough could restrict breathing, could sometimes crack ribs, and was not limited to the Khumbu region; it was also known as the "high-altitude hack." Since it was not caused by infection, but rather from dried-out lung membranes and irritated bronchi, there was little that could be done to treat it other than humidification of the air. Plugging in a humidifier, however, was not a realistic prospect in either a teahouse or a tent. Drinking plenty of fluids, avoiding overexertion, and wearing a bandana over his mouth at night to trap moisture were recommended.

With her reduced kidney function, Erin's body was working overtime to adapt. The increased production of red blood cells, which allows the body to compensate for the decrease in available oxygen at high altitude, begins in the kidneys. Back in Namche, Erin began taking Diamox, a medication that forced the kidneys to excrete bicarbonate, re-acidifying the blood and stimulating respiration, the net effect of which was to accelerate acclimatization. She decided to check in with a doctor at the HRA clinic while in Pheriche. The doctor refilled her Diamox prescription and helped her adjust her daily regimen so she would have the proper dosage to help her kidneys continue to initiate her body's acclimatization throughout the remainder of the trek.

At 3:00 in the afternoon, after their hike and lunch, Dave walked the team over to the HRA clinic for its daily high-altitude medicine lecture. They stepped into a small, bright, primitive, yurt-like structure containing some folding chairs and a small chalkboard. The young American physician scheduled to give today's lecture stood up front and introduced herself to them. An instructor in emergency medicine at Harvard, she was in the midst of completing a two-year wilderness medicine fellowship and had recently begun a two-month stint volunteering at the HRA clinic in Pheriche. A stethoscope dangled over the shoulder of her black down jacket. Her long brown hair was pulled back in a ponytail below a ski hat, and she wore her sunglasses inside the bright structure. Once they had all gathered inside, she invited them to measure their blood oxygen saturation levels by placing a finger in a small blue pulse oximeter, a device that monitors the balance of oxygen in the blood. She informed them that normal oxygen saturation would measure between 95 and 100. Then the doctor began her medical lecture with what she called the golden rule of acclimatization.

"If you are ill at altitude," she said, "assume it is due to altitude unless proven otherwise."

She added: "Remember, there's no way to predict how well your physiology will allow you to acclimate since a body's ability to acclimatize has very little correlation to any other factors, including fitness." She encouraged the climbers to drink a lot of fluids, to take acclimatization hikes, and to take rest days, all of which would help give the body's physiology a much-needed chance to catch up to the demands of altitude.

"Now let's talk about protecting eyes . . ."

Bonny, an acupuncture provider, was intrigued by the physiological impacts of altitude. She was surprised to learn that the lack of oxygen and the greater ultraviolet radiation at high altitude could result in changes in the thickness of the cornea. It could also cause cataracts and the formation of benign growths on the clear tissue that covers the eyeballs. Polarized or reflective sunglasses were advised.

The doctor went on to warn that, if ignored, the typical symptoms of acute mountain sickness—like headache, insomnia, shortness of breath, lack of appetite, and nausea—could quickly evolve into symptoms of more serious conditions like High-Altitude Cerebral Edema (HACE), a brain injury caused by increased intracranial pressure resulting from swelling in the brain. Its symptoms were similar to those of a stroke. She explained that High-Altitude Pulmonary Edema, when fluid collected in the lungs, was another looming threat. Shallow rattling breaths, blue skin tone, a rapid heartbeat, and a cough that produced pink, frothy sputum were symptoms that indicated HAPE. When fluid blocked the passage of oxygen into the lungs, she told them, the resulting suffocation was akin to drowning.

"HAPE is rarer than HACE but it's more deadly and kills more people," she noted, adding that both were life-threatening emergencies that would require oxygen, steroids, and immediate descent to a lower altitude. She stressed that Nepali porters and guides, particularly those who lived at lower elevations near Pokhara or Kathmandu, were just as susceptible to altitude sickness as foreign trekkers and climbers. Therefore, she insisted, each team member should remain alert not only to their own symptoms but also to those of their fellow trekkers, porters, and guides.

"Pay attention to the signs of someone not acclimating well, such as dizziness or confusion or a lack of coordination. Never ascend with symptoms. Descend if symptoms increase. Look out for each other," she concluded.

After the lecture, the team meandered back to the lodge. They passed the rest of the afternoon eating; reading worn paperback books and abandoned; outdated copies of *Time* magazine; and visiting with climbers and trekkers from other teams, including a group who had just made the seven-hour, twelve-mile trek down from Base Camp and were now delighting in the relatively thick air in lower Pheriche. While they all relaxed together in the common room, one of the trekkers in the lodge snapped a photo of Dave on her phone.

"I recognize you. You're Dave Hahn, right?" she said. "You sure look an awful lot like him," she added, looking past him.

Dave turned around. The woman explained that she was aware of Dave's record number of Everest ascents. She had also noticed the remarkable resemblance between Dave and the portrait of Sir Edmund Hillary that was hanging on the wall behind him. In the portrait, Hillary sat in the foreground of Everest, his large hands resting on the head of his ice axe, his climbing rope hanging over his left shoulder. Hillary's long, angular face, strong jaw, mop of brown hair, large hands, weathered complexion, and serene yet intense expression were, she insisted, the spitting image of Dave. Dave felt a little embarrassed by the attention and politely shrugged off the comparison to perhaps the most famous mountaineer in history, but he couldn't entirely deny the likeness.

Dave was focused, as always, on his team. He encouraged them to snack as much as possible to keep calorie intake up and energy levels high. Here in Pheriche, it was still possible to buy much-coveted, familiar American junk food like Snickers bars and Coke, although they cost more at this higher end of the valley. Having witnessed the porters on the trail carrying heavy loads of such goods on their backs all the way to remote settlements like Pheriche, it was easy to see why, and most climbers were more than happy to splurge on such comforting indulgences while they still had the opportunity. Dave also kept an eye on the weather, hoping they wouldn't get too much snow during the night. He aimed to be in Lobuche, their last stop before Base Camp, by tomorrow afternoon, and he felt eager to get going.

12 ⛰ THOK LA

April 2, 2015

Posted by: Dave Hahn, JJ Justman

Categories: Expedition Dispatches; Everest

Elevation: 16,000 feet

RMI EXPEDITIONS BLOG

Conditions were nice enough for walking, but it was a little
on the cool side and not conducive to hanging out for long.
The first glance at the sky today had us thinking we'd be walking
in another snowstorm, but things cleared up well enough while
we ate breakfast. We had fine views of Taboche, Cholatse,
Pumori, Nuptse and Ama Dablam along with a half dozen
other Himalayan giants . . .

The team moved out of Pheriche on a brisk morning and headed toward
Thukla, or Dukla as some preferred to call it, hiking on a narrow trail
that hugged the mountain on one side and dropped off steeply on the
other. They shared a chuckle when they reached a painted yellow sign
proclaiming "Welcome to Thukla & Dukla" hanging below the skull of a
long-horned yak on the side of an old teahouse made of earthen bricks.
The huge piles of rough rocks they noticed near Dukla marked the terminal moraine, or edge, of the Khumbu Glacier and represented the
extent of the glacier's advance during the last Ice Age. From there, they
began a long, steady climb up the hill toward the glacier's prominent
lateral moraine, or side, which would be home to those of them climbing
Everest for the next seven weeks.

After two hours of hiking up vast, gravelly terrain, they reached
level ground atop the Thok La pass, where they came upon an other-
worldly panoply of stone memorials to fallen Everest climbers in the
foreground of a panorama of white clouds hanging low in the vast sea

of snow-covered peaks, which were so near now and stunning they did not seem remotely real. The dozens of remembrance chortens of varying shapes and sizes, some marked and others unmarked, formed what looked like a sprawling graveyard. It was apparent that the bewildering number of stacked-stone towers had been erected by hand, stone by carefully stacked stone. Colorful strings of prayer flags connected one monument to the next, one soul to another.

For Dave, the chortens at Thok La always served as a sobering reminder of Everest's human toll, at a point in the journey when he was typically chomping at the bit to climb the very mountain that had exacted it. As they wandered between the monuments, he, JJ, and Chhering remembered the friends who did not make it home.

JJ reached out to touch the engraved brass plaque on a chest-high table and rubbed his forefinger across the indentations of the words *Late Babu Chiri Sherpa*. Layers of weathered and torn prayer flags were wrapped around the wide chorten like a fluttering patchwork quilt. He read the rest of the epitaph, composed in slightly broken English:

> Babu Chiri Sherpa was born on June 22, 1965 in Taksindu,
> Chhulemu, Solukkhumbu. At the very young age of 13, he started
> his career as a climber. By the age of 36, he had summit Everest
> 10 times, twice in two weeks, spent an unprecedented 21 hours on
> the summit without the aid of auxiliary oxygen and became the
> fastest climber of the world highest peak climbing in 16 hours 56
> minutes, thus creating two unique world records on Everest. On
> Sunday the 29th of April, 2001, while on his way to summit of
> Mt. Everest for the 11th time, he fell into a 200 ft. deep crevasse.
> This extraordinary cimber left this world. May his soul rest in
> peace and his dream be fulfilled.

JJ admired Babu, not just for his astounding mountaineering feats but also for his shattering of Sherpa myths and his ambitions to modernize the way Westerners viewed the Sherpa people. Although he died at the young age of thirty-five, Babu Sherpa had put his six daughters through private school in Kathmandu and had built a school in his home village to fulfill his dream of creating more educational and career opportunities for Sherpa children. He had worked tirelessly toward cultivating greater respect for Sherpa mountaineers.

JJ had narrowly escaped death himself on Everest in 2006, when a massive serac, or a block of glacial ice, fell in the Khumbu Icefall shortly after dawn, crushing sherpas Ang Phinjo, Lhakpa Tseri, and Dawa Tempa. JJ had been just ahead of them on the trail. He was haunted by the notion that he had cheated death by what he estimated to be one minute. At Thok La, he valued the opportunity to pay his respects to the men who had not survived.

Ang Phinjo was fifty years old and on his forty-ninth expedition to an 8,000-meter peak when he was killed in the Icefall that day. Runners had been sent down the valley to deliver the devastating news to his family and friends in his home village. Dave felt the loss acutely. Phijo had been a friend, a coworker, and a comrade who had looked after him in the mountains for fifteen years. They had shared a blissful summit on Cho Oyu, the world's sixth-highest peak, in 1995. It had been Phinjo's first summit, but Dave knew that he had been capable of many more; Phinjo had simply deferred his own summit opportunities in order to aid others in attaining theirs. Ever after their shared summit, Phinjo had greeted Dave with a cheerful and affectionate "Attu tambu," which Dave understood roughly translated to "Hello, brother." Dave could still see Phinjo's bright smile, and he wished he had hugged Phinjo when he last saw him, at Base Camp, on the night before he died. He cherished the photos he had of them standing together on top of Cho Oyu in the sunshine. One of the photos in particular remained imprinted on Dave's mind, and as he stood among the chortens, the image appeared to him as if he were watching it being exposed in a darkroom. It was a snapshot of himself, bearded and sweaty in a purple-and-red down suit, standing beside Phinjo, who wore a green suit and red goggles and held a Nepalese flag in one hand. They both beamed euphorically. In the landscape of Ang Phinjo's selflessness and generosity of spirit, the image was a close-up of camaraderie and joy.

Dave thought of Thok La as both a solemn place of remembrance and an unofficial boundary between the inhabitable valleys below it and the more inhospitable terrain of rock and ice above it. He gazed back toward Pheriche and rested his eyes on the hastening, silver Dudh Khosi River twisting through the valley below as it flowed down toward the Bay of Bengal in the Indian Ocean. It brought Dave comfort to know the Dudh Khosi would merge with other rivers along its thousand-mile journey. From Thok La, they proceeded quietly, still tethered to spirits and memory, toward Lobuche, hiking the last hour on relatively flat, snow-covered ground.

At 16,000 feet, the small, grim settlement of Lobuche sat frigid and still. Everything seemed to move slower at this end of the valley, including their minds and bodies. As they entered Lobuche, they followed a train of massive yaks en route to Base Camp, burdened with cumbersome loads wrapped in nylon tarps. As the laden yaks lumbered up the trail, their hooves clicking against rock, the bells around their brawny necks jingled and jangled in chorus. The yak drivers yipped and whistled. The team followed the noisy procession until they reached their final teahouse, which appeared from the outside to be the most primitive yet. Inside it felt cold and damp, but they were delighted to find themselves back in the land of Internet, with a squat toilet down the hallway and hot lemon tea to boot.

The next morning, Larry was woken by a worsening cough, which he attributed to both the new altitude and the smoke in the lodge from the yak dung that was mixed with kerosene and burned in a potbelly stove in the common room for heat. Here above the tree line in the Khumbu, patties of yak dung were pressed to the outsides of the homes and lodges, facing the sun, to dry. While trekking up to Lobuche, Larry had noticed children in the fields collecting them in baskets. The dung provided a cheap and readily available source of fuel but produced particulate matter that could cause respiratory irritation when inhaled.

The team minus Peter, who was still suffering from a gastrointestinal infection, spent part of the morning exploring. They scrambled over the rocks and sediment deposited along the side of the Khumbu Glacier, on its lateral moraine. Vertiginous Nuptse stood directly ahead of them, but their eyes kept straying toward Everest Base Camp.

"It isn't very far now," Dave said. "We'll be there tomorrow with any luck." He pointed out the peaks surrounding it, identifying them wistfully: "Pumori, Lingtren, Khumbutse . . ."

"Well, first things first," he interrupted himself. He led the team on a short hike to the nearby Italian research pyramid, a gleaming glass structure situated incongruously in the remote landscape. The pyramid was home to an atmospheric and glacial science lab and observatory, otherwise known as Ev-K2-CNR. As they hiked up to the highest research station in the world, seated in a rocky pocket of mountainside, they noticed the rectangular solar panels used to power it, tilted upward toward the sky. On the south side of the isolated pyramid was a simple stone building, resembling the lodges where they had been staying, which provided accommodations for up to twenty researchers, technicians, and logistical staff. One of the staff, an Italian scientist, came out to greet them and offered to give them a tour of the facilities.

"It all started in 1986," he began, "when an American expedition declared K2 was taller than Everest . . ."

The scientist went on to explain that Italian geologist and cartographer Ardito Desio and climber Agostino da Polenza could not resist the challenge and launched the Ev-K2-CNR Project in collaboration with the Italian Research Council. Together they put mountaineering at the service of science and organized expeditions to re-measure both mountains using traditional survey techniques and the latest GPS technology. After verifying Everest's title as the world's tallest mountain, they went on to form the Ev-K2-CNR committee with the goal of continuing scientific research at high altitude.

Some of the hundreds of studies conducted at the pyramid laboratory since its inception in 1990 included the development of new technologies to thermally treat waste in high-mountain parks in order to reduce the environmental impact of waste disposal, a monitoring program on the endangered snow leopard and its prey species, and research on the impact of altitude on human cognitive abilities. Another involved a tectonic evaluation of the Himalayan mountain chain.

Since the Himalayas were being pushed higher at a rate of 1.77 inches per year by the collision of the Indian subcontinent into Asia, friction between the plates continued to build up energy along a thrust fault, where one part of the earth is pushed up and over another segment of the earth. In neighboring Kashmir, a 2005 earthquake killed 75,000 people and left millions homeless. In Nepal, there had been 4 significant quakes in the last 205 years. The most recent one, a 6.0-magnitude temblor, killed 1,500 people. In 1934, Kathmandu was nearly destroyed by an 8.0-magnitude earthquake that killed more than 16,000 people. Its epicenter was about 5.9 miles south of Mount Everest. This was, however, the first time any member of the team had even remotely considered earthquakes since arriving in Nepal.

When the tour concluded, the team walked the fifteen minutes back to their teahouse under the gathering snow clouds. After lunch, as snow started to fall, Bonny challenged Dave to another round of Scrabble in the sparse common room, which felt about as cold inside as it was outside. Peter joined them. Bonny delighted in her Scrabble matches with Dave.

"He's a pro and you don't even know when he's going to go in for the kill!" she told Peter. Dave had earned Bonny's deepest respect. She considered him to be an introvert, but through the quiet play and gamesmanship she felt she learned more about how his mind operated. His observant nature, his strategic thinking, his intelligence and seriousness, and his wry sense of humor were all on display during a game with him. It was through such quiet moments that she felt she got to know Dave best.

The team passed the rest of the quiet afternoon, wearing their hats and jackets inside the cold lodge, keeping themselves distracted with Scrabble, cards, and chess. "Books and naps work pretty well, too," Dave suggested before retreating to the twin bed in his room for a while. Eventually, their thoughts returned to Base Camp. This would be their last night in a teahouse. By the evening, Peter's gastrointestinal symptoms and Larry's cough had continued to worsen. Tent life, they all knew, would begin tomorrow.

13 ⛰ MOUNT EVEREST SOUTH BASE CAMP

April 4, 2015
Posted by: Dave Hahn
Categories: Expedition Dispatches; Everest
Elevation: 17,575 feet
Satellite phone transcript

RMI EXPEDITIONS BLOG

This is Dave Hahn calling from Everest Base Camp, 17,500 feet on the Khumbu Glacier. Well, we made it. We came up from Lobuche today, the entire team—six climbers, two trekkers, and two guides. Chhering Dorjee Sherpa, our sirdar, leading the way, brought us up to Base Camp. . . . And at our base camp, incredible progress has been made. Our Sherpa team has done great work setting our camp up and Mark Tucker, our base camp manager, has been here the last couple of days and got things buffed out just perfectly for us to move in. We started up from Lobuche at 8:15. We got to Base Camp at 1:15, so we made good time and great progress. It was a beautiful day with just a little cloud cover, and it was just about perfect for walking. Tomorrow we'll get squared away and get internet capabilities again, and get back into written distractions, but just wanted to bring you up to date for this evening. Bye now.

Entering Base Camp felt like descending into another universe: a vast quarry of rock-strewn glacier bustling like a massive beehive, enclosed by cavernous walls. Speckled by yellow and orange tents, like the hexagonal cells of a honeycomb, the rolling, mile-and-a-half long tent village pulsed with the energy of an international climbing club. Although they were among the first climbing teams to arrive this season, Base Camp was already abuzz with early-season adrenaline that Dave knew would only grow stronger as the season moved into full swing and as Base Camp burgeoned into a glacial metropolis.

Base Camp was louder than Erin had expected. The popping of the glacier's shifting ice sounded like gunshots. A few helicopters reverberated overhead on sightseeing tours. The hike from Lobuche had been grueling, and the altitude had pushed her to the outer reaches of her physical limits. Her pack had never felt heavier. As they trudged through Base Camp, it took all of her mental attention to stay focused on the loose scree beneath her feet and to continue to put one foot ahead of the other. They passed other hikers bent over their trekking poles, gasping to catch their breath in the thin air.

Once they reached RMI's camp, Erin recuperated with a cup of hot grape Tang and a warm meal in the mess tent. When she felt recovered enough, she found her way to her own tent in the neatly arranged RMI camp and crawled into it. It was only after a rest that Erin was able to appreciate the fact that she had made it to Base Camp. She forced herself back up and went outside to take some photos.

Around her sprawled a bright encampment sitting in a wide expanse of snow and rocks. RMI's Sherpa team was building a stone altar for the puja ceremony that would take place in a few days. She heard Nepali music humming on tinny FM radios, the sounds of shovels scraping gravel, and the sharp chopping of vegetables in the kitchen tent. Occasionally, a male voice burst into song. From Base Camp, she could not see Everest's peak since the view was blocked by Everest's formidable west shoulder, but there was no missing the mammoth jumble of giant ice chunks looming not far above the camp.

The notorious Khumbu Icefall, much like a massive waterfall in slow motion, was constantly moving. The glacier migrated downward toward Base Camp at an estimated 3 to 4 feet per day. Unlike a waterfall, however, the rapid flow of glacial ice over a steep drop-off or through a narrow passageway often fractured, causing the formation of deep crevasses. Intersecting fractures formed massive columns of ice, or seracs, which sometimes broke off. The maze of the Khumbu Icefall gaped and yawned. Erin now viscerally understood that for those moving through the Icefall, there was no way to control the various and unpredictable threats it posed. The only way to limit the risk would be to pass through it as quickly and cautiously as possible.

That night they were all woken by storm winds and the thunderous claps of several avalanches in the amphitheatre of mountains around them as blocks of ice the size of railroad cars broke off the edges of the glacier and plummeted below. Dave, Tuck, JJ, Chhering, Hao, and the others who had been to Everest Base Camp before were accustomed to this noise, and not especially bothered by it since the camp felt safely removed from the vertical walls of the enclosed valley. For the newcomers, however, the nighttime clamor was a startling and sobering reality.

It snowed through the night, but by the morning the sun peeked through the clouds, and each climber and trekker awoke to find chocolates and Easter eggs that Dave assured them the Easter Bunny had left when he had hopped through Base Camp during the night. "We couldn't hear the rabbit over the noise of the storm winds and those ice avalanches thundering down around us," he explained.

The team's cook, Kumar, prepared a hot breakfast of eggs, potatoes, pork, biscuits, and coleslaw that left everyone feeling full and warm. Dave reminded them that it was a holiday and that nothing more strenuous than "a series of naps" and a walk out to the "Icy Cyber"—a spot out on the edges of the Khumbu Glacier with semi-dependable 3G cell service—would be required of them as they adjusted to the higher altitude. Rest would be the day's most important work.

For Dave, Everest Base Camp felt like home. He had spent as much time there over the last couple of decades as he had at his own house in Taos, New Mexico, and by this point in the trip he was more than ready to be finished trekking, relieved to no longer be sharing germs in common spaces and to no longer being woken during the night by the sounds of coughing fits through thin walls or of heavy boots clunking down the hallway to the latrines. He was glad to have the space and privacy of his own yellow tent to spread out his gear, and he was content to sleep without a roof over his head, in the comfort of his down sleeping bag with moonlight streaming through his tent ceiling. More than anything, he felt eager to get climbing.

Dave thanked the Sherpa team for the weeks of labor that had gone into assembling their distinctly nonprimitive accommodations: individual tents for each climber, a dining tent, a couple of shower tents, toilet tents that enclosed 50-gallon blue plastic barrels fitted with toilet seats, and a communications tent from where they would establish a radio base station. Dave still regarded the shower tent as a luxury. Such comforts would have been inconceivable during his first Everest expeditions. Now it was considered typical for a team to set aside one propane tank for an on-demand heater attached to a barrel full of water connected to a tiny electric pump that squirted a thin stream of hot water from the showerhead. It was a popular improvement and a generally welcome extravagance.

The Sherpa team had also built a kitchen out of stones they had quarried and installed propane stoves within it. They had carried hundreds of gallons of water from an underground frozen lake bed, far enough from Base Camp to avoid contamination from waste, to the kitchen where they had boiled and treated it for consumption. And now they were again hard at work constructing the puja altar.

The puja ceremony was important to Dave precisely because it was so important to the Sherpa team. Dave knew the Sherpas would never conceive of climbing Everest before performing this traditional prayer ritual, conducted by a lama from Pangboche, invoking the goddess Chomalungma's blessing to climb the mountain. The Sherpas looked to the puja to make a spiritual connection with the divine, to discipline the mind, and to energize both the deities and themselves.

Prior to the expedition, Chhering had consulted with his uncle, the reincarnated monk, to determine a *mahrat*, or an auspicious date, for the team's puja according to the Tibetan calendar. The date of a team's puja was largely determined by the birthdate and birth year of the team's sirdar. Since Chhering, the sherpa sirdar of the expedition, had been born on March 3, 1989, the Year of the Dragon, his uncle had calculated that April 7 would be the most favorable date for their puja. He had taken into consideration the activity to be commenced, namely climbing Mount Everest, as well as Chhering's horoscope, the planetary positions, and the lunar calendar day. The entire expedition had then been planned around it.

Erin and Bonny would miss the puja since they would be leaving Base Camp in the morning. They had both originally planned on trekking back down to Lukla with one of the sherpas from RMI; however, Bonny had grown concerned that the trek down could prove even tougher on her knee than the trek up had, and she didn't want to risk a significant injury that might thwart her upcoming climb on Mount Kilimanjaro in Africa. When she had overheard Hao reminisce about flying from Base Camp to Lukla the previous season, it had planted the idea in her head. Tucker helped her arrange a helicopter flight from nearby Gorak Shep. It would have been possible, albeit more expensive, to have arranged a helicopter from Base Camp, but Dave mentioned he felt the flight would be safer from the lower Gorak Shep, since every bit of altitude made takeoff and landing that much more dangerous. Plus, he added, "Helicopters tend to crash up here in the thin air and hard rock, and we all live in soft shelters that perform poorly when subjected to shrapnel."

Bonny was quoted $900 for a one-person flight and $1,100 for two people. She offered to pay for Erin's flight so Erin wouldn't be left to hike down to Lukla on her own, and Erin gratefully accepted. Erin was feeling both relieved and anxious. She had accomplished her mission of making it to Base Camp in spite of her kidney condition, and she felt confident she was leaving Robbie in good hands. She had the utmost faith in his guides. However, she had something she felt she needed to tell Dave before she left.

That night, Erin and Bonny's second and last at Base Camp, it was so cold that the only way Bonny could get her laptop to hold a charge was to sleep with it in her -20-degree down sleeping bag. She wore a wool hat and several layers of polypropylene, wool, and fleece clothing while she slept, but nevertheless, the cold penetrated her bones. To make matters worse, her bladder felt like it might explode from the copious amount of fluids she had ingested that day in order to contend with the altitude. Bonny tried to will the aching discomfort away since she desperately wanted not to have to leave the relative warmth of her tent in the middle of the frigid night. She silently cursed the men for their ability to use pee bottles. Eventually, she could not hold out any longer, and she forced herself out of her sleeping bag. Trying not to wake Peter, she felt around the darkness for her headlamp, slipped her arms into her down jacket, pulled her boots onto her feet, and darted out of the tent.

Bonny braced herself as she plunged into the colder air. Her physical relief after a quick trip to the toilet tent was soon replaced by a sense of wonder and astonishment while heading back to her sleeping tent. She stopped, took a breath, and tried to absorb the scene around her. An obscenely full moon hung in a wide, violet sky. The Icefall glowed white in the moonlight. Avalanches sloughed off the walls of the valley, but they sounded far enough away that Bonny did not feel threatened. Instead, she became enveloped by a sense of peace, transfixed by the majesty of her environment. Standing beneath a sea of stars at the foot of Everest in the middle of the inky night, she felt, for that one precious moment, like the only person in the world.

April 6, 2015
Posted by: JJ Justman
Categories: Expedition Dispatches; Everest
Elevation: 17,575 feet

RMI EXPEDITIONS BLOG

Hello RMI Blog Enthusiasts!

It's another sunny day here in Everest Base Camp. Of course, our team is doing great. However, all of us are a little sad. This morning our two trekkers that followed along with us parted ways and started their return journey back to Kathmandu.

I have to tell you that it was a lot of fun having Bonnie and Erin along giving our climbing team support. I am sure they are already trying to figure out what kind and how many pizzas they will order at Fire and Ice Pizza.

As for the rest of us we got down to some business today. The team went over and rigged their climbing equipment. Now, crampons are fitting snug, ice axe leashes are set and ascenders are set to the perfect length. There's no doubt, we are ready to do some practicing to work out any kinks before we actually get busy with the real deal.

It's now time to relax, drink a few more cups of tea and put on our dinner attire.

Most importantly though!! How bout them Wisconsin Badgers! This Wisconsin native cannot remember the last time The Badgers were in the finals. So without further hesitation . . . WISCONSIN!!!

"Goraks are those big black birds we've been seeing up high, the ones that look a lot like ravens," Dave said to Bonny, Erin, and Robbie at the start of their two-hour trek down from Base Camp toward Gorak Shep, pointing upward at the dark silhouettes soaring against the sky. "So Gorak Shep roughly translates to Dead Raven, which doesn't really do the place justice."

"Or maybe it does," he said, on second thought. "Anyway, we gotta be fast to reach that helicopter on time."

Gorak Shep, a frozen lake bed covered with sand, served as the original base camp for Everest climbers in the 1950s before Base Camp had been moved to a spot significantly closer to the base of the mountain. Dave and the entire RMI team had trekked through the dusty settlement that sits on Gorak Shep's edge during their hike to Base Camp from Lobuche. On their way up, they had snapped photos at its famous yellow trail sign marked with a red arrow and the words "WAY TO M.T. EVEREST B.C." planted in a pile of rocks in the foreground of the giant white Himalayas.

It wasn't much of a village, had no vegetation, and was only inhabited during climbing season, but "The Shep," as Dave liked to call it, remained an important place for trekkers. Home to a cybercafe with temperamental internet and a few trekkers lodges, it was also a jumping-off point for the short acclimatization hike up to Kalapathar, the 18,300-foot ridge perched above it. Gorak Shep would have felt like a desert if it weren't for its freezing temperatures and the white summit of Pumori—a much steeper, sharper, technical climb, towering above it.

Erin felt relieved for the opportunity to swap the 36-mile trek back to Lukla with a short helicopter ride, and she was glad for Bonny's company. Peter, still fighting his intestinal bug, had stayed behind. He and Bonny had spent part of the previous evening reading some of the letters their friends and family had placed in a gift box, which they bestowed upon them at the airport, just before Peter and Bonny departed Washington, DC, for Nepal. Tears had streamed down their faces as they read the letters in their tent, and after thirty minutes of it, they had grown too emotional to continue and they stashed the letters away. When the group was a few hundred yards away from Base Bamp, Dave glanced back.

"Hey, Bonny, stop. Turn around," he said. "Peter's saying goodbye."

Peter stood at the top of a hill behind and above them. He was smiling, waving broadly with his trekking pole. A bright smile spread across Bonny's face. Bonny thought Peter had seemed unusually reserved and distant for much of the trek, weakened by his GI infection, preoccupied and anxious about the Everest climb ahead. She took a mental picture of Peter with his loving expression in that moment as she waved back enthusiastically. She was not able to know for sure if she would ever see her husband again.

"Thank you, Dave," Bonny said, still waving. "I'm so glad you noticed him on the ridge. I wouldn't have otherwise thought to turn around."

They hiked quickly, with Chhering leading the way. On the uphill stretches of the descent to Gorak Shep, the purse-lipped *phoooo* sound of Dave's exhales reminded the rest of them to do the same. Dave had reviewed with them the technique of pressure breathing early on during the trek, but more often he led by example rather than reminding them outright. The simple act of exhaling forcefully, lips pursed, as if blowing out a series of birthday candles on a cake, forced more carbon dioxide out of the lungs and made it easier to inhale more oxygen. Since the lack of atmospheric pressure at altitude caused oxygen molecules to be farther apart, making it more difficult for lungs to take in oxygen, pressure breathing became a critical habit to bring the oxygen saturation of their blood back up to a more normal level. Back in Pheriche, Bonny had been amazed to watch the numbers on the monitor of the pulse oximeter she slipped on her finger at the HRA clinic rise from 83 to 93 with just a few pressure breaths. As the small group followed Chhering and Dave out of Base Camp they were all soon exhaling with audible *phoooo*'s.

As soon as she began pressure breathing, Bonny's body remembered to make use of the rest step, another technique modeled unconsciously by Dave, one she found provided significant help hiking with her knee issues. After each forward step, she paused momentarily on her rear leg, allowing her knee to straighten for a fraction of a second. This enabled her skeleton, instead of oxygen consuming muscle, to bear the load and gave her glutes and quadriceps a brief rest during every step. It slowed down her heart rate and prevented fatigue.

They made it to Gorak Shep with enough time to grab a snack and a hot lemon tea at a crowded teahouse. Robbie and Erin took a moment alone to say goodbye to each other, and afterward, Erin pulled Dave aside. She inhaled deeply, squinting her eyes a bit, before confiding in Dave that she had been in one other serious romantic relationship before meeting Robbie. She explained that her previous boyfriend, Kahlil, had been killed in a motorcycle accident. He was twenty-seven years old when he lost control of his bike on the ninth turn of the road course at the Spokane County Raceway. "His skull was fractured upon impact. He died later that same day in the hospital. I was at his bedside," Erin said. She told Dave she could not bear the thought of enduring another similar loss.

"I need Robbie to come home," she said, almost in a whisper. "Please take care of him."

Dave did not know exactly how to respond, and he found himself at a loss for words, unable to guarantee Robbie's safety. He felt a sense of relief when their conversation was quickly interrupted by the loud *thwapping* sound of an approaching helicopter. Erin exhaled. She felt content that she had told Dave enough. She had the utmost faith in him as a guide and she had not experienced any frightening premonitions, like she had before Kahlil's race, about the rest of their expedition. She felt confident that Dave would look out for Robbie on Everest.

"Let's go," Dave said, as he led the group up to the ridgetop where the chopper landed, spewing dust across the stone helipad. Erin and Bonny ducked their heads as they darted across the circle and climbed in. The helicopter immediately lifted upward and tilted sideways as it sped through the canyon. Robbie, Dave, and Chhering waved as they watched the helicopter shrink into the distance, like a gorak soaring against the sky.

While trekking back to Base Camp, Dave found the sweet melody and melancholic lyrics of a familiar song stuck in his head. He could hear the Memphis blues guitar strumming and John Prine's gravely voice. The sunny chorus, lifting over a church organ, haunted him: "Somebody said they saw me, swinging the world by the tail, bouncing over a white cloud, killing the blues." Dave thought about what Erin had told him and recalled the sight of Peter waving goodbye to Bonny.

Dave had never been married. He didn't have children. He had always checked the single box on Miss Hawley's forms. He recognized that guiding was something of a selfish pursuit. He had seen repeatedly that leaving someone to go away on long expeditions put that person through hell. He thought about what he had told Bonny when she had asked him about his personal life: "I never intended to avoid marriage and family. I figured I'd do it all when I grew up, but, sure enough, growing up has turned out to be more tedious and time-consuming than I had anticipated." The answer seemed to satisfy her and was generally true, he rationalized. He found it was easier than explaining that he feared he wasn't suited for a real relationship. In any case, he had shaped his life around his work, and he found he was more likely to feel lonely at a big party or while driving around suburbia than when alone in the wilderness.

The toughest thing about packing up for Everest every spring was the prospect of leaving his cozy adobe home and his community of friends during the social end of his ski-patrol season in Taos, New Mexico. Every year, just as the daffodils began to push up through the soil in his yard after a snowy winter in the Sangre de Cristo Mountains, and when the birds began to sing again, he would head off alone for ten weeks of cold and mean Everest weather. He never complained because he knew he'd be excited once he got there, and he reconciled it with simply being one of the inconveniences of turning his passion into a job. He buoyed himself with the notion that soon enough, he'd get back home to slide both his backpack and the responsibility of other people's lives off of his shoulders, to mow his lawn, and to spend some time not being scared of dying for a while.

April 7, 2015
Posted by: Dave Hahn
Categories: Expedition Dispatches; Everest
Elevation: 17,575 feet

RMI EXPEDITIONS BLOG

It was cloudy overhead this morning, threatening another pulse of snow. We'd enjoyed yesterday's calm sunshine and hoped for one more day of the same, but that didn't seem likely. The snow held off nicely for our Puja ceremony though and we even got a couple hours of sunshine. The climbing Lama had made his way up from Pangboche for the event. . . . Ours was the first in camp other than the one for the Icefall Doctors (who have been hard at work building the climbing route for the past two weeks already). We sat and listened to the prayers and chants as our Sherpa team attended to all of the mechanics of the ceremony, distributing offerings and building the prayer mast with colorful flags radiating out in five directions. The idea is that we want the blessing of the gods before we put any of our team at risk on the mountain. Having watched a gargantuan avalanche come down over the icefall around seven this morning, we all hoped the gods were paying attention to our pleading. . . . We all wished each other good luck and careful climbing and then toasted with beer, coca cola, whiskey, rakshi and chang. (It wasn't a require-ment that any individual have each and every one of those . . . we are at 17,500 ft and it really doesn't take much sipping to feel an amplified effect.) After lunch, we walked out onto the lower section of the Khumbu Glacier to stretch our legs and explore as the storm moved in. . . .

   Best Regards,
   RMI Guide Dave Hahn

The three-hour puja ceremony sometimes reminded Dave of sitting through church as a kid, but as restless as he sometimes felt throughout it, he had told his team beforehand, "I'm always grateful for the opportunity to contemplate the gravity of an undertaking dangerous enough to warrant so much blessing." His thoughts, however, had strayed ahead. "Tomorrow, when we resume our training at the foot of the Icefall, we'll be rested, blessed, and ready."

As the woody aroma of burning juniper branches wafted through the air, the team placed their crampons, ice axes, helmets, and offerings of whiskey and fruit on the stone altar to be blessed. They sent their prayers for Chomolungma's protection, like the flags on the prayer mast, in all directions. With the flapping of the flags in the wind, they sent off to the gods their requests for permission to climb the sacred Chomolungma and their pleas for forgiveness for any damage their climbing might cause the mountain. They held each other's chins in their hands as they smeared gray *tsampa*, a barley flour, across each other's tanned and smiling faces. In doing so, they committed themselves to each other's care on the expedition and invited the hope that they might live to see each other grow old and grey.

The massive avalanche that had unleashed itself in the Icefall earlier in the morning, prior to the puja, made the blessing feel all the more imperative. When Dave heard the sound of its roar around 7:00 a.m., his mind flashed back to the avalanche that occurred at the same time of day on April 18 of the previous year. Today, when he stuck his head out of his tent and watched the avalanche crash down the Icefall, intently studying its path, he was almost certain there was no one in it. April 18, 2014, however, had been different.

On that day, a scheduled rest day for the RMI team, Dave and JJ had been asleep in their tent at RMI's Everest Base Camp when a 2.2-million-cubic-foot, 64,000-ton chunk of blue ice calved off Everest's west shoulder, a mile-high face rising directly above the Icefall, at 6:45 a.m. It exploded upon impact and pushed a wall of wind before it, gaining momentum and accumulating daggers and bullets of ice debris as it hurtled through the Icefall. The avalanche swept across the route that the Icefall Doctors had established through it for the 2014 season. Some of the dozens of sherpas working their way through the maze of the Icefall at that moment, most of them carrying supplies to Camp One, had time to throw themselves behind the shelter of seracs. Some had found themselves safely outside the margins of the ice avalanche's path as they watched their friends, cousins, and brothers disappear in its powder cloud. All of them were coated in a ghostlike layer of white pulverized ice.

Dave was well accustomed to the sound of ice collapse at Base Camp and had not felt especially worried at first on that April day in 2014. He knew at the time that all the members of RMI's team, including their entire sherpa team, were safe and together at Base Camp. However, when he glanced out his tent flap, he noticed that an unusual number of people were gathering in the Icefall, as JJ was realizing the same. They turned on their radios and glanced at each other with furrowed brows as they absorbed the gravity of the situation; guides from other teams had witnessed the avalanche engulf the Icefall's route with the sickening realization that members of their sherpa teams were in it.

"Shit!" JJ shouted.

Dave, JJ, and Chhering began to stuff their packs with rescue gear. They decided that Chhering would helicopter with others up to the Football Field, a relatively safe section of the Icefall, where a rescue operation was being staged just below the accident scene. Meanwhile, Dave, JJ, and two sherpas from their team, Rinjen Bhote and Galden Sherpa, would climb the 1,600 vertical feet to the site, as an insurance policy should the helicopter encounter any mechanical issues or otherwise be delayed in getting there.

Dave and JJ had climbed up and down through the Icefall with their team just the previous morning, April 17, 2014. They had woken at 3:00 a.m.; slipped on boots, jackets, helmets, and crampons; and led their clients toward the Icefall, following the shafts of light from their headlamps and the moon through the darkness. The giant cathedral of ice shimmered and gleamed as morning's earliest light hit it, but the climbers were too focused on navigating its maze of daunting obstacles to become entranced by its beauty. Over the next several hours, they climbed halfway through it to the Football Field and back again as planned, crossing its deepest chasms and scaling its towering ice walls on series of quivering aluminum ladders roped together. It had been a successful, albeit tiring, dry run.

However, on the morning of April 18, 2014, Dave, JJ, Rinjen, and Galden faced over an hour of fast, treacherous climbing on the damaged Icefall route to reach the Football Field. As they raced up, they lifted their heads toward helicopters dangling lifeless bodies in backward arches over them in the wide blue sky. Given the size and force of the avalanche, the cold temperatures, and the amount of time that had passed since the initial blast, they came to the grim realization that their rescue efforts would most likely become body retrieval. They offered water to the dazed sherpas descending. By the time they reached the Football Field, ten men had been confirmed dead. A guide from another team who had been helping in the evacuation of three seriously injured survivors pointed them in the direction of an area where a glove and backpack attached to a body had been found, at the lowest portion of the avalanche debris, and told them that a second body had been spotted above the ladder.

When JJ and Dave came upon the first sherpa's body, they were struck by the extent of the blunt-force trauma. All that was left of the climber's helmet was a plastic headband. They did not know his name. The snow around him was stained red with blood. JJ, overcome by the sight and the scope of the tragedy, wept.

They pulled out their ice axes and got to work freeing his body while fellow guides from other teams including Andy Tyson, Garrett Madison, and Ben Jones climbed the triple ladder to the cliff above it, where they found a boot sticking out of the snow. The severely fractured leg inside of it belonged to Dorje Khatri, the forty-six-year-old sherpa sirdar for Madison Mountaineering. The rest of Dorje Khatri's body was encased in ice, facing head down in a crevasse. The guides began to chip away at the ice entombing him.

By 2:10 that afternoon, Dorje Khatri's body had not yet been extracted, but the day's bleak work was suspended when it was determined that the warmer afternoon temperatures would make the Icefall even more unstable, and that the worsening weather would make helicopter evacuation flights too risky. As desperately as the guides wanted to bring Khatri's family an opportunity for peace and closure, especially in light of the Sherpa belief that the spirit of the deceased lingers close to the body for three weeks, they resigned themselves to the reality that they would have to leave Khatri's body until the morning. Dave guided in the last of the body retrieval flights, his arms uplifted in the shape of a V. He and JJ tied the broken body they had extracted, still in a climbing harness, to the cable and watched it rise.

They then retreated to the Football Field, where a red H, poured from a sports drink on the snow, demarcated a landing pad. They learned from the others there that eleven of the dead had been killed in a single spot while waiting for their turns at a ladder. Chhering had been put in charge of identifying their bodies since he personally knew most of those killed; some were his best friends. Most Sherpas shared the belief that touching a dead body was an invitation for bad luck, but Chhering, reeling from shock and flooded with grief, quietly helped with the dreadful task anyway. Three other climbers were still missing and presumed dead. The seriously injured had been stabilized and were en route to hospitals in Kathmandu.

The helicopter pilot wordlessly transported the rescue workers, two by two, back to Base Camp. Dave went last, and since they were an odd number, he found himself sitting in the phantasma of the Icefall alone except for the restless spirits of those left behind. When the helicopter returned for him, he jumped into its doorless, bare belly, slid precipitously across the metal floor in his crampons, and grasped for something to hold.

April 8, 2015
Posted by: Dave Hahn
Categories: Expedition Dispatches; Everest
Elevation: 18,200 feet

RMI EXPEDITIONS BLOG

Great day for hiking. Now that most of the team are feeling more or less adjusted to the 17,500 feet of Basecamp, today seemed like the day for walking higher. Our choices are limited in this dead-end valley since going up through the Khumbu Icefall for exercise is too spicy a proposition for most reasonable folks. Our solution is to backtrack a bit, following the trail part way back down toward Gorak Shep and then branching off to gain some elevation. The goal today was Pumori Camp One at about 18,200 ft of elevation. We like this particular stairmaster of a hike because the boulder-hopping is pretty similar to the ice-chunk hopping we'll do in the Icefall. As a bonus, we gained stupendous views of Everest (from North Col to South Col), Lhotse, Nuptse and those distant peaks like Ama Dablam and Thamserku that we used to see so regularly while trekking. We could also see the sprawl of tents down on the Khumbu, growing by the minute. Sure enough, when we reached the main trail during our descent, it was like getting on the interstate highway back home. Hundreds of trekkers, climbers, porters and yaks are now flowing in and out of Base. Tents are going up everywhere, helicopters are buzzing around like flies. . . . The climbing season is cranking up quickly. We walked the half hour or so from downtown Everest Base Camp to our exit in the upper midsection and sat down for one of Kumar's great lunches. Afternoon is for resting, relaxing and re-hydrating. We've got plans for cranking things up another notch tomorrow.

Dave prepared the team to edge from the hiking world into the climbing world as they feasted on a hot lunch prepared by RMI's renowned chef Kumar and sipped lemon tea in the dining tent following their morning hike up Pumori, or "Mountain Daughter" in the Sherpa language. Dave had observed each of them as they scrambled across Pumori's cold boulders, getting a sense of their health, their acclimatization, their fitness, their climbing skills, and their overall readiness to climb through the Icefall, a route which he reminded them was unlike any other route in the world.

"I've climbed on plenty of glaciers, but climbing through the Icefall, where the glacier drops off a steep slope, picks up speed, and breaks into crevasses you can fall in, and into ice towers, or seracs, that can fall on you, well it is not a normal or common thing, even for a mountain guide. Experienced technical climbers and those who have experienced glaciers elsewhere have not have seen anything like it before," he said, cradling a warm mug in his large hands. "It's the major leagues. We need to be ready and on our game. Practice is a good thing. Tomorrow we'll get comfortable with ladders, rigging, and systems. We'll take it one little step at a time."

Larry felt stressed. He had hobbled into breakfast using trekking poles as crutches after throwing out his back while unzipping his tent after dinner the previous night. He had managed to crawl into his tent to sleep but was in so much pain by the morning that he had required help pulling on his boots. It had forced him to stay behind when the rest of the team headed to Pumori. By lunchtime, his back was still throbbing and he was growing uneasy about missing out on more critical Everest "boot camp" opportunities with his teammates.

After lunch, they all retreated to their tents. Peter wrote in his journal. He was still somewhat weakened by his gastrointestinal bug but could feel that his body was on the mend. He had been anxious about his illness but had tried to remain patient, aware that it took longer to heal at such extreme altitude, and he could finally notice his strength returning.

His consuming worry was being replaced with rising anticipation and a thrilling sense of astonishment realizing, as he described in his journal, that he would soon be climbing in "the footsteps" of legendary and historic climbing giants like Whittaker and Gombu, Hillary and Tenzing, and Mallory and Irvine.

The next morning, the team rose early in the cold and quickly donned layers of warm clothing, mountaineering boots, crampons, harnesses, and helmets. Larry would rest another day to allow his back to heal. The rest of the team headed out with their ice axes into the lower reaches of the Khumbu Glacier, just below the Icefall, to explore its ice walls, pinnacles, and frozen streams. Dave led them into folds of the glacier for a scavenger hunt in an area where he had previously found wooden ice axes and old oxygen bottles from some of the earliest climbing expeditions to the south side of Everest, as well as old logs that had been used as crevasse bridges in the Icefall in the days before metal ladders.

"They still bear the crampon scars of the climbers who scrambled across them," Dave said as they worked their way across frozen ponds of meltwater to the start of the climbing route at the base of the Khumbu Icefall.

Dave had watched the glacial surface change dramatically since he had first come to this side of Everest in 2000. During his first several seasons here on Everest's south side, he had become familiar with its landmarks—the boulders, ridges, and ice towers that tended to remain roughly the same each season. However, beginning in 2009, he was startled to notice that large, flat, frozen ponds were sitting where familiar 60- to 70-foot ice ridges had once reached upward. New stream courses seemed to appear everywhere.

It was clear to Dave by now that his eyes and memory had not betrayed him. Science confirmed that there was no longer an accumulation zone left on the Khumbu Glacier; no part of the glacier was receiving more snow than was melting in a given year. During the years that he had been coming to Everest, the glacier had, in fact, been melting before his eyes.

In the afternoon Dave and the team moved to a nearby obstacle course on the lower stretch of glacier, constructed by RMI's sherpa team, with skill stations for practice. With the Icefall hanging over them, they played in a jungle gym of ladders, fixed ropes, rappel stations, and ice walls simulating the conditions and tasks they could expect to encounter in the Icefall. Under the watchful eyes of their guides, Robbie, Peter, HP, Larry, Hans, and Hao practiced properly clipping into fixed ropes with ascenders—mechanical ratchet devices that slid up the fixed rope and gripped it with metal teeth. They worked on rappel procedures. They rehearsed the awkward balancing act of walking across a shaky metal ladder, just a few feet off the ground, while wearing metal plates with spikes fixed to the bottoms of their boots. Then they crossed a ladder tilted at a 45-degree angle. Their crampons scratched and clanked on the metal and their ascenders jingled like bracelets. Next they tried to climb a short vertical stretch of ladder, protecting themselves from a fall or ladder collapse by attaching themselves to safety lines.

"For me," Dave offered, "it helps to keep one chunk of my brain concerned with risk and hazard, while another chunk of my brain enjoys the playground."

Dave wanted all these skills and safety systems to become as rote and as natural as possible for each of them so his team could be quick and efficient in the Icefall. He could tell they were eager to kick their crampon points into ice, to pull ropes, and to enter the world of climbing. They did lap after lap on the course, with and without packs, with and without ice axes, until they all felt weary and satisfied.

Dave couldn't predict what surprises this year's new Icefall route might hold. The only climbers to have been through it already were the Khumbu Icefall Doctors, the team of Nepalese workers tasked with forging and maintaining a rope-and-ladder passage through the constantly moving Icefall every season. They were hired by the Nepal government through a nonprofit environmental protection organization called the Sagarmatha Pollution Control Committee (SPCC), founded by Khumbu locals in 1991 with the goal of tackling the significant problem of trash and waste disposal in the Khumbu Valley. In a departure from their original mission, the SPCC took over the maintenance of the Icefall route in 1997 as a way to help fund the management of the approximate 30,000 pounds of human waste and 50,000 pounds of burnable waste generated each year by trekkers and climbers in the Khumbu.

This year the Icefall Doctors had built the Icefall route to the right of where it had snaked through the Icefall during the deadly 2014 season, shifting it toward the center of the Icefall in an effort to avoid some of the threat posed by the hanging seracs of Everest's west shoulder. A week before the disastrous avalanche in 2014, still quite early in the season, Dave had requested that the Icefall Doctors improve upon the route by doubling up ladders in the choke points most threatened by avalanches, which would allow for passing and would prevent potentially deadly traffic jams in such precarious sections of the route.

"This route is a good start," he recalled saying, as Lam Babu, RMI's sherpa sirdar that season, translated for him, "but it will need double ladders at the choke points before we get too far along."

Dave's impression was that the response to his suggestion had been positive. There seemed to be agreement among the Icefall Doctors and their administrators with his assessment that more ladders would be beneficial, and he was left with a general sense that such improvements would likely come in time. The avalanche, however, had struck first.

Dave, Chhering, and JJ knew well that climbing sherpas on Everest had the most dangerous job in the world, statistically far deadlier than Alaskan bush pilots, American miners, or US soldiers in Iraq during the height of the Iraq War. Climbing sherpas might make thirty to forty trips through the Icefall during a single season, carrying loads of oxygen bottles, tents, food, water, and fuel to higher camps. Since the Icefall Doctors spent even more time in the Icefall than other climbing sherpas did, their job was considered the most perilous of all.

Dave believed the Icefall Doctors, who risked their lives to find safe passage for climbers through an infamous stretch of moving mountain glacier, deserved and required the best of equipment, resources, and training. He was concerned that circumstances had not allowed for that in recent years, in spite of the fact that the SPCC had charged each Everest climber $500 for the maintenance of the route. Last year's tragedy had raised questions about the distribution of that revenue since the SPCC used excess funds to finance their garbage program initiatives, which were much needed in the Khumbu and only minimally subsidized by the Nepalese government. While the number of climbers on Everest had doubled, funding for the route setting had not increased as more resources were required to maintain it.

This year the fee had been raised to $600 per climber and Dave hoped the previous spring's tragedy would result in a greater investment in the maintenance of the Icefall and in the Icefall Doctors themselves, in terms of their training, gear, and compensation. He hoped the SPCC had fielded the best-equipped, strongest, and most experienced Icefall Doctor team possible this year for the critical and dangerous work. However, during any season, given the inertia of bureaucracy and the mercurial nature of the Icefall itself, he never knew exactly what to expect in it or what forces of man and nature would conspire there. Only time in the Icefall would tell.

April 10, 2015

Posted by: Dave Hahn

Categories: Expedition Dispatches; Everest

Elevation: 17,575 feet

RMI EXPEDITIONS BLOG

One of the finer days we've seen on the trip, weatherwise. Clear skies and calm as anything in the morning, which made us forget the cold. We were out in the glacier again, at our jungle gym of ladders and fixed lines and ice walls. . . . In the afternoon on this fine day, our Basecamp Manager, Mark Tucker, took a foursome out for the first day of a planned four-day golf tournament in the mellow section of glacier close to camp. Tuck showed his party around the Khumbu Country Club, scoring a hole-in-one in the process. (His partners now each owe him 100 rupees.) Newcomer Robbie came away with the low score for the round however, with a nine under par performance.

Best Regards,

RMI Guide Dave Hahn

Glacier golf, chess, scrabble, and various versions of poker became popular ways for the team to unwind at Base Camp after mornings of concentrated activity. Peter enjoyed learning to play poker when he wasn't writing in his journal. Robbie was a natural on the "golf course." Hans loved a good book. Dave's favorite game was Scrabble; he had carried a pocket dictionary with him to Base Camp. On the dry-erase board used to communicate messages to the team each day, he scrawled today's message in red marker: "Learn your two-letter words." Hao especially liked playing chess when he didn't have a strong enough Internet connection to get work done on his laptop.

Though 3G cell service had arrived at Base Camp in October of 2011, coverage could be weak and spotty. Climbers waved their cell phones in the air while wandering up its rolling hills of rock and boulder in hopes of gaining a signal. Tsering Gylatsen Sherpa, who grew up in Namche Bazaar, first dreamed of providing fixed wireless access to the Khumbu Valley in 2000 when his mother was diagnosed with breast cancer and flown to Kathmandu for treatment. Coping with his family's medical crisis made Khumbu's isolation feel more profound and impressed upon him the need for reliable communication between Kathmandu and the small villages of his home valley. By late 2014 he fulfilled his dream when he founded his company Everest Link, bringing wireless Internet connectivity to the Khumbu by establishing thirty-six solar-powered towers at high points all the way up the valley. As a result, there was now Wi-Fi at Base Camp so long as there was enough sunlight to generate power.

At Base Camp, the team also enjoyed visits from Momo, a tail-wagging black dog who became a familiar visitor. Momo was from one of the Khumbu villages but took up residence at Base Camp during the climbing seasons. JJ told the group that once, during a previous season, Momo had followed an expedition team through the Icefall, managing to cross the ladders, and made it as far as Camp One. When Momo couldn't negotiate the ladders on the way back down, a guide strapped Momo to his backpack and carried him back to Base Camp.

Dave had been ramping up the group's activity level on a daily basis as they had grown more acclimatized to the altitude of Base Camp. If he were guiding them on Rainier, he would take some time to review ice-axe arrest, practicing what to do if a slip became a slide. He had taught self-arrest hundreds of times.

"First," he would instruct them, "yell 'Falling!'" He'd explain that this was done to alert teammates of a potential death slide into a crevasse.

"It's not enough to just yell it," he would add. "You have to yell it with some fear included."

Then Dave would gamely fling himself down a serac with his ice axe in hand, demonstrating the proper, awkward technique of self-arrest. While sliding downward head first, he'd cover the spike of the axe with his left hand, lock his elbows, lower his head, and draw his shoulder up over the head of the axe. He would flip over onto his stomach, swing his legs below him, and anchor himself with the axe, coming to a gradual stop while still clinging to the axe that was now dug in above him on the hill.

Self-arrest, however, was considered a basic "snowschool" climbing skill; each of his Everest climbers was expected to be proficient in it already. Instead, he continued to review the more advanced expedition climbing skills they had been practicing, including techniques used for climbing fixed lines (bolted ropes) and for using caribiners (D-shaped rings with a spring catch on one side) to anchor themselves, in order to ensure that their first trip through the Icefall was a successful one. On other big mountains, they would have the chance to more gradually warm up, sharpen their skills, and streamline their systems as they went, but the nature of climbing Everest demanded that all these procedures be exact, right out of the gate. Honing the smallest details, like their ability to get their crampons and climbing harnesses on quickly and their ability to keep their equipment meticulously organized while climbing in order prevent their gear and ropes from getting tangled, could make all the difference.

That evening, worn out from several more hours of such concerted effort in the obstacle course followed by an afternoon of glacier golf, they all retreated to their tents earlier than usual after dinner. Dave was pleased by how enthusiastically the team had embraced the rigors of training. He was growing excited about what they might be able to accomplish on Everest together.

The following morning, after enjoying breakfast together in the dining tent, Dave said to the group, "Let's go for a walk," and proceeded to lead them back down the valley for another training hike on Kalapathar, veering off the main trail soon after leaving Base Camp to avoid the increasing traffic of yaks, trekkers, climbers, and porters as Everest's pre-monsoon climbing season ramped up. They plodded through a rugged, back path of snowfields across Everest's original, abandoned base camp in Gorak Shep, and then rejoined the popular trail to Kalapathar.

It was a cloudless day, and Dave promised epic views of surrounding peaks. He figured their "walk" would take about five and a half hours round trip, and it would entail some good distance as well as vertical gain and loss. When they reached Kalapathar, the 18,200-foot bump in the ridge a mile below the summit of Pumori, they shot dozens of digital photos until their hands grew too numb to continue. The freezing temperatures and gusting winds compelled them to retreat back toward Gorak Shep. There they headed back up the popular route to Base Camp, all glad and satisfied to realize their acclimatization efforts were paying off as they easily passed at least a hundred unacclimatized trekkers stopping to gasp for air.

They spent what was left of the afternoon playing golf and Texas Hold'em. Colorful tents and puja flags began to spring up around them in all directions. As climbing teams from around the globe entered Base Camp, it grew into an international, multicultural tent village and hummed with the musical chatter of many different languages. Indian Army Camp was their nearest neighbor. Old friends and fellow guides stopped by to visit and exchange handshakes, backslaps, hugs, and radio frequencies with Dave, Mark, and JJ, all of whom were happy for the chance to catch up with plenty of friends they giddily referred to as "the usual suspects" over steaming cups of milk tea.

Since tomorrow was slated to be a designated rest day for their team, Dave predicted they would sleep soundly, with none of the anticipatory anxiety commonly experienced before a training or climbing day. They all smiled gladly when he reminded the team that tomorrow would also be their weekly shower day.

They were still at least five weeks away from the summit. Their rotations on Everest would repeat a now-familiar "climb high, sleep low" pattern of climbing, acclimatizing, descending, and repeating at higher and higher camps and elevations until they were eventually poised for a summit bid. Experience had taught Dave that each challenge they faced would help ready them for the next. Whether it be the Icefall, the Lhotse Face, the Yellow Band, the Geneva Spur, the Balcony, the South Summit, or the Hillary Step, Everest provided a veritable treasure trove of exposed ice and rock wall trials straddling the edge of the Earth's atmosphere.

"There will be no shortage of tests," he reminded them.

Dave, Chhering, and the sherpa team planned to make their push through the Icefall on April 13, the day after tomorrow's rest day, to check out the route and establish Camp One at close to 20,000 feet. If the weather should cooperate, it would be business as usual. They would set their alarms for 4:00 a.m., encircle the puja altar to light juniper incense and send up a prayer, hike to the base of the Icefall by the light of their headlamps and the moon, climb through the ice towers to the Popcorn Field (named for its SUV-sized chunks of glacial ice rubble that made it resemble a giant bowl of popcorn), up to the wide and relatively flat Football Field, across the Ballroom of Death where seracs hung directly above, and dump their loads at Camp One. Meanwhile, JJ would take the rest of the team hiking. They would reunite at Base Camp in the afternoon. "That's the plan, anyway," Dave said quietly, wishing them "Sweet dreams!" as he stepped out of the dining tent into the dark, frigid night.

By the time Dave got into his sleeping bag, snow had begun to fall. When he poked his head out of his tent at 3:30 a.m. on the morning of April 13, it quickly became apparent that the snow had not quit and would not allow him to proceed with his plan for the day of climbing through the Icefall. By breakfast, it had snowed a foot, so instead, during the afternoon, Dave led the entire team, including the RMI sherpa team, in an avalanche-rescue training class beneath overcast skies. They all slid the straps of their transceivers over their shoulders and set their beacons to transmit mode. JJ snapped some photos of Dave (who was wearing a red jacket, tall red Millet mountaineering boots, and a Taos Ski Patrol cap) as he stood before the group reviewing the techniques of using transceivers to locate and rescue teammates caught in a slide.

As the team set out to find the transceiver that Dave had hidden several feet beneath the snow, they switched their transceivers to receive mode, in order to pick up the pulsed radio signal being emitted by the buried beacon, and searched for a signal. When they determined the general area, indicated both by numbers on the LCD screen of their devices and the frequency of the beeps, they lowered their beacons to the ground and combed the area in a grid pattern. They honed in on the site, then probed the snow and dug with shovels until they successfully located and uncovered the beacon.

The team's initial enthusiasm was somewhat muted when Dave reminded them, "While a victim's chance of survival is certainly greater if their teammates are trained in the use of transceivers, we're still unlikely to save the lives of those who've been buried by an ice avalanche." He explained that asphyxiation, physical trauma, and hypothermia were common, quick, and often combined causes of death, ultimately influenced by the force of the avalanche's impact, the depth of burial, and the time required to locate and extract a victim.

"The transceivers are critical regardless though, especially since they facilitate the process of locating bodies . . . This helps reduce the inherent risks for those trying to find and retrieve them."

Experience had taught Dave that every avalanche has its own personality. Avalanche specialists use nine distinct "characters" or "problem types" of avalanches to express with more nuance an avalanche's nature, depending on their snow type (dry, wet, soft, hard, surface hoar, depth hoar, graupel, consolidated, unconsolidated, etc.), associated weather conditions, predictability, triggers, and degrees of danger and destructiveness. Most avalanche types fall into one of two more general categories: "loose snow" avalanches sometimes called point-release or sluff avalanches and "slab" avalanches that occur when a field of snow suddenly detaches from an underlying bed surface and slides away.

A species of avalanche that exists outside these two common categories is an ice avalanche, where a frozen glacier hanging over the edge of a cliff collapses and plunges downward. An ice avalanche can trigger slab avalanches by the force it unleashes on unstable snowpack or by the reverberations its impact generates.

To be caught in a slab avalanche, according to survivors, feels like being slammed by a monstrous wave traveling at the rate of a speeding car that hits with the force of a freight train.

An avalanche victim's first indication that something is wrong is a loud crack or a deep *wumph* from above. He might have a second to glance upward and notice cracks in the snow surface as the slab, likely the size of half a football field, suddenly begins to slide downward. The avalanche doesn't give him long to react. After five seconds, the avalanche is traveling at 40 to 80 miles per hour. The victim in its path is hit, swept up, and hurled downward, tumbling furiously head over feet, unable to discern bottom from top. His hat, mittens, and goggles are stripped from his body. He sucks in a snow-air mixture that forms an icy plug in his throat.

His "fly in the toilet bowl" plunge continues until the avalanche reaches its run-out zone and gradually comes to a stop. At this point, the victim, if he has not been killed by trauma already, finds himself in total darkness and in pain from snapped limbs and head injury incurred during the descent. He is totally immobilized, encased in the snow that has set up like concrete around him. There is not even enough room for his chest to expand and take in a full breath. If he can wiggle his fingers or thrash around with his body, he may try to create an air pocket in front of his face. Otherwise, suffocation is imminent.

The victim's skin turns white and his lips turn blue, but he does not feel cold as hypothermia sets in. The hypothermia slows his metabolism and reduces his brain's need for oxygen, which will give him a few more minutes before his brain begins to die. He is wheezing now.

Claustrophobia and panic take hold as the victim, in shock, attempts to process the reality that he is completely hidden from the view of anyone who might be near enough to help. As he rebreathes the carbon dioxide trapped in the snow around him, he begins to lose consciousness. Brain damage commences within fifteen minutes, as the electrical activity in his brain begins to weaken.

If the victim is wearing a transceiver or if a witness saw him go under, he might be found, dug out, and rescued. However, within 25 minutes, half of all completely buried victims not already killed by trauma will be dead. The vast majority (85.7 percent) of slab avalanche deaths are due to asphyxiation; 5.4 percent are due to trauma alone, and 8.9 percent are due to a combination of these two factors.

An ice avalanche is a different beast. Like the more common slab avalanche, the first signal of an ice avalanche might be an ominous crack, in this case when a giant, overhanging chunk of ice calves off the snout of a glacier and drops. The chunk of ice, which might be the size of a building, shatters upon impact. This may trigger secondary slab avalanches all around. The ice accelerates down the steep mountain slope, pushing a massive powder cloud of snow, rock, and ice pellets ahead of it. Ahead of the powder cloud, an invisible and immense air blast travels fast enough to easily uplift and overturn a train car.

A victim of an ice avalanche is lifted from the hurricane-wind force of the blast and then hurled back down onto the ice, rocks, and glacial moraine. He may suffer broken limbs, a broken pelvis, a broken back, and/or a fractured skull. He may be killed by ice and rock transformed into daggers and bullets by the force, or impaled by objects caught in the air blast, such as tent poles. He is much more likely to die from trauma than asphyxiation, as Dave had witnessed in the Icefall the previous season. A beacon might help to locate the body, but, as Dave conveyed to the team, it would be unlikely to help save the victim.

April 14, 2015
Posted by: Dave Hahn
Categories: Expedition Dispatches; Everest
Elevation: 17,575 feet

RMI EXPEDITIONS BLOG

This is Dave Hahn with the RMI Everest Expedition calling in. We are without internet . . . due to forces beyond our control, so we'll have to do a voice dispatch. We are doing fine. Nobody wants to push through the Icefall right now with the possibility of more snow coming . . . that doesn't seem worthwhile at the moment but maybe in another day or two. We'll see. Everybody is doing well. We'll let you know what happens. Thanks.

On April 14, the team again woke up to thick and soupy clouds, deep snow on the ground, and the threat of more snow falling. The storm blocked all solar gain and caused them to lose Internet connectivity. "I wonder if it might be oversimplifying things to say that those bound for the summit just need to mix up intensely hard work and ample rest, time at extreme and less extreme altitudes, and endure terror and boredom for two months . . . but it does run something like that," Dave said, over a breakfast of coffee and hot rice porridge in the double-walled dining tent insulated from the weather.

After a second helping of breakfast, this time scrambled eggs and fried potatoes, Dave decided to take the team out for ninety-minute climb to give them some exercise and some more training. They trudged through the snow, explored narrow passages in ribbonlike folds of the glacier, and negotiated frozen stream crossings until they reached the face of the first steep portion of the Icefall. For a moment, the sun even made a veiled appearance behind a thin layer of clouds. Dave pulled his camera out of his pack to snap a shot of a circular halo that shone around it. The ethereal rainbow-like ring around the sun was caused by ice crystals reflecting and refracting light in the upper atmosphere. The ice crystals in the troposphere behaved like prisms and mirrors, reflecting and redirecting light, creating the extraordinary circle. In Nepal, such a 22-degree circular halo around the sun was called *Indrasabha*, a connotation to the court of Indra, the Hindu god of thunder, lightning, and rain. The Indrasabha confirmed the most recent weather reports. Dave did not want to make a push through the Icefall with the threat of more weather, so they returned to camp and spent much of the cold, cloudy afternoon playing football in the snow and relaxing with hot tea, worn-out magazines, and poker in the dining tent.

The next day, April 15, the snow kept up, on and off. Again, the team ventured out to the base of the Icefall and back, as Dave wanted to keep their legs stretched and their reflexes tuned. Back at camp, they used the time to review their gear and become acquainted with their down suits. They snapped photos of each other in their puffy First Ascent one-pieces, some red and some blue, their bulky forms resembling astronauts in space suits. The Sherpa team did the same, posing more formally in two rows for a group photo. Nima Wangchu Sherpa, Pasang Temba Sherpa, Chetan Bhote, and Rinjin Bhote stood with Chhering smiling in the center, arms draped around each other, while Yuba Raj Rai (Camp Two cook), Lapka Gyaljen Sherpa, Densa Bhote, Fura Sonam Sherpa, and Pasang Bhote (Camp Two cook assistant) kneeled below them. Climbing Sherpa Pemba Norbu Sherpa was the only one missing from the impromptu photo op.

Later, JJ worked with the team on further streamlining their systems for climbing fixed ropes in which the anchored ropes were bolted in place to provide safety to climbers in exposed and difficult terrain. While some argued that fixed ropes reduced the skill level required to climb Everest, they helped reduce bottlenecks on the most technical sections of terrain and allowed expedition members and sherpas to progress up and down the route more quickly and more safely. Practicing clipping into and using such rope systems down at Base Camp would help the team to safely and efficiently advance across shared rope on much steeper terrain up higher on the mountain, where mittened hands, nerves, and lack of oxygen to the brain made even simple tasks much trickier.

Dave later took advantage of the opportunity to have the team practice with their oxygen apparatus. "We'll practice with it more at Camp Three, on the Lhotse Face, but I also like doing this sort of run-through down here in the thicker air on a rest day," he told them. "That way when we have to get up in the cold at a bajillion feet above sea level with cold hands and dim brains, we can maybe muddle through and get our hookups and flow rates right."

They familiarized themselves with the systems by attaching the regulators to the metal bottles, the hoses to the regulators, and the black masks to their faces. Dave informed them they would begin to use their oxygen at 24,000 feet and throughout their summit bid. They would put on their oxygen apparatus at Camp Three, sleep with it there, and continue to use it while moving to the summit.

"I think people back home have some misconceptions about supplemental oxygen," Dave told them. "Oxygen certainly helps but it doesn't bring you down to the beach. Oxygen is awkward as anything; having a mask with a big hose on it on affects your ability to see where you're putting your feet. The benefit is similar to putting oil in your car. It runs without it but it runs a lot better and faster with oil. One of the underappreciated benefits of oxygen is it keeps you warmer, especially your extremities like your fingers and toes. Another is that it helps with the decision-making process. You get oxygen to your brain and, well, turns out you do a much better job of thinking." He smiled.

Dave recalled to them an angst-ridden experience he had once had with oxygen while working as the lead guide for the American Women's Everest Expedition in 2002. He still felt withered by the memory of

Miss Hawley, her ankles crossed while sitting on a scarlet, velvet love seat in the lobby of the Hotel Tibet, commenting to him, "That is rather unimpressive, don't you think?" after she had compared the number of climbers listed on his Everest permit with the number of climbers who had reached the summit during the expedition.

"Well, we tried pretty hard," Dave remembered replying meekly during their post-trip interview.

Dave had, in fact, been quite impressed by his team that season, which had been composed of five women ranging in age from twenty-five to fifty-eight and had included an investment banker, an ER nurse, and a breast-cancer survivor. Along with their highly capable sherpa team and skillful assistant guides, Lisa Rust and Ben Marshall, they had climbed well and strong to the South Col at 26,000 feet, with only one climber having turned back the day before, at 24,000 feet, as a result of becoming claustrophobic from her bulky O2 mask. She had never used supplemental oxygen before and the steep and icy Lhotse Face turned out to be a tough place to learn. Then, on the day of their summit bid, Dave made a series of decisions, based on the mystifying and rapid mental and physical decline of another one of the climbers, that led him to turn around their team of sixteen climbers just short of Everest's summit. When he later discovered that the valve on the distressed climber's oxygen bottle had been jostled shut during a rest stop, causing her sudden symptoms, he felt sick about it. In spite of the closed valve, its gauge had showed the correct psi and flow rate. Dave was relieved to see the climber begin to recover within seconds after he opened the valve, as if having surfaced from the bottom of a swimming pool, but, as a guide, he couldn't help but regret the mistake that had proven frustrating and costly.

Practice, Dave advised, would help RMI's 2015 team avoid such agonizing and potentially life-threatening errors. They all took turns strapping the black masks to their faces and, to lighten the mood, swapped fighter pilot and Darth Vader impressions, repeating "Luke, I am your father" to one another. With their brains and bodies engaged in such meaningful and exhilarating rehearsal, the day passed relatively quickly for the team.

Dave's longtime friend and mentor, and a legendary climber, Ed Viesturs liked to call Dave "the King of Patience," but by April 16, even Dave had to admit that it was beginning to feel like Groundhog Day. Once again, Dave, Chhering, and the sherpa team were ready to embark on their recon mission in the Icefall, and once again they realized by 3:00 a.m. that the weather would not allow it. Snow continued to fall and the clouds looked to Dave to be as thick as clam chowder. Still, just to maintain mental and physical readiness, they geared up and plodded through the whiteout to the base of the Khumbu Icefall, finding the route by feel more than by vision. As they broke trail through the snow, the ice towers occasionally drifted into view through the dense, ghostly veil of clouds. Dave thought they looked eerily beautiful.

Later in the afternoon, Tuck tried to lift the groups' spirits by plotting out a snowy baseball field for what JJ deemed The Khumbu World Series. "Batter up!" JJ shouted to the group as he passed out balls and bats that Tuck seemed to have produced magically out of thin air. They played until it grew too dark to see the ball.

"Tomorrow, for sure," Dave said at dinner. "Up and at 'em."

That night the storm persisted and they lost all power and cell service. The clouds had blocked all solar gain and their reflector dishes were wrecked by winds. Dave, Chhering, and the RMI sherpa team managed to climb partially up the Icefall in the early morning in spite of the weather, but they were forced to turn around, along with approximately seventy sherpas from other teams, at a point where the route had collapsed. Vertical ladders destroyed by shifting ice would need to be replaced in order to make it passable. Winds from the storm persisted up high. They were back at camp before breakfast time.

"Bad weather and shifting glacial ice are perfectly normal in this game," Dave reassured his team. "Realistically, there will be more waiting to endure. The Icefall Doctors need to do a fair bit of work to make the route passable. We're in the same situation as the few dozen other teams at Base Camp . . . so we'll wait, and we'll be ready when our chance for climbing comes."

By the next morning, April 18, it appeared the storm might finally be passing. The sun peeked out from behind the clouds at Everest Base Camp, but Dave knew there would be no climbing on what was the grim anniversary of last year's Icefall tragedy, out of respect for the sixteen Nepali men who had lost their lives that day. The atmosphere at Base Camp felt heavy with grief and memory. Chhering found there were no words to describe the now-familiar pain the horror of that day—and the sudden, violent loss of so many friends—caused him. It was tethered somewhere deep inside of him to the unfathomable sorrow of his only brother being forever swept away.

Following April 18, 2014, a day that marked the worst loss of life on Everest since climbing expeditions first came to the Khumbu, with the Sherpa community mourning an unprecedented loss, the Nepali government had offered 40,000 rupees (about $413) to the families of each of the victims. The amount was not enough to cover the cost of a funeral, much less to ease the enormous burden left by the loss of a breadwinner on his immediate and extended family. Frustrated by the meager compensation for such dangerous work that was the backbone of a multimillion-dollar industry, which net the government three to four million US dollars per year from climbing fees and poured money into the local economy, the sherpas' resentments boiled over. Well aware that no commercial expeditions would succeed on Everest without sherpa support, they felt their critical roles were unacknowledged. In shock and in grief, at the foot of Chomolungma, the sherpas organized what in an industrial setting would be called a labor dispute and strike, effectively shutting down the rest of the 2014 climbing season and creating a list of demands in a thirteen-point charter. On April 24, 2014, Bhim Prasad Acharya, Nepal's Minister of Tourism, had been flown by helicopter to

Base Camp to reassure the expedition outfitters that the $10,000 climbing fee permits they had already purchased would be rolled into the 2015 season. While breathing oxygen through a nasal cannula, he also met with a rainbow sea of Sherpa mountaineers wearing a colorful array of down jackets and ultimately promised to bring their charter to the cabinet for consideration.

When the government later announced it would meet many of the sherpa requests—including raising their minimum life insurance to about $15,000, erecting a memorial to the beloved men lost that day, providing a pension for older sherpas and educational assistance to the children of sherpas, and creating a relief fund from the climber fees to help support families of the dead—the local Sherpa people were skeptical of the government's concessions, not believing it until they could see evidence of it. In the meantime, mountain guides and climbing companies made donations to nonprofits such as the Juniper Fund, established by Dave's friends and Everest guide colleagues Melissa Arnot and David Morton in 2012 to provide a safety net for Nepali workers in the climbing industry, and The Khumbu Climbing Center, a climbing and mountain rescue training center for local Nepali workers established in the memory of Dave's friend Alex Lowe. Guides and climbers also contributed to funds set up in the tragedy's aftermath by several different organizations and individuals (including the American Alpine Club; the American Himalayan Association; a Japanese climbing team;, a group of photographers from *Outside Magazine* and *National Geographic*; and Joby Ogwyn, an American climber who had planned to attempt the first wingsuit jump off of Everest before the season came to a halt when his entire sherpa team was killed in the avalanche). Together they had raised nearly one million dollars for the sixteen families.

In spite of these goodwill efforts, Dave worried whether or not the trauma, anguish, and friction revealed by the tragedy could be healed. He still believed that mountain guiding on historic and stunning Everest could be a noble profession, one that could be achieved without exploiting workers or insulting the traditions of mountaineering. He knew that ultimately their lives depended on it—and on each other.

Weather delays and Icefall repairs were to be expected on Everest, but in the wake of the previous year's devastating season, making it through the obstacle of the Icefall to the Western Cwm felt to Dave like a more formidable task than ever. He was sure the route would need to be repaired after the storm made its exit and that there would be more waiting to endure, which would further tax the team's patience, stamina, and nerves. It would have been a major morale boost to the team, Dave thought, if he had made it up to Camp One yesterday. All things considered, Dave decided it might be best to give the team their freedom today. Some of them chose to hike down to teahouses in Gorak Shep and some to spend the day with showers and good books at Base Camp.

During the night, fierce winds blew the storm out of Base Camp. In the morning, bright, strong sunshine shone, and it was T-shirt weather by midday. Internet was restored. The Icefall Doctors worked diligently to fix ladders while various climbing teams scrambled around the lower flanks of the Khumbu glacier, trying to stay out of the way of the Icefall Doctors as they practiced climbing techniques in their own obstacle courses. Tuck organized an impromptu horseshoe tournament, complete with an awards ceremony. "Ladies and gentlemen, I present to you the RMI 2015 Sherpa World Champion Horseshoe Team!" JJ declared. By late afternoon, word had spread around camp that the route to Camp One was nearly repaired. Dave took the delighted team for an afternoon "cruise" away from the tents and through labyrinthine ice towers and ridges in a relatively safe section of the glacier well below the mouth of the Icefall.

The following morning, on April 20, Dave, Chhering, and the sherpa team departed Base Camp in the pitch-black darkness of 4:30 a.m. and made another attempt to accomplish a recon/carry mission through the Icefall. As the sun began to rise, the sky was lit up in an azure-blue, crepuscular glow. The weather and visibility were perfect, but they encountered a traffic jam on the route at 7:00 a.m. For ninety more long minutes they inched upward in the Icefall, which was especially frigid since the sun had not yet hit it. They stomped their feet to keep warm while anxiously glancing back and forth from the ice towers hanging above them to the nearby site of the previous year's avalanche. Dave estimated that between them and an imposing wall climb ahead were at least one hundred sherpas, all forced to a standstill. He decided they had pushed their luck far enough. Thwarted again, they cached their loads at the midpoint of the Icefall and reached the relative warmth and safety of Base Camp soon after the rest of the team had headed out on another Pumori training hike with JJ. On the whiteboard was a message: "Don't feed Momo."

Dave and Chhering had made it far enough through the Icefall that morning to determine that the route was, in general, a safer path than the routes of the previous few years, veering "climber's right" near Nuptse and avoiding the hanging ice on Everest's west shoulder. However, it was also clear to them that the route would require more work and more ladders in order to handle the traffic of the sherpas and the conga lines of less-skilled, non-Nepali climbers who would soon be snaking through it. Back at Base Camp, the growing population of which was approaching 1,000 people, Chhering and Dave shared their assessment with the Icefall Doctors and their administrators.

Tomorrow, they would try again.

April 21, 2015
Posted by: Dave Hahn
Categories: Expedition Dispatches; Everest
Elevation: 17,575 feet

RMI EXPEDITIONS BLOG

Finally, a breakthrough day. Our excellent Sherpa climbing team
ran up to the midpoint of the Icefall where we'd cached our gear
yesterday. They put all of that on their backs and busted on up
to establish Camp 1 at approximately 19,800 ft. Two of the guys,
Rinjin and Sonam then cruised on up to Camp 2 (Advance Base
Camp), claiming our campsite—which will be crucial with the
mountain as busy as we expect it to be—and retrieving our ABC
gear from last year ("abandoned" when the season came to an
unexpected end last year). Meanwhile, Chhering, JJ Justman
and I guided the climbing team on our much anticipated "dress
rehearsal" for the Icefall. We were up at 3:30 AM, eating at
4 AM, and walking by 4:30 AM. The intention was to travel
smoothly and efficiently to the midpoint of the Icefall and return
to base . . .as a check that the entire team would be ready for
the committing step of moving to Camp 1. We did just that on
another perfect weather morning. It was encouraging for all of
us, and a little awe inspiring when three of the Icefall Doctors
caught up and passed us as if we were standing still—all while
carrying heavy and cumbersome sections of ladder to put in
place at yesterday's trouble spot near the top of the Icefall. About
two hours into our climb, we hit our own first real ladders and
shadows and then got set for the equally challenging descent
to Base. The team cruised through this test, showing the
advantages of two weeks of training and acclimatizing. We were

Perched on the second-to-highest rung of three ladders stacked and tied one on top of the other, diagonally spanning the yawning mouth of a crevasse and a vertical wall of ice, Dave felt elated to finally get the team up into the Icefall for a "dress rehearsal." He was relieved to see the Icefall Doctors moving more ladders upward through it, which he suspected they would install in the bottleneck section he had encountered higher up yesterday. Dave figured one advantage of their longer stay at Base Camp was that the team had grown better acclimated and more eager than they might have been with an earlier push to the Western Cwm, the glacial valley basin located above the Icefall at the foot of the Lhotse Face. The extra time had also given Peter's body an opportunity to recover fully from his GI infection and Larry's back a chance to rest and heal. Larry's cough, however, had not improved with the extended time; it had, instead, continued to worsen.

Larry found he was lagging behind the rest of the team. His persistent cough interfered with the rhythm of his breathing. He needed his body to function as a synchronized machine in the Icefall, with no wasted effort or energy, but it was impossible to breathe smoothly and efficiently while bent over coughing. His coughing fits forced him to stop several times, and he felt painfully aware that pausing in the Icefall and therefore spending more time in it would only increase the inherent risk that being in it posed, for himself and for the others. He also knew his cough would not get any better as they climbed higher on Everest in the following days and weeks. Larry had experienced enough years of climbing to come to a prudent decision. He would sleep on it, just to be certain.

The next morning, after a night of fitful hacking, Larry pulled Dave aside before breakfast.

"Dave, I've decided that I'm not going up," he said.

Dave appreciated that Larry had been climbing hard and pushing himself to extremes in the face of a number of physical setbacks. On just his second night in Nepal, Larry had slipped in the bathroom at the Yak and Yeti, slamming his toe into the wall and breaking his toenail. He had meticulously rewrapped it with gauze, bandaged it, and taped it every day since. The subsequent back spasms and bronchitis had tipped the scale. Having climbed with Larry before, Dave recognized that Larry had always been an asset to his climbing teams and would never allow himself to become a potential liability to his teammates.

"Well, I understand," he said gently to Larry, as he laid a hand on his shoulder.

Larry announced his decision to the rest of the team at breakfast.

"I'll stay here, pack up, and wait for you guys to come back from Camp One," Larry told them. "We'll say our goodbyes then, before I head back to Kathmandu."

His teammates felt disappointed for Larry and regretted losing a teammate, but like Dave, they applauded him for what they viewed as a wise and conscientious decision. They were experienced enough climbers, one and all, to recognize the importance of knowing when to turn around.

The team spent the rest of their designated rest day selecting food and gear they would require for what they hoped would be a three-night stay at Camp One. Tomorrow they would make their push through and above the Icefall toward the Western Cwm. The Cwm, a Welsh word for a bowl-shaped valley, was so named by British mountaineer George Mallory, one of the first explorers of the upper reaches of Everest, when he first saw it while searching for routes to the summit during a British reconnaissance expedition in 1921.

Mallory was perhaps best known for uttering the three most famous words in mountaineering: "Because it's there," when a reporter asked him, "Why do you want to climb Mount Everest?" He and his climbing partner, Andrew "Sandy" Irvine, both disappeared during their historic attempt to make the very first ascent of Everest in June of 1924. Their expedition colleague, the geologist Noel O'Dell, believed he had last spotted them about 800 vertical feet from the summit. O'Dell later recounted:

> At 12:50, just after I had emerged from a state of jubilation at finding the first definite fossils on Everest, there was a sudden clearing of the atmosphere, and the entire summit ridge and final peak of Everest were unveiled. My eyes became fixed on one tiny black spot silhouetted on a small snow-crest beneath a rock-step in the ridge; the black spot moved. Another black spot became apparent and moved up the snow to join the other on the crest. The first then approached the great rock-step and shortly emerged at the top; the second did likewise. Then the whole fascinating vision vanished, enveloped in cloud once more.

Seventy-five years later, in 1999, Dave was the climbing leader of the team that made the stunning discovery of George Mallory's remarkably intact body at 27,000 feet, lying on the windswept scree of Mount Everest's North Face. Dave had been brought aboard the Mallory and Irvine Research Expedition by his friend and colleague, Eric Simonson. The goal of the expedition, advised by German researcher Jochen Hemmleb, was to discover evidence of whether Mallory and Irvine had made it to the summit of Everest before they disappeared. Based on his investigations of earlier sightings by a previous expedition, Hemmleb had identified the general vicinity of a body on Everest, believed to be Andrew Irvine's since it lay directly below his found ice axe. The hope was to find both the body, presumably preserved for decades by the cold, and a camera belonging to Mallory and Irvine, the film in which might reveal photographic evidence of a summit.

Ever since he was a young boy, Dave had felt intoxicated by the prospect of search and discovery. He still remembered the twinge of excitement he had felt in his stomach, at the age of eight, upon finding a treasure in the coin change given to him when had paid a secret visit to a candy store in Kingston. "Hey, you gave me an 1841 dime!" he had happily exclaimed to the unimpressed merchant. Dave could still remember the way the storekeeper had shrugged and mumbled something in reply about the coin being good enough for change. Dave also treasured a vintage camera he had found on the Nisqually Glacier when he first climbed Rainier, and he delighted in hunting for oxygen cylinders from historic expeditions on the flanks of Everest whenever he could sneak away long enough to do so. When Dave was invited to help form the Mallory and Irvine Research Expedition, he was easily convinced. He felt tugged by the mystery of the disappearance of Mallory and Irvine and thrilled by both the prospect of climbing Everest with such strong climbing partners (including Andy Politz, Jake Norton, Tap Richards, and his friend Conrad Anker) and the possibility that they might discover the coveted camera or stumble upon other clues that could help solve the puzzle of how far Mallory and Irvine had ascended.

The expedition was marked by typical Everest challenges, including battering winds, insomnia, impossibly steep slopes, and high-altitude-induced ills. However, from the moment Conrad Anker came upon a well-preserved alabaster-colored body wearing the hobnail climbing boots common before World War II, the expedition began to feel like stepping through a portal of time into another era. With labored breath from the extreme altitude, Conrad called in the rest of the team, who had spread out in their search across uneven and sharply sloped terrain, over the radio. Despite some initial miscommunication, the team eventually converged with Conrad as he stood beside what most of them assumed was Andrew Irvine's body. Andy Politz's intuition told him otherwise. Fingering through layers of ragged remnants of clothing left on the body, they were at first confused when Jake flipped over a fragment of a laundry label on a shirt collar marked "G. Leigh Mallory." Then they found another identical label on another layer of clothing, and then another.

"Oh my God. Oh my God," Dave said as the revelation began to take hold. He felt a surge of adrenaline rise up in him from the surprise.

"Maybe it was the altitude and the fact that we'd put aside our oxygen gear," Dave would later recall in a written dispatch, "but it took a while for the realization to sink in. Finally it hit us. We were in the presence of George Mallory himself. . . . We weren't just looking at a body. We were looking at an era, one we'd only known through books. The natural fiber clothes, the fur lined helmet, the kind of rope that was around him were all so eloquent. As we stood there, this mute but strangely peaceful body was giving us answers to questions that everyone had been asking for three-quarters of a century: the fact that a rope had been involved, that there was no oxygen apparatus…"

Mallory had suffered a broken leg and a golf ball–sized fracture in his skull. His arms were outstretched, as if attempting to break a sliding fall, and his fingers were dug into the scree, presumably in an effort to self-arrest. His exposed back revealed strong musculature. On his body and in the pockets of his clothing, they found an altimeter, a pocketknife, and snow goggles, but no camera. Remnants of a climbing rope still encircled Mallory's waist, which was marked by a rope-jerk injury. Anker had found the body about 300 meters below and 100 meters across from where an ice axe had been found in 1933, the one believed to have belonged to Irvine due to the mark on its shaft. The combined evidence suggested that Mallory and Irvine may have been roped together when Mallory slipped and fell, snagging the rope and sliding to his death.

Dave documented Mallory's remains with photographs. The team took a collection of artifacts, clothing samples, and a small sample of skin from Mallory's forearm for DNA analysis (as requested by the families of both Mallory and Irvine prior to the search). Then they covered Mallory's body in a layer of stones, and Andy Politz read Psalm 103 in a brief ceremony.

...The life of mortals is like grass,
they flourish like a flower of the field:
the wind blows over it and it is gone
And its place remembers it no more...

While thrilled by their historic discovery, the group felt a collective sense of grief when it came time to leave George Mallory's body. Even in death they were awed to be in the presence of this pioneer of high-altitude exploration. Renowned for his exceptional agility, grace, and grit, as well as his route-setting ability, Mallory was considered widely to have been the best mountaineer of his time. They identified with him, as fellow climbers, and with another, lesser-known answer of his when asked the question of why he climbed Everest: "For the stone from the top for the geologists, the knowledge of the limits of endurance for the doctors, but above all, for the spirit of adventure to keep alive the soul of man."

The mystery of whether Mallory and Irvine reached Everest's summit would remain a source of debate and curiosity in the climbing world. All that was certain was that they perished in the attempt. Dave and his teammates sometimes wondered just how much the question of the summit really mattered, given the epic scale of their achievement and the relatively primitive resources available to them at the time. Even in death, George's physical strength, his fierce tenacity, and his unquenchable desire to climb were palpable. Perhaps, Dave thought, that was what mattered more.

20 ▲ THE VALLEY OF SILENCE

April 23, 2015
Posted by: Mark Tucker
Categories: Expedition Dispatches; Everest
Elevation: 17,575 feet

RMI EXPEDITIONS BLOG

The 2015 Mt. Everest season has been a tough start with big snowstorms here at base camp, but full steam ahead right now. The snow that kept us from moving up earlier has blossomed to some nice days. You would be amazed at the difference on the glacier since last week. Rivers running, pools forming and a route through the Icefall that has allowed a reasonable ascent to Camp 1, where the team is at this very moment. I just got off the radio with Dave and word is, all well. I was able to follow the team's climb up the ice fall with my tripod-mounted spotting scope. They were at times obscured from view by huge ice towers and the route taking them down into the depths of the glacier, out of sight, and then minutes later they would they pop back into view. Their training, adjusting to the altitude and experience at this sort of wild climbing paid off with what I can guarantee you was one of the most amazing and memorable days in these mountaineers climbing careers. So proud of this group as I watched them progress through the Khumbu Icefall working the mountain, assisting each other, and sticking together in pure style and grace. Way to go team!
    RMI Guide and Everest Base Camp Manager
    Mark Tucker

As Tuck trained his eyes on the team with his spotting scope, he could see the climbers work their way through the Icefall on a route that appeared steeper to him than last year's route. A half-moon hung above them in the cerulean blue of the early-morning sky. He watched their tiny shadowy figures move through what looked at dawn like the giant, frozen waves of an ice-blue sea. The higher peaks glowed white, as if emitting a light from within.

Just after 11:30 a.m., Dave's voice came across the radio. Tuck held his breath until Dave reported that they had safely reached Camp One at an altitude of 19,990 feet. Tuck exhaled and grinned as he listened.

"It's so nice to be out of Base Camp and climbing on the mountain," Dave told Tuck. "Everybody did a great job coming through the Icefall. It was, uh, rough going. It's a steep route. It has some big, hairy ladders . . .but everyone did really well."

Dave's voice radiated relief. Tuck understood, in the shadow of last season's tragedy and with the weather delays they had recently endured at Base Camp, just how heavily the prospect of the Icefall had weighed on Dave. When Tuck inquired about their sherpa team, Dave confirmed that five of RMI's sherpa team had gone as far as Camp Two to drop off valuable loads there before heading back to Base Camp. Four others from their sherpa team had reached Camp One ahead of Dave, Chhering, JJ, Hans, Hao, Robbie, and HP, as planned, and had already built camp for them.

"Those guys did great work for us," Dave said. "We're very grateful. But we're going to have to move our tents."

The tents had been set up against a wall below the west shoulder, which was loaded with ice and snow. Dave had seen avalanches wash down the wall before, destroying tents, so he didn't feel comfortable with the spot. He realized that his climbers and his sherpa team were physically and mentally fatigued after a five-hour climb through the Icefall but felt convinced they would have to rally to move the tents about one-quarter of a mile toward the center of the bowl, away from the threat of a potential slide.

Nowhere in Camp One could be considered entirely innocuous. The Western Cwm was a vast, 2.5-mile-long, gently undulating glacial valley basin of endless snow and deep crevasses, with Everest's west shoulder to the east, Lhotse to the south, and Nuptse to the west. The giant snow-covered basin reflected and amplified radiation, acting like a solar oven. Temperatures could become uncomfortably hot by midday, then plunge to below freezing in minutes when sun turned to shade. Beneath tiny fissures in the snow hid the gaping mouths of large crevasses. The Western Cwm was sometimes called the Valley of Silence, since it was protected from the wind. However, crevasses opening and closing deep down beneath it, inside the glacier, made the sound of a crackling murmur far below tents at night.

They moved camp inward, trudging across the expanse of whiteness, to a spot located on the fin of a glacier between two crevasses. For the remainder of their expedition above Base Camp they would share tents. They lined their yellow tents up in a row, with Robbie and Peter sharing the first, Dave and JJ in the next, Chhering and HP in the third, and Hans and Hao next to them.

Breathing at this new altitude felt like sucking air through a straw. The atmospheric pressure at nearly 20,000 feet was about half of that at sea level. Although the percentage of oxygen in the air remained the same as it was at sea level, the number of molecules of oxygen in each lungful of air was reduced by half. Pounding headaches began to set in. They rested and hydrated with snow they melted on their camp stoves, while they grew acquainted with their new home.

Eventually they began to mentally process the experience of their climb through the Icefall. Peter and Robbie talked it over with each other in their tent. The route, as expected, had been crowded with local sherpa teams and foreign climbing teams. What surprised both Robbie and

Peter, however, was the number of underprepared and unacclimated foreign (non-Nepali) climbers they observed in the Icefall. Robbie told Peter he had taken the job of preparing himself for Everest seriously. He had trained at his local YMCA for thirty-two weeks and had saved up for five years to pay for the trip. He had sought out a guide service with a stellar reputation, known for vetting its climbers based on previous, documented high-altitude climbing experience. As a team, they had taken the time to acclimate appropriately. He was stunned to see climbers who appeared out of shape and others who seemed to be unfamiliar with their equipment here on the world's highest mountain.

"I met a guy down there who told me he hadn't trained one day," Robbie said.

Peter concurred. He had scheduled several ice-climbing and rock-climbing trips with RMI guides during the year leading up to this expedition in order to work on specific techniques he would need on Everest. He had already climbed four of the Seven Summits, most recently Vinson Massif (the highest peak in Antarctica), which he felt would prepare him to cope with Everest's steep terrain and bitter cold. He knew that acclimatization gained on Vinson would last only two to three weeks after returning to sea level, so he strived to get into the best cardiovascular shape possible before Everest, believing it would enable his body to use more energy toward the acclimatization process that would begin once he reached Kathmandu. He had worked on cultivating greater core strength, balance, upper-body strength, and leg strength. After all, he reminded Robbie, at sixty-three years old he was more than twice Robbie's age. The Icefall had been even tougher than he had expected, but he also felt he had been able to deal with it better than he had anticipated.

"I came away from it feeling like I had earned the right to be there," he said.

They were both awed by the strength and stamina of the sherpa teams who often passed them smiling and cheerfully wished them "Namaste" while carrying heavy loads on their backs through the Icefall, a place where Robbie and Peter agreed even rest took enormous effort.

They were still four weeks away from a potential summit. On this first climbing rotation they would spend a few nights at Camp One and a few nights at Camp Two before heading back to Base Camp to rest. During their next rotation, the plan would be to make it as far as Camp Three. Ideally, their summit push would occur during an anticipated opening in the weather window.

Summiting was not an option when the winds roared like a jet engine, often with a force of more than 100 miles an hour. Everest was raked by cold, jet-stream winds through much of the winter and spring. The summer monsoon would arrive in June and bring with it huge amounts of moisture that would arrive in the form of snowstorms, and subsequent avalanches, on Everest. The expedition had been planned with the idea that the team would complete their acclimatization cycles during the tail end of the windy season. This would set them up to use the window of relatively calm weather that typically opens for a week or so sometime during the second half of May, when the jet stream would pull north away from Everest and before the monsoon season moved in from the Indian Ocean's Bay of Bengal, to make a push toward the summit.

The exhausted team settled in for a cold night at the higher altitude. Dave told them his plan was to hike them halfway to Camp Two, also known as Advanced Base Camp, in the morning so they could "stretch their legs," acquaint themselves with the lay of the land, and accelerate their unavoidable acclimatization process.

"The first night at Camp One is usually good for . . . let's see . . . a headache, some more insomnia, and more of everything that is uncomfortable and mean about new altitude," he said to them as he bid them good-night.

Their tents glowed like fireflies in the vast snowfield beneath the inky, starry sky. The moon illuminated the snowy, rock-face walls of Nuptse to the west, the west shoulder of Everest to the east, and Lhotse dead ahead.

April 24, 2015
Posted by: Dave Hahn
Categories: Expedition Dispatches; Everest
Elevation: 19,900 feet
Satellite phone transcript

RMI EXPEDITIONS BLOG

Hey, this is Dave Hahn calling from Camp 1 on Mount Everest. A good day for us up here. We got up this morning at about 6:00 in the morning and set out at 8:00 to explore the last couple of ladder crossings in the Western Cwm. They go about halfway to Camp 2. Our intention today was just exercise and getting to know the lay of the land. Our hope is tomorrow to get a good acclimatization hike in going all the way to Camp 2 and then coming back down here to Camp 1 for that next night. The afternoon today after we get back to camp was pretty quiet. It was snowing lightly, kinda socked in. We just took the opportunity to rest and recuperate inside our tents and continue our acclimatization process. Thank you.

RMI Guide Dave Hahn

The team gathered around 6:00 a.m. at Camp One on April 24, their mouths dry and their heads pounding after a cold, fitful night of tossing and turning and something vaguely resembling sleep at close to 20,000 feet. They all wore their down suits, since the Western Cwm was still deep in frigid shadow at such an early hour, while they sipped instant coffee and warm Tang they had made from snow melted on their camp stoves. "My friend Conrad calls it 'rotisserie sleeping,'" Dave said. "There are a lot of reasons to feel shitty up here," he added as he gazed longingly up the vast, dead-end valley toward the steep face of Lhotse, the fourth-highest mountain in the world, "but sure enough, the big mountains have a way of organizing your mind." He pointed out a series of frozen ice waves originating near Lhotse's base that were cascading slowly, imperceptibly, pulled by gravity toward the cliff below their campsite. As the glacial ice waves flowed over the cliff and across steep bedrock, at a rate of 3 to 4 feet per day, they created the chaos of the Khumbu Icefall. Dave noted the striations of annual snowfall in the exposed sections of seracs. They resembled the rings on a tree trunk.

Dave explained that the entire climb to Camp Two, clipped into fixed rope due to the heavily crevassed terrain, would generally take between two and three hours to cover its distance of 1.74 miles with an altitude gain of 1,500 feet. They could expect a combination of large lateral crevasses—hundreds of feet deep—transecting the route, as well as smaller, more dangerous ones hidden beneath thin bridges of snow formed over them by drifting snow and cornices. Dave's acclimatization goal for today was for the team to make it about halfway to Camp Two, crossing over the remaining few ladders, and return to Camp One before the midday sun made the temperatures in the Western Cwm unbearably hot for climbing. With the sun reflecting off the snow-covered slopes of Everest, Lhotse, and Nuptse, temperatures could easily climb to 100 degrees Fahrenheit in the basin. Then again, should clouds gather, wind pick up, and snow begin to fall, it could also turn bitterly cold.

"Layer up. There's no such thing as the wrong weather, only the wrong clothes," Dave reminded them.

At 8:00 a.m., they set out toward Camp Two, which sat at the base of Everest's southwest face. In spite of their sleep deprivation and altitude hangovers, they agreed it felt liberating to be out of Base Camp and thrilling to be climbing above the Icefall. The impossibly steep face of Lhotse at the other end of the Cwm was intimidating even from afar. As they climbed, they squinted behind their sunglasses and strained their necks to try to take in the 5,000 feet of vertical terrain above them. Soon they faced ladder crossings composed of two or three ladders strung together with frayed rope, spanning crevasses that appeared bottomless. Though their legs still shook as they walked across the ladders, clinging to the ropes on either side with their gloved hands, these crossings somehow felt slightly less terrifying and more routine than the first ones yesterday in the Icefall had.

On the relatively less treacherous terrain, they stomped up the glacier in their crampons.

Along the route, they ran into many sherpas from various climbing companies, some who were carrying substantial loads all the way up from Base Camp to Camp Two, and others who had emptied loads at Camp Two and were descending back to Base Camp, smiling and relaxed from having been so unburdened. Dave continued to steer his team toward Lhotse until he announced they had gone far enough, and then, after a quick break, they did it all again in reverse, attempting to maintain steadiness and focus over the shaky ladders. They clomped back into Camp One by 11:00 a.m. and eagerly retreated into the shelter of their tents. It had started to snow lightly.

The team passed the rest of the day hunkered down, melting snow on their camp stoves, resting, and rehydrating. Their appetites were lagging, but they continued to force down whatever calories they could at the high altitude to fuel their bodies and help pass the time in the tents. They snacked on small bites of energy bars, oatmeal, instant soups, and ramen noodles. Hao was experiencing some stomach cramping for the first time on the expedition. Between the altitude, exertion, nerves, and the array of viral and bacterial gastrointestinal ills common on Everest, he wasn't sure exactly what was causing it. He pulled his journal and a pen out of his backpack and began to document the morning's events.

HP enjoyed listening to the Nepalese music that Chhering played on his iPhone 5 in their tent. Chhering was especially fond of a genre of Nepali song called Dohori, a rhythmic musical debate between two groups, usually men or boys in one group singing in response to girls or women in the other. The songs ranged from traditional folk to more synthetic-sounding pop. HP was delighted to realize he could make out some of the lyrics, since his Indian heritage and language were so closely related to Nepali: "My heart is flying like a silk in the wind. I cannot decide whether to fly or sit on the hilltop. Our love is waiting at the crossroads."

The next morning, on April 25, the team fired up their stoves in the dark of 4:30 a.m. and departed camp at 6:00 a.m. in order to give themselves enough time to complete a full circuit to Camp Two and back to Camp One before the Cwm heated up. Then, if all went according to plan, they would spend one last night acclimatizing at Camp One before heading back to Base Camp, which would complete their first rotation on Everest. Dave assured them that both the air and their sleeping pads would feel thicker back down at 17,500 feet. "After being up here, Base Camp will feel like the land of good naps," he said.

Though it was no longer snowing, the white blanket of yesterday's snowfall made the crevasses appear less deep. This was a welcome optical illusion as they steeled themselves to walk across the shaky ladders yet again. They also noticed there were no headaches today. The two nights at Camp One had given their bodies a chance to acclimatize. As they trudged upward to Camp Two, the thin carpet of fresh snow made it easier to find their footing.

With their team focused on Lhotse, which often felt like a distant mirage never getting closer, Dave and Chhering paid close attention to the weather. Puffs of clouds were gathering above Lhotse. Within three hours, they made their last push up a steep pitch and had reached a rocky patch at the foot of the icy, 1,200-feet-high Lhotse Wall. There sat Camp Two at the base of the wall and the head of the Western Cwm, on the rocky moraine overlying dense glacial ice. More clouds had rolled in, up the valley, and into the camp. The skies appeared full of moisture.

Hao noticed that Camp Two felt distinctly less primitive and more established than Camp One. With its mess tents, cook tents, and sleeping tents, Camp Two's accommodations were deluxe by Camp One standards. He also thought it felt safer than Camp One. It seemed the gigantic crevasses surrounding them like moats would likely swallow any avalanches that unloaded off the vertical faces. It was easy to see why Camp Two was often referred to as Advanced Base Camp, and it made sense to him that it served as a staging area and launching point for the upper parts of the mountain. In spite of Camp Two's protection and comforts, however, the impending weather kept them from lingering.

As they clomped back down the moraine, Dave pointed out remnants of old stoves, pots, pans, boots, and shredded tents mixed in with the rock and ice. "Over sixty years of Advanced Base Camp in this place . . . and a number of those decades of mountaineering occurred before any ethics existed governing which items should or should not be left in the hills," he said.

Chhering explained that in 2014 the Nepalese government had established a rule that each member of an expedition would be held accountable for bringing back at least eight kilograms of garbage, in addition to their own trash, from Mount Everest, Mount Lhotse, and Mount Nuptse expeditions.

"Each expedition now pays a $4,000 deposit, which is refunded once we show that we have brought back everything we have taken up the mountain," JJ added.

"Yep, and since there's little to no snow left on Everest from recent winters, the glacier surface is down to old snow and ice, which reveals the old trash . . . and occasionally some treasures," Dave said.

"You should see his oxygen-bottle collection," JJ chimed in.

Dave grinned. "Yeah, it's junk to most people, but it's treasure to me," he said. He had always enjoyed searching for old bottles and then matching them to legendary expeditions and climbers of the past.

"I call it *goraking*, after the big black birds around here that go around looking for leftovers and food. I have to remind myself that it's not everybody's thing, but for me, it's a little bit like being a kid treasure hunting. I guess some of the canisters from the more memorable expeditions will eventually end up in museums, instead of in my living room. No goraking today, though," he said, looking upward. "I want us to get back down to Camp One. It looks like a storm is gathering."

Dave, JJ, and Chhering knew that members of the sherpa team had left Base Camp before dawn and had begun heading up through the Icefall in the dark carrying loads consisting of twenty-two oxygen bottles, food, tents, and other supplies. Each of their loads weighed a minimum of 14 kilograms (approximately 30 pounds) and up to 24 kilograms (about 53 pounds) if they were carrying double loads, for which they were paid more. They were bound for Camp Two, where they would stash the provisions before turning around and heading back to Base Camp.

When possible, Chhering had his sherpas travel in teams of three, mixing up speed and experience. Lapka Gyalgen, Rinjin Bhote, and Fura Sonam Sherpa had just passed Camp One. The rest of the climbing team, including Densa Bhote, Chetan Bhote, Pemba Norbu Sherpa, Nima Wongchu Sherpa, and Pasang Temba Sherpa, were nearing the top of the Icefall.

When Dave, Chhering, JJ, Hans, Hao, HP, Peter, and Robbie had descended halfway back down to Camp One, they stopped for a rest and noticed more low clouds building. Dave, Chhering, and JJ discussed the weather together, briefly, and made a joint decision to turn around their sherpas. Chhering radioed his team.

"It's getting pretty cloudy," Chhering told them, in Sherpa Nepali. "We want you to all turn around and go back down, please. Lapka, Rinjin, and Fura, store the gear by our tents, and then return to Base Camp so you won't get stuck in the Icefall during a whiteout. Check in with me when you get back to Base Camp."

For Dave and Chhering, turning the sherpa team around was a decision made out of an abundance of caution, just one of countless such decisions made during the course of an expedition. They had no way of knowing how impactful this particular decision would prove to be. After dropping off their back-bending loads, the sherpas who had reached Camp One bounded quickly down to Base Camp, where they would take shelter from the impending storm. The others, still carrying heavy packs, reversed themselves in the Icefall and headed back to Base Camp. Dave, Chhering, JJ, Hao, Hans, Robbie, and Peter rolled back into Camp One at 11:15 am, lips and throats parched, their minds and bodies thirsty for both fluids and rest.

For the time being, standing on the tallest mountain top,
For the time being, moving on the deepest ocean floor,
For the time being, a demon with three heads and eight arms,
For the time being, the golden sixteen-foot body of a buddha,
For the time being, a monk's staff or a master's fly swatter,
For the time being, a pillar or lantern,
For the time being, any ordinary person,
For the time being, the entire earth and the boundless sky.

Dogen Zenji, "For the Time Being"

A low cloud ceiling hovered over Base Camp, making the titanic mountains invisible. The smell of chicken soup and the murmur of voices over the clanging of pots and pans reminded Larry that it was lunchtime. Sitting in his tent, he pulled on his boots. He was still coming to terms with his thwarted climb, but he had woken on this quiet, grey morning with a sense of serenity that matched the weather. He had begun to accept that with his injuries and illness, this was simply not meant to be his year to climb Everest. He had no regrets. He laced up his boots and stood up to head over to the dining tent. Just then, the ground below him began to shake.

Larry had grown accustomed to the constant movement of the glacier beneath him as it shifted, but that now-familiar sensation typically felt like a quick jump or a jerk. As the ground continued to rock below him, Larry's stomach dropped. Time began to slow down, to feel almost gelatinous in its consistency. Through the open front flap of his tent, he could see Mark standing about 20 feet away.

"Mark, what the hell is going on?" he called out, dropping to his hands and knees inside the tent.

"It's an earthquake," Mark said, stunned. Born and raised in California, he instantly recognized the sensation.

Larry heard a rumbling like a freight train in the distance, but he couldn't see anything through the low-hanging clouds.

"It's a big one!" Mark shouted.

They were jolted by the sound of an explosion. Larry's first thought was that it sounded like a cannon booming.

"Shit! Get behind something!" Mark screamed to Larry

Mark began to run for shelter. Larry stuck his head out of his tent and looked toward the deafening roar coming not from Everest, but from behind Base Camp. Suddenly, an avalanche broke through the cloud cover in the distance, a monstrous wave of snow and debris. He watched the immense powder cloud, thousands of feet tall, hit the Indian Army Camp, instantly engulfing it. There was no time to run or hide. He instinctively backed himself into his tent and lay flat on his stomach. The thought flashed through his mind that he hadn't put on his avalanche beacon and that there would be no way for anyone to find him when he was buried. And then, before there was time for another thought or another breath, the avalanche was upon him.

The air blast enveloped his tent and flipped him on his back. A vapour of fine snow crystals surged into the tent, like an aerosol mist, chilling his throat. He struggled to breathe. The churning mass of snow, rock, ice, and air scraped loudly across the outside of the tent as it passed over him. He crawled back up on his hands and knees and hit and punched the tent walls to try to avoid getting buried. And then, as suddenly as it had come, it was gone. It was over.

Mark yelled over to him. "Larry are you alright?"

Larry's heart pounded in his ears and he was breathing loud and fast. He coughed and yelled back, panting, "Yeah . . . I'm fine. Are you okay?"

"Yeah, I'm good."

Larry lifted himself up off the ground and peered anxiously out of the tent. Their campsite had been flattened by the aerosol blast's explosive force. Strings of prayer flags, tent poles, sleeping bags and pads, cardboard boxes, folding chairs and tables, and backpacks had been churned up and spit out. The radio mast and puja pole had been bent like fish hooks. Snow and ice debris blanketed everything. Mark ran over to the Sherpa tent.

"They're OK!" he called out to Larry.

The communication tent had been razed. Mark ran to it and began to search through the debris for the radio. He could think of only one thing in that moment: he had to find a way to reach Dave at Camp One.

The phone rang in Miss Hawley's office as the ground rolled and rocked. Miss Hawley answered it, her tone unflappable. It was Billi Bierling, a journalist and mountaineer from the Bavarian Alps of Germany, who Hawley had brought on board as an assistant in 2014 to help with the high volume of mountaineering expedition interviews. Typically, Billi would be in Nepal during April, either climbing on an expedition herself or tracking down climbers to interview in Kathmandu. This year, however, she happened to be in Europe celebrating a friend's wedding as a bridesmaid when she received a text message from her friend Monica who was climbing on the north side of Everest in Tibet. She glanced down and read the message that appeared on her cell phone: "Billi, the earth is moving and I have a feeling that it's really bad in Nepal." Billi hung up and called Miss Hawley to check on her, growing anxious as she struggled to get a call through the congested phone network. She finally answered.

"I am sitting at the very table I was sitting when the earth was shaking in 1960," Miss Hawley told her, unfazed.

"Perhaps you should get underneath the table for safety!" Billi suggested emphatically.

"There is no space as my staff is underneath the table. And if I go there I will never get out again!" Miss Hawley replied, annoyed. "Don't worry about me; my house is safe," she added as she began to methodically move her Himalayan Database files into a tin box so she could quickly flee out the back door of her house with them if necessary. Outside her window, the ground rolled. A groundskeeper holding a rake leaned drunkenly to the left, trying to find his footing. Goldfish in a nearby pond were thrust into the air momentarily before gravity pulled them back into the water.

Billi, who also served as a member of the Swiss Humanitarian Aid organization, jumped at an opportunity to join their Rapid Response Team on a flight back from Bern to Nepal at 5:30 a.m. the following morning. When she expressed her disappointment to her friend Chrissie about feeling compelled to leave in the midst of her weekend nuptials, the bride reassured her.

"Billi, we met in Nepal and the country is very dear to both of us. Go to Nepal, and go for all of us," she said.

Figure 24. Mark Tucker plays football at Base Camp.
Courtesy of Robert Massie.

The Icefall. Courtesy of Robert Massie.

Momo greets climbers returning from the Icefall. Courtesy of Dave Hahn.

Icefall ladders. Courtesy of Dave Hahn.

Ladder crossing.
Courtesy of
Robert Massie.

Crossing a crevasse. Courtesy of Robert Massie.

Climbers in
Icefall. Courtesy
of Robert Massie.

JJ Justman, Hao Wu, Peter Rogers, Robbie Massie,
and HP in the Icefall. Courtesy of Dave Hahn.

top Camp One. Courtesy of Dave Hahn.
bottom Nearest neighbors at Camp One. Courtesy of Robert Massie.

JJ Justman at Camp One. Courtesy of Robert Massie.

Chhering attends a meeting with
other guides after the earthquake.
Courtesy of Dave Hahn.

Climbers gather at Camp One
after the earthquake.
Courtesy of Dave Hahn.

Rescue helicopter
casts a shadow on
Camp One. Courtesy
of Dave Hahn.

Helicopter touches down at Camp One. Courtesy of Dave Hahn.

RMI Base Camp after the earthquake. Courtesy of Larry Seaton.

Rescue helicopter. Courtesy
of Robert Massie.

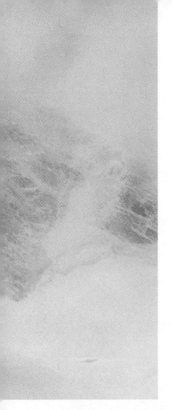

Base Camp after the earthquake.
Courtesy of Hao Wu.

Base Camp rebuilt after the earthquake.
Courtesy of Dave Hahn.

Gorak. Courtesy of Robert Massie.

Prayer flags at Base Camp
after the earthquake. Courtesy
of Robert Massie.

Destruction in Deboche.
Courtesy of Robert Massie.

Facebook
Everest ER
April 25, 2015

There has been an earthquake in Nepal, and a huge avalanche off Pumori covered many tents in base camp. Many of our friends in base camp have been seriously injured and killed and we are taking just a few moments away from our work with the suffering to let our personal friends and families know that the Everest ER team are all safe. With the help of nearly every able bodied friend in base camp, we moved our clinic to the IMG camp where we are caring for patients. We [have] very limited communications at the moment. Pray for Nepal, friends. Namaste.

In Plano, Texas, in a stately, suburban, brick home on Vermillion Drive, the phone began to ring just after midnight. HP's wife, forty-six-year-old Nomita, and their two sons, seven-year-old Shayan and twelve-year-old Shaan, were all asleep in their beds, until the ringing woke Nomita. She rolled over and felt for the phone on her nightstand, which was crowded with framed photos of their family and friends wearing bright saris and sherwanis, smiling widely at glamorous Diwali celebrations, weddings, and birthday parties. In the images, Nomita's round face, big liquid brown eyes, wild curly hair, and vibrant garb lit up her husband's handsome features and quiet elegance.

"Hello," she answered, reaching over to turn on her bedside lamp. Her voice, normally lilting and velvety, was raspy from sleep.

"Nomita, something has happened." Nomita recognized her friend Sonali's voice. "Get up and switch on the TV. I just hung up with my mother in Kolkatta. While we were talking she felt the ground jolt. It was a tremor, from an earthquake."

"What?" Nomita said as she tried to make sense of what Sonali was telling her.

Nomita was born in New Delhi, India. She and HP, Hemanshu to her, attended elementary school there together. They had moved to the United States in 1997. Nomita's parents, who were none too pleased about their son-in-law's dangerous Everest expedition, still lived in New Delhi. Nomita knew how close Kolkatta was to Everest — just under 400 miles. Glancing at the clock on her nightstand, Nomita made mental time calculations. It was midday in India and Nepal, ten hours and forty-five minutes ahead of Central Time in Dallas, Texas.

Nomita told Sonali she had last spoken with Hemanshu on the phone early on the evening of the 21st, which was the morning of the 22nd in Nepal — the date of their twentieth wedding anniversary. Hemanshu had called to wish her a happy anniversary and had mentioned that he would be heading up on a rotation to Camp Two the following day. He told her he wouldn't be able to call her again until they returned to Base Camp in a few days.

The next morning, a bouquet of a dozen red roses, in a glass vase with a helium "Happy Anniversary" balloon bobbing from a ribbon tied around it, had been delivered to the front door. Otherwise it had been an ordinary day. Nomita had dropped the kids off at school and had gone to work.

"Where was the epicenter?" Nomita asked Sonali.

"They're saying Nepal but there's not much information yet. It just happened."

"Hemanshu's at Camp One or Two now but the earthquake was probably too far from Everest to impact them. I mean what are the chances?" Nomita said as she pointed the remote at the flat-screen TV and turned it on.

Nomita considered herself a realist. In her mind, there was nothing romantic about climbing Everest. She and Hemanshu had discussed the fact that everything and anything could go wrong. During Hemanshu's previous summit of Aconcagua, one of his teammates died from altitude sickness.

"I don't wear rose-tinted glasses," Nomita had told her husband. "You are not the first one to climb Everest and you won't be the last! Nepal really needs the money so I will support you, but remember you will be able to do only as much as the mountain allows you and as much as your endurance allows."

Of the countless dangers that Everest posed, one neither she nor Hemanshu had ever considered was the possibility of an earthquake. Nomita grew exasperated as she flipped through the channels. "I can't believe it," she said to Sonali. "All they're covering is Bruce Jenner's gender transformation! There's nothing about the earthquake."

"Try the Indian TV!" Sonali suggested.

Nomita flipped over to the few Indian TV channels to which they subscribed as part of their satellite TV package. Suddenly she was watching scenes of destruction in Kathmandu. Hundreds of people streamed out of shaking, collapsing buildings into the middle of the city streets. The Indian news station reported that the epicenter of the earthquake was located in Nepal. Initial reports suggested that the earthquake had registered a 5 or 6 on the magnitude scale.

"They're showing Kathmandu. It looks really bad!" she blurted.

Nomita flipped back to the American news stations to see if they had more information, but they were not yet reporting on the quake. She hung up with Sonali after promising to keep her posted, called her parents in New Delhi to check in on them, and then returned to watching the Indian news stations, growing more anxious by the minute.

At 1:30 a.m., one of the news anchors reported that Everest had been impacted by the quake. Nomita's stomach dropped. A series of maps and colorful graphics flashed on the screen, showing that the earthquake was more severe than initially reported, registering between

7.8 Mw (moment magnitutde) and 8.1 Mw on the magnitude scale with the maximum Mercali intensity level—a measurement of the intensity of the shaking produced by the earthquake—of IX, or Violent.

Magnitude expresses the amount of energy released by a quake. Each whole number increase in magnitude means a 32-fold increase in the amount of seismic energy released. A 7.0 Mw quake, therefore, produces 32 times more energy than a magnitude 6.0 quake. A 7.9 Mw quake releases 700 times the power of the atomic bomb dropped by the United States on Hiroshima.

According to the map on the screen, the quake's epicenter (the point of origin from where the shock waves radiated) appeared to be in the Ghorka District, located about 50 miles northwest of Kathmandu. Then Nomita heard the anchorman say, "According to tweets out of Base Camp, the earthquake triggered avalanches all around Everest. . . . Camp One and Camp Two on Everest have been completely destroyed."

Nomita felt nauseous. Her hands were shaking as she called her brother Nilesh, who lived nearby in Dallas. "It looks like it's all over!" she said when he picked up the phone, growing distraught. "Everest has been hit by an earthquake. The camp where Hemanshu is . . . it's gone! God forbid he is no more!" she cried.

"I'm on my way over," he told her.

"What do I tell the children? How am I going to tell the boys?" she sobbed.

Nomita tried to absorb the news. Her youngest son, Shayan, was just seven years old and was far too young to even fathom the perils his father faced on Everest. All he really knew was that his father had gone on a climbing trip. Her fourteen-year-old son Shaan, however, understood that his father was on an extreme and perilous expedition. He felt proud that his father's upcoming Everest trip had been featured on a local TV news program a few weeks earlier. His middle school classmates were excited about it too.

I'm going to be a single mother, Nomita thought to herself. *I cannot afford this house. We'll have to sell it.* As her mind raced to comprehend the realities of a life without her husband, she held out hope that the news was wrong or that she could somehow help Hemanshu.

Nomita called RMI's office in Ashford, Washington. It was two hours earlier there but still late at night. No one answered. She left a frantic voicemail message as she let her brother into the house. Then, at 3:30 am in Dallas, the Indian news station began to conflict their earlier reports with an update that it was Base Camp that had been destroyed by an avalanche off of Pumori, not Camps One and Two. An image of a tweet from a Romanian climber named Alex Gavan flashed on the TV screen: *Everest base camp huge earthquake then huge avalanche from Pumori. Running for life from my tent. Unhurt. Many people up the mountain.* She flipped back over to CNN. By now they were covering the earthquake in Nepal but had few details to report.

Nomita called the Embassy of Nepal in Washington, DC, searching for more information. The female staff member who answered the phone told her, in a flat and officious manner, "It just happened. We don't have any more information than you yet. The landlines in Nepal are dead and the cell phones are not working. I'm sorry but I am as clueless as you."

Since Nomita didn't have a Twitter account, she and Nilesh opened HP's. Several climbers at Base Camp were tweeting out news of the disaster, including names of the dead. She tweeted to the community of climbers, explaining that her husband was climbing with Dave Hahn's RMI team, based out of Seattle. "Any survivors? When was he last seen alive?" she asked.

Almost immediately, she received a reply from one of the climbers: "Yes, I last saw them at Camp 2. No news. If I hear of anything I will tweet."

Heartened by the climber's response and desperate for more information, Nomita sent out a flurry of tweets to Hemanshu's climbing community. She tweeted the Indian Army: "Any news? Wounded? Dead?

Alive?" She scoured through the tweets of other climbers and trekkers describing the destruction.

"They say there's blood everywhere. People have been thrown from their tents. They're saying the Icefall route has been broken. Entire Sherpa villages have vanished from the face of the Earth," she said, hunched over her cell phone, to her brother.

Nilesh put his hand on her shoulder. "Nomita, drink this," he said, handing her a mug of warm milk. "And take this," he added, handing her a sleeping pill. "You need to get some rest. There's nothing we can do now. We'll know more in the morning."

Nomita peeked in at her children, still asleep in their pajamas, through the open cracks of their bedroom doors as she retreated down the hallway to her bedroom. She laid down, closed her eyes, and slept fitfully for a couple of hours until she was woken again by the phone ringing. She answered it as Nilesh entered the room.

"No. I still don't know if he's alive or dead . . ." she said. When she hung up, she explained to Nilesh, "It was someone from *Good Morning America*. They saw my tweets and wanted to know if I'd give them an interview." Then she leaped out of bed.

"I have to go tell the boys," she told Nilesh, just before Shaan walked in the room.

"What is it? What's wrong, Mom?" Shaan asked her. Shayan, sleepy and bed-headed, trailed behind his older brother. He climbed onto the bed and into his mother's lap. His skin was warm and he smelled like shampoo.

"There's been an earthquake near Everest," Nomita said as calmly as she could. Shaan looked at her with furrowed eyebrows and a pained expression.

"Is Daddy OK?" he asked, searching his mother's face with his brown eyes.

"We think so but we don't know for certain yet. I'm working to get more information." Her tone was matter of fact.

Nomita hugged her shocked sons and then, while their uncle reassured them, she returned downstairs and sunk into the brown leather couch in her living room in front of the television. She surrounded herself with her laptop, her iPad, her two home phones, and her cell phone, creating a makeshift command center. On Twitter, a clearer picture of the disaster was taking shape. Most tweets radiating out from Base Camp were confirming that the Icefall route had been destroyed, as had sections of Base Camp, and that Camps One and Two were still standing. Climbers from Indian Army Camp, who were now deeply involved in rescue operations, were particularly responsive to Nomita's tweets, but there was no news of Hemanshu or his team yet.

The Romanian climber at Base Camp tweeted, "Many dead. Much more badly injured. More to die if not heli asap." The dismal tweet filled Nomita with hope. If Hemanshu was still alive, she would find a way to get him evacuated to a hospital by helicopter. One after another, she called friends in Dallas, relatives in India, anyone she thought might possibly have influence, connections, or information, pleading, "Have you heard anything? Can you pull some strings? Do you know anybody I can contact to find out more?"

A blog post appeared on the *International Mountain Guides* Facebook page:

The earthquake caused a huge block of ice to fall from the ice cliff in the saddle between Pumori and Lingtren. This saddle is at 20,177 feet and Everest Base Camp is at 17,585 feet, so the difference is 2,592 feet. The tons and tons of falling ice going this vertical distance created a huge aerosol avalanche and accompanying air blast that hit the upper part of Base Camp and blew many tents across the Khumbu glacier towards the lower Icefall. Apparently the air blast and earthquake also caused many big rocks to shift, which were the cause of some of the crushing injuries suffered by climbers in the upper section of Base Camp.

The camps farther down the glacier (like the IMG camp) were untouched. It is worth noting that, over many expeditions, we have never seen an avalanche in this area that was even remotely of this scale. It was truly a freak event caused by a tremendous earthquake. . . . IMG Base Camp has been turned into a triage center and our big dining tents are now being used as hospital tents.

As the sun rose in Texas, the phone rang again. It was the *Plano Star* reporter who had interviewed HP before he left for Everest. "Nomita, you're going to have news vans lining up outside your house. If you don't want to talk to them just put up a sign saying 'No press please' on your front door."

Her brother interrupted the call to read Nomita a tweet from another climber. "5 RMI climbers safe at Camp One."

"Five?" she asked Nilesh, even as a wave of relief swept through her. "But there were seven of them!"

Nomita got off the phone and began to reach out to the family and friends of Hemanshu's RMI teammates. She messaged base-camp trekker Erin Machinchik on Facebook: "Do you know anything? Do you know if anyone on the team has a personal satellite phone? Is there a way to get a number for RMI's sat phone directly?"

Eventually, she reached one of RMI's staff members, Autumn, at her personal cell phone number. Autumn told Nomita that they had not heard anything from Dave yet. "But no news is good news," she added.

At 8:00 a.m. the phone rang again, and Nomita saw the RMI office phone number appear on the screen of her cell phone as she answered it. "I have an update," Autumn said. It sounded like she was crying; Nomita braced herself. "We were able to retrieve a sat phone message that Dave left us right after the earthquake struck. The message said they're all OK. They're at Camp One, waiting out a snowstorm."

"Thank God!" Nomita said, throwing her head back and looking up at the ceiling, although part of her remained unconvinced. She felt she could not totally trust the news until she spoke to HP herself. "Now they have to get down."

Nomita turned to her brother and children and shared the news. She fed the boys breakfast and drove them to school, figuring it was best to try to keep their routines in place. For the rest of the day, Nomita remained glued to her living room command station, watching news of the quake radiate around the world like the shock waves from its epicenter. She made frantic calls inquiring about booking private helicopters from Base Camp to Kathmandu. At her request, Nilesh stayed home from work to be with her.

The boys took the bus home from school that afternoon. When Shaan walked in the front door, he dropped his backpack on the floor and shouted at Nomita, "He's dead!"

"What?" Nomita asked.

"You didn't tell us, and we went to school!" he said.

"Who told you this, Shaan?"

"One of the kids at school. He saw it on the news!"

Nomita reached out to comfort her son but Shaan recoiled in anger.

"It's not true. I've told you everything I know. He's alive, Shaan, but Daddy hasn't called yet. I don't know anything more yet," she said. Her cell phone began ringing on the couch. "And I promise, in a worst-case scenario, I would do my best to be Mommy and Daddy to both of you."

She answered the phone. Shaan watched his mother's face, frozen by stress, melt with relief and then flood with emotion. He listened for clues in her half of the conversation. "Thank you. . . . We'll do anything. . . . Yes. . . . Please keep us updated."

She hung up and looked at Shaan. "That was the RMI office. They were able to speak directly with Dave. Daddy and all of the RMI climbers and Sherpa team are accounted for. They're stuck at Camp One still but they're alive and they have food. They're working with Dave on an evacuation plan to get Daddy and everyone down safely."

Then, she posted an update on her own Facebook page and to a Facebook page that Hemanshu had established for friends and family to follow his climb. She typed, "Everest 2015 Update: HP and Team 2015 are at Camp 1. Communication towers are down. Route completely destroyed. It's a rescue mission now."

Saturday, April 25, 2015, Day 36, Camp 1 (Hao's Diary Entry):
2015年4月25日,星期六,第36天,第一营地(吴皓日记)

We got up at 4:30am. Today we would walk to Camp 2. We started the stove, melting snow to make breakfast, same as yesterday. I went to poo in the open pit bathroom before gearing up. We left our tent at 6:10am.

The round trip took about 5 hours. We were back to our tents by 11:20am. It has been snowing all along. After we crawled into our tents to relax, I felt the tent rumbling—it was moving! I never thought Himalayas would have earthquake. Then it's avalanche. The ice dust swept through our tents . . .

When their tents stopped flapping and shaking at Camp One, HP felt paralyzed by the fear that even the slightest shift in his weight could cause the ice shelf below them to give way and send them hurtling downward. He said a silent prayer as he and the rest of the team, their bodies still frozen in terror, began to comprehend that they had dodged a bullet. They had been hit by a foot of snow and ice pellets without significant rock or ice debris. Its force had been bearable, and the ground had stopped rocking below them—for now, anyway. The roar had silenced. They had survived.

Still, Dave didn't like anything about their predicament; they were profoundly isolated in the middle of the biggest mountains on Earth and he was certain that while they were alright, there had to be plenty wrong. At 20,000 feet on Everest, they might as well have been on the moon. JJ and Chhering darted out of their yellow tents to check on everyone while Dave reached for the radio and the satellite phone. Robbie listened through the tent walls as Dave radioed Tuck.

"Everything's OK up here! We were in the right place. Avalanches came off the shoulder and Nuptse, but we only got dusted, over."

Tuck exhaled an audible sigh of relief.

"OK Dave. Listen, we got hit real bad by a huge air blast of ice debris down here. It's like a bomb went off. Looks like it might've come off Pumori. We're all OK. Camp is flattened. It must've been moving at about 150 miles per hour. Cell service got knocked out. Larry's OK. Our Sherpa team's OK. It's snowing pretty hard so it's tough to see. I gotta go try to figure out what the hell's going on . . . see if anyone needs help. I gotta go . . . "

Dave tried to wrap his mind around Tuck's news. He had urgently wanted to let Tuck know that they were alright. He had also been worried about those up higher at Camp Two and about the greater situation in Nepal, but the possibility that things could be worse at Base Camp than they were at Camp One had not even occurred to him until now. Base Camp was considered safe from avalanches, insulated by distance and buffered by ice ridges and lateral moraines. The concept of an ice avalanche and its accompanying air blast sweeping from east to west, originating on Pumori and hurtling all the way into Base Camp, was mind-boggling. What troubled him most was that by this point in the season, he figured the population of Base Camp had likely swelled to around 1,000 people.

"Copy that Tuck, I understand. Keep me posted on the situation down there. It's snowing pretty hard up here too right now. We're gonna have to ride this storm out. Make sure you take care of yourself," Dave said.

With the spotty communication, Dave understood it was going to take time to figure out just what had happened at Base Camp, up higher, and throughout Nepal—or what might still happen. Two things were clear: they had to stay put for now, and all their priorities had changed.

The radio crackled again. "Dave, do you copy? It's Tuck, over."

"Tuck, it's Dave. Go ahead."

"It's really fucking bad!" he said. Dave and JJ glanced at each other. The profanity was unlike Tucker. They had never heard him so agitated. "Lots of hurt people. Head injuries. Loss of life. Blood everywhere. The middle of Base Camp is decimated, unrecognizable. Over."

Staring at his tent walls and grinding his teeth, Dave listened to the ensuing rescue efforts over the radio, helpless to do anything and with growing concern for his friends at Base Camp. He knew that for Chhering and the sherpa team, the situation was far more torturous as they worried about their families in the remote villages of the Khumbu, which were susceptible to deadly landslides, and in Kathmandu—a city of nearly a million—where buildings were not constructed to resist seismic forces. Nepal's poverty and lack of infrastructure made its population especially vulnerable to natural disaster. Dave felt pained as he watched Chhering, ever stoic, try to reach his pregnant wife, Yanzee, on the sat phone.

"No luck?" Dave asked gently, although Chhering's silence made the answer obvious to him.

Chhering shook his head. "It seems the phone network is down in Kathmandu," he said.

Chhering then tried to make contact with his mother and sisters on the only phone in their small village, but again he was unable to get a call through. The silence on the line was deafening. He closed his eyes and dropped his chin to his chest for a brief moment. Then he called Tuck and spoke with his sherpa team and kitchen crew at Base Camp. Dave couldn't understand what Chhering was saying to his distressed team as he conversed with them in the Nepali Sherpa language, but the tone of Chhering's quiet voice was somehow steady and reassuring.

Dave plunged outside of the tent into the driving snow and paced back and forth irritably, clutching his radio in a gloved hand. As he listened to the frenetic Base Camp chatter, it became clearer to him that the middle third of Base Camp had been hit the hardest and that Tucker was emerging as one of the leaders of the rescue operation. He listened in as Tuck gathered other rescuers and coordinated search efforts between different climbing teams through the devastated camps. He heard the urgency in the voices of Tuck and the others as they called for stretchers and manpower.

The RMI Sherpa team, anxious about the fate of their own families in the nearby villages, worked with Tucker to help pull the wounded out of the avalanche debris and carry them to the IMG camp where, from what Dave could make out over the radio, the Himalayan Rescue Association (HRA) had been forced to move their rescue operations, since their iconic Everest ER tent, white with a red cross, had been shredded by the blast.

Everest ER, the highest emergency room in the world and a satellite clinic of the HRA in Pheriche, had been established at the base of Everest in 2003 by emergency-room doctor Luanne Freer in an effort to benefit sherpas and foreign climbers in an underserved area. Dave thought of his friends working there this season, like Rachel Tullet, a thirty-three-year-old ER doctor from New Zealand, as he heard her name called over the radio and occasionally made out her voice amid the multilingual commotion. Rachel sounded calm and clear. Dave could hear boots crunching on snow and someone moaning in pain in the background.

What Dave wouldn't know until later was that Rachel had already been awake for over twenty-four hours. She and Meg Walmsley, a thirty-two-year-old soft-spoken anesthesiologist from Australia, had spent the night caring for two base-camp trekkers with severe altitude sickness in the metal-structured ER tent. In the morning, just when Rachel was about to leave Meg and twenty-four-year-old Aditya Tiwari, who had recently graduated medical school in Kathmandu, to oversee the ER so she could take a nap, a sherpa experiencing severe abdominal pain had walked into the tent at 9:00 a.m. Since the patient's condition was possibly life-threatening, and required an ultrasound and IV pain meds, Rachel had stayed to help.

Rachel was standing outside the ER, on a slope just above the dining tent, when the earthquake struck. Ten seconds afterward, she heard the avalanche begin its descent. When she turned and faced it, it looked to her like a tsunami wave. She estimated it was moving at about 200 miles per hour. She assessed instantly both that it would reach the ER and that it had the potential to kill them. Then its force threw her over a ridge and against a rock. Her knee was gashed and twisted and she was buried beneath a thin layer of ice and rock debris. Nevertheless, in spite of a cracked patella, torn knee ligaments, and a gaping wound, she stood up and brushed herself off, found a trekking pole to support herself, and, while limping, worked to triage and treat the wounded being carried to her, many of whom were her friends; their head trauma and internal injuries were consistent with a bomb blast. She also worked to certify the dead, tenderly kissing the forehead of one of the climbers she examined before she looked up at his best friend and said, "He's gone." Along with Meg and Aditya, she led an ad hoc team of nine medical professionals, composed of expedition team doctors and climbers, in a makeshift clinic tent with the help of Tucker and other guides. She would stitch up her own leg the following day without anesthetic after having saved the lives of twenty-three of the twenty-five seriously and critically injured patients she treated. Two would later die in a hospital in Kathmandu.

By Dave's calculations, it was the middle of the night in Ashford, Washington, but he called the RMI office there anyway to leave a sat-phone recording that could be posted on his blog on the company's website. He wanted to ensure that friends and family of the RMI team got word that he and his team were safe. His voice was composed and measured as he spoke into the sat phone:

This is Dave Hahn with RMI's Everest Expedition. This morning,
early this morning we got up from Camp One: five climbers,
Jeff Justman, Chhering Dorje and myself. We completed a good
circuit, climbing up to 21,300 feet Advance Base Camp and back

to Camp One. We were here about 11:30, 11:15 this morning. And then shortly after that, at about noon, there was a major earthquake and resulted in avalanches off of all the mountains around us. Our camp was in a good place; we got dusted but here at Camp One we were just fine. Our concern then shifted to Base Camp. We are hearing reports of some pretty destructive action down there, injuries and loss of life. Our entire team is okay. We have talked with our Sherpa team down below and with Mark Tucker. And so our team is okay. About the same time as the earthquake a pretty good snowstorm commenced up here in the Western Cwm and down at Base Camp. We're sitting things out safely at Camp One. But we don't have the ability to travel right now; good mountaineering sense dictates that we stay put and ride this storm out. This may take a little time to ride the storm out and that's what we'll do. It may take this a little time but we are okay. We are self-sufficient up here and our concern is with our friends at Base Camp. We're hearing the strenuous efforts that our Sherpa team and Mark Tucker are going through down there trying to help with the injured and those who haven't fared so well. We'll try to be in touch. We obviously are in a situation where we won't have great communication. It's likely that the earthquake destroyed any cell service around the Base Camp area. We are calling you on a satellite telephone; we've got some batteries and we will nurse those batteries to make them last.

Dave was worried. Their ability to retreat from the mountain would depend on both weather and the condition of the Icefall, factors which were entirely beyond his control. In the meantime, they would need to ration both food and fuel for melting snow into water. Base Camp, which typically served as command central, a communications hub, and their primary source of logistical support, was, for all intents and purposes, gone. A distant yet familiar and vaguely sickening sensation spread inside of him, as if emanating from a vestigial organ; there was no one to protect them now.

He and Chhering went to meet with the other expedition leaders at Camp One, including Argentinian Damian Benegas of Benegas Brothers Expeditions and Justin Merle of International Mountain Guides, to share information and solidify an escape plan. When they returned they gathered the RMI team outside their yellow tents. Standing in the white vastness of the Cwm, they had never felt so small. Their vulnerability was undeniable. They were entirely at the mercy of Mother Nature.

"Look, you guys need to know it's bad down at Base Camp. An avalanche came down Pumori and killed sixteen people. . . . The cloud cover is too low to get helicopters in to evacuate the injured. That will have to wait until the morning," Dave said.

He explained that if the weather cleared up by the morning, a helicopter would fly over the Icefall to inspect it and, if possible, to drop Willie (Guillermo) Benegas at Camp One to supply his twin brother Damian Benegas and Justin Merle with rope, ice screws, and snow pickets; they would use these to try to get down through the Icefall from the top to determine if it was passable. While they climbed downward, Chhering would send two of the RMI sherpa team, Rinjin Bhote and Furba Sona Sherpa, up from Base Camp to see how far they could get through the Icefall from the bottom.

"Then again," he added, "if this stormy weather persists, we'll have to wait."

Afterward, Hao picked up his journal to add to the entry he had started earlier. He wrote, in neat print, "We were told later that it was a 7.8 magnitude earthquake. It's likely that the Icefall route was damaged. . . . We might need to stay at Camp 1 for a couple of more days. The food is limited as we were prepared only for a three-day trip . . ."

That evening, their nerves raw, the team wore their helmets and boots when they crawled into their sleeping bags at Camp One. Their minds raced and they struggled to fall asleep in the thin, frigid air.

As night descended upon Base Camp, survivors tended to the wounded; due to the snowy weather, helicopters had been unable to fly in and evacuate them. Climbers made homeless when their tents were shredded by the blast found refuge in those of neighboring climbing companies. Weather models on EverestWeather.com forecasted snowfall all around the mountain on April 26, in a pre-monsoon pattern that would worsen throughout the day and further deteriorate over the next two days. Meanwhile, flights were being diverted from the single-runway, nine-gate Tribhuvan International Airport due to the disaster. Trauma patients flooded Kathmandu's medical clinics and hospitals.

Around the world, international aid agencies and global rescue services scrambled to deploy resources and hoped that Kathmandu's airport would be operational by daylight in order to support emergency flights and disaster relief. *U.S. News and World Report* ran the headline "Nepal Earthquake: Experts There a Week Ago to Plan for Earthquake." The article featured the meeting of about fifty earthquake scientists and social scientists from around the globe held in Kathmandu a week earlier, quoting a seismologist who attended the conference from the University of Cambridge in England: " It was a nightmare waiting to happen," he said. "Physically and geologically what happened is exactly what we thought would happen." They just hadn't expected it so soon.

The following morning, April 26, dawned sunny and clear. A message greeted the team on the dry-erase board, scrawled across it in HP's handwriting: "Count your blessings." HP felt fortunate and grateful; they still had food, enough fuel to melt snow into water, and oxygen, and they had remained safe through the continued aftershocks that had caused avalanches to persist in crashing down every steep mountainside. Hans also felt lucky. He knew that if the quake had occurred an hour or so earlier, it would have caught one of them on a ladder over a bottomless crevasse. Robbie wondered aloud if they'd still be alive had they not moved their tents when they first arrived at Camp One. HP told his teammates he felt optimistic. "My feeling is if you can get up, you can get down."

Dave heard the first pulsating, echoing reverberations of helicopter blades at 6:15 a.m. when a Fishtail Air B3 helicopter pilot made the most of the narrow opening in the weather to begin evacuating the seriously wounded from Base Camp to the HRA clinic in Pheriche. From there, many of the patients would be further evacuated to the overwhelmed hospitals in Kathmandu. The casualties, wrapped in orange tents and lined up next to the helipad at Base Camp, would have to wait.

Dave listened to the rescue operations on the radio as the Swiss pilot of the Fishtail Air helicopter, Maurizio Folini, made loop after loop, carrying two patients at a time from Base Camp to Pheriche. Other helicopters, including a Russian Mi-17, a beast of a machine that could transport fifteen patients at a time from Pheriche to Kathmandu, were still trapped at Lukla Airport, socked in by clouds. As Maurizio unloaded his first two patients at the rudimentary, two-room HRA clinic in Pheriche, he told the young doctor there, in a tone so calm it could have been mistaken for nonchalance, "I'll be bringing you about fifty-one more." The doctor, bent over the two patients, glanced up at him to make sure he wasn't joking. With communications down, the doctors in Pheriche had received only spotty information from Base Camp. By midmorning, as the weather lifted for a little while in Lukla, a few more Eurocopters made it out to aid in the evacuation loops to Pheriche.

In the meantime, Dave, Chhering, and JJ supported the Icefall reconnaissance mission over the radio from Camp One. Willie Benegas had successfully been lowered down to them, with supplies, on a cable. The two sets of guides planned to meet in the middle of the Icefall, somewhere near the Popcorn Field. Damian and Justin Merle began their descent from Camp One down through the Ballroom of Death, while Rinjin Bhote and Furba Sona worked their way up from Base Camp through the bottom of the Icefall. When they reached points about one-third of the way down the Icefall and one-third up it from the bottom, both teams described that the ladders had been broken and twisted beyond repair and that the quake had created massive, gaping crevasses that would allow them to go no farther.

"There's no way we can get down through the Icefall. The route is gone," Damian reported. Then, at 1:00 p.m., as both teams cautiously worked their ways in opposite directions out from the Icefall, the ground shook violently again. The massive aftershock tossed them like rag dolls. Rocks and ice crashed down around them.

"You guys gotta get outta there!" JJ shouted into the radio.

Measuring 7.3 on the magnitude scale, the aftershock felt nearly as powerful and intense as yesterday's quake and even more unnerving. Damian and Justin escaped the top of the convulsing Icefall without a scratch, leaping across the mouths of crevasses as they opened up around them, and returned to Camp One, frazzled. Chhering confirmed that Rinjin and Furba had also somehow managed to emerge from the mouth of the Icefall and had returned, rattled but unscathed, to Base Camp.

Dave and JJ began to reluctantly discuss the idea of a helicopter rescue. The quake's unpredictable aftershocks were bound to continue. As long as Chomolungma shook, the Icefall could not be repaired. Then again, if the snow continued to fall, as was forecasted, flying would be impossible.

By late afternoon, after a day of careful watching and waiting, Dave reached the inescapable conclusion that they had run out of options. He radioed down to Base Camp to attempt to coordinate an unprecedented helicopter rescue of what he estimated to be between one and two hundred stranded between Camps One and Two—there was no official count of how many climbers were on the mountain when the quake hit—from 20,000 feet on Mount Everest. The logistics seemed as daunting and unlikely as the Apollo moon landing he had watched as a kid from the Holiday Inn in Kingston, New York. He was surprised to suddenly feel the collective weight of all of their lives on his shoulders. "We're trapped," he said. At 4:00 p.m., the RMI team walked out on the glacier and stomped out a 50-foot helipad in the snow. Then they retreated to their tents for the night, where they tossed and turned in their sleeping bags, wearing helmets and boots, their bodies braced for more aftershocks.

25 ⛰ LANGTANG

April 27, 2015
Posted by: Dave Hahn, JJ Justman
Categories: Expedition Dispatches; Everest
Elevation: 17,575 feet

RMI EXPEDITIONS BLOG

At Camp One, we were up before dawn, boiling cups of instant coffee and hurriedly packing. It wasn't going to be an ideal scenario, by any means. . . . Being "rescued" from 20,000 ft on Mount Everest, along with perhaps 140 of our closest friends. . . . But we weren't likely to get any better offers . . .

On the second morning after the quake, a thin, snaking line of climbers from Camp Two descended through an ethereal sea of whiteness to join the climbers at Camp One as they formed polite, nervous queues at each of the snowy helipads. Dave felt certain that a helicopter evacuation was their best bet, but he also expressed concern to his fellow guides. It seemed unlikely to him that over ninety helicopter landings and takeoffs at such extreme altitude could be accomplished "without chaos or catastrophe or at least some kind of unworkable delay," such as weather or mechanical issues. He worried about panic setting in among the climbers waiting for rescue at Camp One. "We don't want a helicopter mob scene a la Saigon '75," Dave told his fellow guides. "I think all of our clients should understand the need for superior social skills today. There's only one way out of here and I'm sure no one wants to end up on the 'no fly' list."

The idea of being plucked off the mountain was a tough pill for Dave to swallow. He felt a surge of gratitude for the pilots, fueled by adrenaline, daring to attempt the largest high-altitude rescue in history. However, he found it was an unfamiliar and distinctly unpleasant sensation to be in need of such a rescue. He much preferred the role of rescuer. At the very least, he would have liked to climb down and get off of Everest on his own two feet. Instead, it felt to Dave that Everest, after all of his decades of climbing and guiding, was bucking him off.

To make matters worse, the very thought of high-altitude helicopter flight made Dave anxious. Back in 2002, the 31-foot Bell 206B-3 Jet Ranger carrying him and a National Park Service ranger to rescue an injured and unconscious nineteen-year-old climber on Washington's Mount Rainier crashed when its tail rotor struck the sloping surface of Carbon Glacier at 8,800 feet. Dave, Park Ranger Chris Olson, and the pilot all managed to escape serious injury, even though the million-dollar helicopter was destroyed in the crash. After they extracted themselves from the wreckage, Dave and Chris continued on foot to reach and help evacuate the Pennsylvania teenager who had been hit on the head by a falling boulder while climbing Liberty Ridge. While Dave and Chris were able to reach the injured teen and successfully complete their rescue mission, for which they were later awarded a Citizen's Award for Bravery and a Valor Award, respectively, from the US Department of the Interior, the experience had left Dave with an indelible, somatic impression of the dangers of high-altitude helicopter flight. He felt a pit in his stomach.

Dave had learned the hard way that the lower density of the air at high altitudes reduced both aircraft and engine performance. Lift, the force that acted in opposition to gravity and kept helicopters airborne, was generated by the rotors pushing air downward. Less air density meant less lift and therefore reduced a helicopter's takeoff, climbing, hovering, and landing performance and impacted its weight and balance limitations. When Dave factored in the dangers posed by crevasses, steep slopes, and hanging glaciers, in addition to the extremely high altitude—over 11,000 feet higher than the incident on Rainier—he felt almost as dizzy as he had during those moments in June of 2002 when his helicopter spun wildly after its rotor blades were sheared off. It had been all he could do to hold on.

Let the great Everest Air Show begin, he thought to himself as the first B3 helicopter powered from Base Camp toward Camp One at 6:00 a.m. For three hours, the RMI team watched the red-bellied B3 birds make loops as they picked up and ferried climbers, two at a time, over the massive crevasses that had opened in the Icefall, down to Base Camp, transecting what was arguably the most treacherous stretch of climbing in the world in just minutes.

Veteran forty-six-year-old pilot Jason Lang, from Queensland, New Zealand, worked for the Nepali airline Simrik Air. He had learned to fly in the Swiss Alps and was one of only a handful of pilots willing to conduct rescues at an altitude that most pilots would not dare approach, one that would have been impossible for any helicopters built just two decades earlier. He had pushed his B3, its flank marked with the slogan "Follow your dreams," to its limits in 2014 to help recover the bodies of the sherpas killed in the avalanche.

Jason was one of the first pilots to be airborne in the area the day after the quake, and he was the first to arrive on the scene in the nearby Langtang region, a U-shaped, glacially carved valley located just north of the Kathmandu Valley, marked by small farming villages and the tightly terraced fields that clung to its mountainsides. Home to an idyllic farming village and known for its welcoming local residents and its fertile April bloom of rhododendron forests bleeding red beneath its snowy white peaks, Langtang had become the third most popular trekking destination in Nepal. During his reconnaissance mission there, Jason was horrified to discover that the Langtang village appeared to have been essentially wiped off the map by a landslide triggered by the quake. Unable to trust his own eyes, he documented the inconceivable devastation with a few aerial photos and sped back to his base to raise the alarm for an interagency disaster response effort to the decimated, isolated village. Jason was certain that hundreds of people had perished.

The photos he took confirmed his sickening revelation that Langtang, buried completely by debris, had vanished.

Today, Jason had been tasked with coordinating the helicopter rescue effort at Camp One. He recruited fellow Simrik pilot, thirty-year-old Nepalese Ananda Thapa, to help him. Flying above Everest, Jason wore a bulky black oxygen mask to avoid hypoxia and pulled a yellow eye shield from his helmet over his brown eyes. Before he had taken off from the Lukla helipad, he had removed the doors and back seats of his helicopter and had calculated the minimum fuel load possible. While his helicopter (an AS350B3E) could typically carry six passengers, he could carry only two passengers at a time in such thin air. There was no room for gear and there was no margin for error. As always, he tried to keep his own emotions at bay and focus on the task at hand. In order to avoid confusion and minimize lag time, whenever he landed the B3's skids on the helipad at Camp One, he took control of the schedule by shouting over the chopper's deafening thrum, "Two from Alpine Ascents!" or "Two from IMG!" Any delay would burn fuel he didn't have. Every time he reached the helipad at Base Camp, he instructed the climbers to drop and roll out of it, military style.

After waiting for three hours in the queue, Robbie and Peter, clutching their packs to their chests, were the first of the RMI team to run low to the ground and climb into the doorless helicopter, its rotors beating full-thrust against the thin air, at around 9:00 am. Robbie tried to capture the chaos of the gaping Icefall with his camera as they flew over it. JJ and Hans were next, followed by HP and Hao, who was still doubled over with painful stomach cramping. By the time Dave and Chhering dropped and rolled out of the last RMI chopper at 9:30 a.m., Robbie felt like the morning had lasted a lifetime. Tucker, Larry, and the sherpa team greeted them at the helipad, swiping the backs of their mittens below their sunglasses to brush away their own tears as they hugged their teammates and passed out Cokes and Sprites.

"It's so good to see you guys. You're safe! You're down!" Tucker said as he embraced each member of the team. Plagued by night terrors, he had not slept since the earthquake. Larry, still coughing violently, dabbed at the wet corners of his eyes. He had spent the days since the quake helping to repair RMI's camp, patching holes in ripped and torn tents, in hopeful anticipation of his teammates' arrival.

Dave's initial relief was quickly superseded by sadness and awe as he took in the scene around him. They had been put down in the epicenter of a disaster. Nothing could have prepared him for the destruction. Looking around at the evidence of the explosion at Base Camp, he could hardly believe his eyes. Large mess tents had been stripped to their steel skeletons. Debris was strewn across the glacier. When JJ saw snow stained by blood, the realization sunk into his body that people had been crushed against rocks by the air blast; that people had been struck on the head by debris; that people had died right there on the ground where they stood. Chhering found it difficult to control his emotions. The scene of the violent blast flooded him with visceral memories of the Icefall after the avalanche in 2014 and the trauma of recovering his friends' bodies. He still did not know whether his pregnant wife or his family were alive or dead.

With the entire RMI team reunited, Robbie took a moment to thank Dave in front of the group. "You managed your own emotions and ours. You were calm with a sense of urgency. You made us feel safe. You made us not panic. I can't tell you how much we appreciate it." Dave, however, was focused on the heroic efforts of Mark Tucker and the sherpa team. As they marched sadly toward RMI's camp through the decimated camps together, they stopped occasionally to try to comprehend the force that had bent steel poles and had thrown helmets, shoes, sleeping pads, and shredded tents across the distance of the glacier. For Dave, the numbers of deaths and the nature of the injuries made sense now. As counterintuitive as it was, he understood just how lucky they had been at Camp One.

When they finally reached RMI's camp, Dave realized that Larry,

Tuck, and the sherpa team, after such an exhausting rescue effort, had managed to find the time and energy to rebuild it for their arrival. He noticed how the floating ice crystals made the air sparkle in the sunlight. The earth abided. Chomolungma, in the midst of sadness, death, and destruction, remained exquisite, but Dave could not help but feel that everything had changed.

April 28, 2015
Posted by: Dave Hahn, JJ Justman
Categories: Expedition Dispatches; Everest
Elevation: 17,575 feet

RMI EXPEDITIONS BLOG

We've come to the inescapable conclusion that Everest summit
for 2015 is out of reach for our team. Besides the rather obvious
and glaring philosophical difficulties of pursuing a recreational
venture in the midst of a national—and local—disaster, there
are the on-the-ground mountaineering realities that will not
permit us to look upward again. We have no viable route
through the Khumbu Icefall and the Earth is still shaking.
We couldn't think of asking anyone to put themselves at
the risk required for re-establishing that route under such
circumstances. The effort at this advanced stage of the season
would normally be focused on building a route to Camp 4 rather
than to Camp 1, nobody will be able to say when the aftershocks
will end, but it will—without a doubt—be too late for fixing the
upper mountain and stocking camps before the normal advance
of the monsoon.
We'll put our efforts into an organized and safe retreat from the
mountain. Nobody harbors illusions that travel in this stricken
and damaged country will be simple, but we'll head for home
now in any case.
   Best Regards,
   RMI Guide Dave Hahn

Back at Base Camp, the RMI team members took turns meandering the twenty minutes out to the Icy Cyber, the spot with semi-reliable 3G cell service located out on the fringe of the valley near the side of the Icefall, where they found a strong enough signal from Gorak Shep's cell tower to call friends and family. They were still astonished to find climbing boots, helmets, tents, and heavy camp gear including barrels and tables strewn in a colorful array hundreds of meters across the glacier.

JJ was standing out on the open stretch of glacial plain trying to reach his parents when Tucker walked by him. JJ had always thought of Tuck as RMI's tank, unremittingly stable and strong, but today, Tuck's eyes were bloodshot and he wandered as if in a fog. JJ had never before seen him look so shell-shocked or vulnerable. He stopped him.

"Hey Tuck," JJ said. "Listen, I know you've seen a lot . . ."

"Yeah, you bet," Tuck said.

"You've been through plenty of rescues and . . ." JJ hunted for the right words. "Well, you've seen worse and dealt with more than I have, but I just don't want you to hide anything. Honestly, how are you doing? Are you OK?"

Tuck stared up at Pumori. "It was horrible . . . " he said, his eyes welling up.. "I've seen a lot up here before, but this has rattled me." He paused, lost in thought, then added, "I'm coping though."

"OK, Tuck. Hey, just know that I care about you, OK? If you need to talk, I'm here."

"Thanks, JJ. Appreciate it," Tuck said, breaking his gaze from Pumori and turning to look at him.

After making his brief call, JJ headed back to camp, leaving Tuck to call his wife. Back at RMI's camp, before he ducked his head into the dining tent, JJ overheard Hao, HP, Hans, and some others talking inside. He could make out a couple of voices searching for possible solutions that might allow them to continue the expedition. It became evident to JJ that a few members of the group wanted to find a way to resume climbing while others were adamantly opposed to it.

JJ knew this was Hao's second season-ending experience on Everest in two consecutive years. Having already successfully reached six of the Seven Summits, Hao felt like he hadn't even had the chance to get past Everest's starting gate. JJ recognized that the climbers had invested significant amounts of time, money, and energy into this expedition. While he liked all of them personally and understood their visceral disappointment as they tried to wrap their heads around the disaster that had upended plans and goals that had been years in the making, he also felt triggered by it. He was upset when he ducked into the tent.

"Just to let you know, guys, I'm not going to climb. I'm done. Thousands of people are dead in Kathmandu. I don't have kids, but I've been thinking about my nephew and my niece, and I imagine somewhere out there, there are a little girl and a little boy sobbing right now because their father was killed in an earthquake. I'm not climbing." He sat down at the table, then added as punctuation, "It's just a mountain."

Later, Hao and HP individually approached Dave for his perspective on the situation. Dave knew there were both practical and ethical obstacles to continuing the climb and figured the team would reach the same inevitable conclusion that he had, on their own, if given the time, space, and relevant information to do it. He didn't rush anyone; these were goal-oriented and accomplished clients who were inclined to finish what they started. He reminded them that the route was destroyed and that the manpower and equipment required to rebuild it were not available due to the scope of the national disaster and the threat of continued aftershocks, not to mention the advance of the normal monsoon season as May quickly approached. He also expressed his own personal concerns about the impact of the disaster on the sherpas and their families in the Khumbu Valley, and then he let it be. It had been a shocking turn of events, and he felt every member of the team deserved a chance to process it.

Later, Hao took some time to journal his thoughts. He wrote:

Monday, April 27, 2015, Day 38, EBC (Hao's Diary Entry):
2015年4月27日,星期一,第38天,珠峰大本营(吴皓日记)

My stomach pain still lingers. It's on and off. But when it's on, it's pretty painful. I don't know what caused it. It's like muscle cramping...

Coming down to EBC, we saw the devastating impact by the earthquake and avalanche. It's like a war zone with debris everywhere: helmets, shoes, sleeping pads and broken tents...

I spent some time to think about the situation in the afternoon and we had more discussion after the dinner. It's obvious the expedition is over.

That night, Dave could hear the zipping and unzipping of tents as he and members of the RMI team, still on edge, woke up with each aftershock, sticking their heads of their tent flaps to try to determine how far every avalanche that rumbled off the walls of cavernous Base Camp would reach. By the morning, it seemed the entire group had come to terms with the fact that the 2015 season, much like the 2014 season before it, had come to an abrupt end. Larry reminded them over breakfast that, in the midst of tragedy, they had been privileged to witness what he believed to be one of mountaineering's "finest hours": 140 mountaineers had been safely airlifted from camps in an unprecedented rescue on the highest mountain in the world. Climbers at Base Camp, many of whom did not share the same language, had worked seamlessly together, in dismal and stressful circumstances, to recover bodies and transport the wounded. In spite of their own injuries and the destruction of the clinic tent, doctors and medic volunteers had stabilized patients, and pilots had safely evacuated them from Base Camp amid aftershocks. "And somehow," he said, "the entire RMI team survived the deadliest day in Everest's history."

After breakfast, Dave announced RMI's decision to begin organizing their team's retreat from the mountain on his blog on the RMI site. They packed throughout the afternoon. Hao and Hans arranged for a helicopter to transport them back to Lukla the following day. HP was tempted to walk back down the valley with the rest of the team, but when he made contact with Nomita, she told him, "Get out right away!" and made clear her concerns about the potential ramifications of the disaster throughout the rest of Nepal, fearing potential shortages of food and clean drinking water. She felt he had pushed his luck far enough already. HP, not wanting to cause Nomita and his family any more distress, decided to depart with Hao and Hans.

In the morning on April 29, Hao, Hans, and HP flew out of Base Camp, joining hoards of climbers and trekkers in Lukla where they began their long journeys home. All three of them hoped to return to Everest one day and agreed that the Khumbu exerted a strong pull. Hans was quick to point out that tourism was one of the largest sources of revenue for Nepal and would help the country recover, yet as much as much as he would like to personally, he told the others, " I don't think I will attempt to climb Everest again." He explained he was not willing to once more put his family, especially his twenty-eight-year-old son Sebastian and twenty-three-year-old daughter Stefanie, through such torment. Hao clung to the hope that he would complete the Seven Summits one day and seemed to reflect their conflicted feelings when he said, while thanking his guides and his teammates earlier that morning, "We all live, in a way, to achieve our dreams."

As they continued to pack up camp throughout the day, Robbie, Larry, and Peter decided they were determined to walk back out of the valley. They all wanted the time to digest what had unfolded and to allow the rest of the experience to play itself out. Peter thought it seemed more appropriate. They continued to contact loved ones and, while resting in their tents during snow showers, spent time reflecting upon their strange and still-surreal circumstances.

Chhering, who had watched the others as they reconnected with friends and family, finally was able to make contact with his pregnant wife for the first time, four days after the quake. Standing alone out on the glacier at the Icy Cyber, he squatted to his knees when he heard Yanzee's voice, pressing his head into one hand and his phone against his ear with the other. Yanzee told Chhering how worried she had been about him when the earthquake struck. She said she had eventually been able to check the RMI website, which had reassured her. The walls of their apartment in Kathmandu had been cracked by the quake, she told him, so she was currently staying on the city's outskirts in a tented camp near Boudhanath, along with most of her family. Thousands of people, she reported, had been killed in Kathmandu. She reassured Chhering that she had received word from his mother and sisters. They had survived the quake and were safe in their village.

Chhering tilted his head back toward the grey sky and closed his eyes as he listened. While physically relieved and emotionally buoyed by this news from his wife, he hated the thought of Yanzee sleeping in an earthquake-refugee encampment while pregnant. He consoled himself with the knowledge that it was safer than sleeping in a building with structural damage. He told Yanzee that he and the RMI team would be heading back down the valley toward Lukla in the morning. They would soon be together again.

That evening, their last in Base Camp, Dave, Tuck, and JJ invited doctors Meg Walmsley and Rachel Tullet to the RMI camp for chef Kumar's farewell pizza dinner. The two doctors were technically homeless, since the Himalayan Rescue Association camp had been decimated. They had lost all of their personal possessions when they were buried by snow. Meg was still limping due to the knee injury she had incurred during the blast, and they were both overcome by sporadic, violent coughing fits ever since inhaling the ice-laden air of the powder cloud that accompanied it. The mood wasn't as exultant as a summit celebration would have been, but the doctors and the RMI team greeted each other with hugs, unanimously glad to see each other safe and sound. Listening to the stories of what their friends at Base Camp had witnessed and endured, Dave and JJ felt paradoxically pained by the trauma and loss their friends had suffered and awed by Meg and Rachel's heroic medical response to the tragedy. Together they took refuge in the simple comfort and pleasure of one another's company and enjoyed the cakes that Kumar had made for dessert, one with flour and the other gluten-free out of consideration for Dave.

The next morning, April 30, the sun revealed itself for the first time in a few days, since April 27. Base Camp had become eerily vacant as the season drew to a rapid end. Dave, JJ, Chhering, Robbie, Larry, and Peter began to break down RMI's camp with the sherpa team, all of whom but one would stay behind at Base Camp with Tuck to complete the job. Then they headed out on the trail of Base Camp at 10:00 a.m. to begin their three-day trek down the valley.

They found the trails to be strangely empty and peaceful, devoid of trekkers and porters. It felt restorative to be hiking in such a stunning and quiet natural environment on a sparkling day, amid majestic snowy peaks, in what was a bittersweet respite. The cathartic value of hiking with ample time and space for contemplation could not be overestimated, Dave believed, but the otherwise sublime experience was tinged by grief, and it was difficult for him to reconcile this with the sobering awareness of the national crisis that had resulted in it. He remained anxious about aftershocks and uneasy about what surprises they might still encounter.

They stopped briefly in Gorak Shep and again in Lobuche without noticing much evidence of damage from the quake, but when they arrived in Pheriche, massive piles of rocks and rubble lay where most lodges had recently stood. They ran into two doctors from the HRA clinic who recalled how they had watched puppies dart to safety from the buildings as they collapsed during the quake. The HRA clinic lost a wall on its southeastern corner but had otherwise stayed intact. The doctors had turned its sun-room, where the RMI team had attended an altitude lecture on their way up the valley, into a makeshift ward while they received, triaged, and reevacuated over seventy seriously injured and bloodied climbers, sherpas, trekkers, and porters delivered to them from Everest. They had moved stable patients to the dining room of the nearby Panorama Lodge. Surveying the damage to the homes and lodges, Dave realized how fortunate it was that the quake occurred during the middle of the day, when most trekkers were out on the trails and most local residents were outside working, which he was now certain had reduced the number of fatalities.

For Larry, the construction of earthquake-resistant structures was a familiar challenge. "It's the same thing California has dealt with for ages," he remarked. He was conditioned to look for reinforcements in stone and masonry. The added puzzle in the Khumbu, he realized, was figuring out how to get materials that could add stability to structures up the roadless valley in a way that was cost-effective enough to make it worthwhile. As he was contemplating possible solutions, Dave asked Larry to check out the teahouse where they had planned to spend the night to verify that the structure was safe. With Larry's blessing, they passed a blissfully uneventful night there and departed Pheriche by 8:15 a.m. on the first of May.

Helicopters buzzed overhead as Base Camp continued to empty out. Dave was glad they had held back at Base Camp for a couple of days while packing, successfully avoiding the crowds of climbers who had flooded the valley earlier. He hoped the same would be true by the time they reached Lukla; they had heard reports of climbers fighting to get on planes. They came across a few trekkers and porters on the trails, but certainly many fewer than was normal for this time of year. The locals they encountered, hard at work moving rocks and plastering walls to repair their severely damaged homes—without any form of insurance to help them with the costs—greeted them with generous smiles and bid them "Namaste" as they passed.

On the trail near Pangboche, they heard traditional Sherpa music, mournful and rhythmic, growing louder as they approached a mangled house. "It looks like it was hit by a bomb," Robbie said. They then noticed flocks of red-robed monks gathering outside of it and the sweet, cedar smell of burning juniper. They stopped to check in on the residents and realized, through Chhering's translation, that they had come upon the funeral rites for a Sherpa cook who had been killed at Base Camp.

In the Sherpa culture, funerals are long ceremonial rituals involving elaborate pujas. The body lays in the home, visited by monks and family members and neighbors, for three days before it is cremated outdoors. Gifts of butter, rice, and money are distributed by the family to their community in order to improve the rebirth prospects of the deceased, who, it is believed, is reincarnated after his spirit undergoes a bardo, the transitional, liminal state of existence between death and rebirth lasting forty-nine days.

Chhering, Dave, JJ, Robbie, Larry, and Peter paid their respects to the man's grief-stricken widow. They took up a collection of cash among themselves and put it in her tiny, sinewy hands before they left, along with some food they had carried with them from Base Camp to distribute on the trek down the valley to anyone who needed it. At first, the widow politely declined, but when they insisted, she eventually accepted their offerings.

From Pangboche, they moved across the river to Deboche and proceeded up the hill to the visibly damaged and momentarily abandoned Tengboche Monastery. They rested near the foot of the grand monastery, taking some time for introspection beneath the unblinking gaze of Ama Dablam, her necklace still intact, before heading down the big hill, out of the alpine zone, and into verdant, tangled waves of blooming pink rhododendrons. Above them, feathery lammergeiers and brown eagles soared on broad wings. Shaggy wild goats known as Himalayan Tahr grazed within view.

They circumvented massive rocks that had fallen on the trail as they worked their way up the big hill and across the traversing trail to Namche. While walking into the village, JJ's face broke into a wide smile when he recognized the same little Sherpa girl who had high-fived them on the their way up the valley. Galloping toward them on the trail in rubber rain boots, a red-checkered skirt, and a blue jacket, her dark hair shorn in a buzz cut, she seemed to recognize them too. They tapped her tiny, uplifted hand again. Then they found lodging at their favorite Namche teahouse, Hotel Camp De Base, and slept more deeply than they had in weeks in the decadently thick, 11,000-foot air.

"I suppose we would never have chosen to be 'tourists' in a disaster area, but here we are," Dave said somberly as the group left Namche at 8:00 in the morning, under more flawlessly blue skies.

Five miles down the trail, in the small village of Monjo located just below the Sagarmatha National Park entry gate, they stopped at the home of the sister of Pasanga Temba Sherpa, a member of their sherpa team. While they sipped cups of warm and earthy-smelling *su cha* (yak butter tea) in the cool, dark dwelling, Pasang turned to Dave and Chhering and said something in Nepali.

"He says, 'Thank you for saving my life,'" Chhering translated. Dave was so startled and confused by Pasang's comment, he nearly spit out his tea. Pasang explained that the decision to have him and the other climbing sherpas turn around, leaving the loads they were carrying for Camp Two at Camp One, prevented them from being in the Icefall when the earthquake struck. "He says, 'Most guides would have pushed us through,'" Chhering said.

Dave, no longer tongue-tied, explained with both words and exaggerated hand gestures, as Chhering continued to translate, that he had made the decision in unison with Chhering and JJ and that they had decided to turn the sherpas around at that point due to the looming threat of possible snow and avalanches off of Nuptse, not due to the unknown threat of an imminent earthquake. While he felt relieved and thankful that their sherpa team had made it back through the Icefall before the earthquake struck, he said he could take no credit for getting lucky.

"I hadn't done the math myself," he added. However, he did feel the team could share "generic credit" for having put safety first, yet again. "It seems because of that we reaped unexpected benefits," he conceded.

After thanking their hosts, Dave and his remaining team continued trekking until 2:30 in the afternoon when, just as they reached Lukla, fat raindrops began to drop softly on the dirt trail. Dave was relieved to see that the town and airstrip appeared largely intact and were absent of the crowds they had heard described as mobs just a few days ago. Perhaps, he thought, their luck would remain with them when they attempted to make their departure in the morning.

"We're tentatively scheduled on the first wave of flights to Kathmandu tomorrow," he informed his remaining team, lowering his index and middle fingers twice to indicate quotation marks as he said the word "scheduled."

27 ⛰ HOTEL YAK AND YETI

> "One generation goes and another comes, but the earth abides."
> Ecclesiastes 1:4

Heavy rain thrummed on the tin roof, thunder cracked, and flashes of lightning illuminated their rooms, keeping the climbers awake well into the Lukla night. By the time their phone alarms beeped and chirped at 5:00 a.m. the rain had ceased. Twenty minutes later, as they dressed, the orange sun began to rise in a pink-streaked sky. It looked like perfect weather for flying.

Dave, Chhering, JJ, Peter, Robbie, and Larry departed their lodge on foot and reached the mayhem of the nearby Lukla Airport by 6:00 a.m. After spending an hour milling around waiting, Dave watched a twin-engine prop plane taxi in. "Well, it's got the right number and letters on its tail—must be ours," he told the group. They pushed their ways through the herd of climbers and trekkers out to the runway and walked up a short ramp into the belly of the small plane.

When they landed at the Tribhuvan International Airport, they were quickly absorbed into swarms of tourists, leaving them feeling strangely anonymous and insignificant. They stuck their heads out of the windows of their hotel van, stretching to observe the quake damage around them in Kathmandu as they were driven to the guilt-inducing comforts of the Yak and Yeti. The gleaming lobby was filled to the gills with journalists, foreign correspondents, camera crews, diplomats, and several other climbers and guides, including a few who would soon be heading out to remote villages to conduct relief work.

Tomorrow Nepal would celebrate Buddha Purnima, a festival honoring the Buddha on his birthday. Thousands of Nepalis would descend upon the iconic, spherical Boudhanath Stupa, one of the largest stupas in the world. From the gold pyramid tower atop its white dome, umbrellaed by a gilded canopy, prayer flags would fan out in all directions.

Giant pairs of blue eyes, painted on all four sides of the main tower, would appear to gaze down on the scarlet- and gold-robed monks who would blow resonantly into conch shells, crash cymbals, beat drums, and swing copper chalices on chains with pungent incense escaping from the vents while they paraded toward the stupa. One of the monks, wearing a headdress resembling the red comb of a rooster, would carry a baby Buddha statue tenderly wrapped in flowered, golden silk. Throngs of quake survivors would come to offer prayers for the souls of the departed and to give thanks as they circled the stupa, some over one hundred times, cultivating consciousness.

Dave retreated to his room for a long-overdue shower and shave. The hot running water felt like an ambrosial delight. Now 5,000 feet lower than Lukla, the oxygen-saturated air was undeniably intoxicating. Inhaling the steam of the shower, he considered the evening ahead. He would share a final dinner with his team on the rooftop of the hotel. They would be safe and warm and comfortable. They'd toast each other and watch a full Flower Moon rise in the May sky. He knew it would all be easy to enjoy. He suspected, however, that reconciling the good fortune they had experienced throughout the disaster with the loss and suffering others had endured would not prove quite so uncomplicated, especially as they scattered homeward around the globe tomorrow. Before dinner, though, he had some business to which he must attend. He dressed in his cleanest clothes and then, while still fastening the top buttons of his shirt, with the thin red string from Lama Geshe visible around his neck, headed back downstairs to the lobby to meet Miss Elizabeth Hawley for their post-trip interview.

Sitting in a quiet corner in a burgundy upholstered chair with her quad-prong walking cane standing next to her like a sentry, Dave thought she looked a little smaller than when he had last seen her in March, but the force of her personality was still tangible. She wore a blue cardigan sweater and pink lipstick. After he sat down in the chair across from her, Miss Hawley peered at Dave over the edge of her glasses.

"How many members at end?" she asked.

Dave looked her in her eyes, which at ninety-two years old appeared more liquid and deeper set than he remembered, and said, "All."

"So, will you be here next year?" she asked him, as she had every year. Every year before he had replied with an unequivocal, "Yes." This time, though, Dave hesitated.

"Will you be here next year?" Dave ventured quietly, deflecting her question. As soon as the words left his lips, however, they seemed to take on a morbid tone and melancholic weight he had not intended. Then, Elizabeth and Dave waited in deference to each other.

"Well, at my age, one never knows," she offered impassively. Dave paused in reverence to it.

"I'm not positive I'll attempt it again," Dave conceded, eventually. "Mount Everest has dished out all I can personally stomach of failure and heartache and death in recent years . . ."

"But I suppose those decisions can wait a little," he added, as if it the future were entirely up to them. They both knew it was not.

"What I know for sure," Dave said, "is that I've about given up on being a control freak. Every expedition leader likes to think they're in control . . . and, well, we turn out not to be."

Miss Hawley folded her arms and nodded several times in understanding. She placed her paperwork beside her on the end table. As expected due to the quake, there wasn't much for Dave to report in terms of climbing goals achieved this trip. Instead, uncharacteristically unguarded, they reminisced for an hour about the challenges and joys of the Everest era they had felt privileged to share. They knew Chomolungma had much to say, and they tilted their heads toward each other as if to better hear what she was telling each of them.

Regardless of when he grew too old to guide, Dave possessed a certainty that, just as sure as the Himalayas would continue to rise imperceptibly and the Dudh Kosi would flow into the Bay of Bengal, he would climb mountains always, until perhaps one day he would find himself in a storm he couldn't handle, alone with himself and his memories.

Something in him would always require the test, and he could trust that every time he climbed, life would distill itself into the sound of his own breath, the familiar burn in his shoulders and quads, and the anticipation of what lay over the next ridge.

As Miss Hawley gripped her walker and rose from her seat, Dave stood up too, unsettled by his sudden premonition that this might be their last farewell. "Goodbye, Elizabeth," he said, and he bent down to hug her.

"Nice to see you," she said, accepting his embrace, her eyes beaming at him over an almost shy, closed-lip smile. Then she linked her right arm in the bent left arm offered to her by her driver, Suban, and Dave watched the two of them walk out of the dark lobby of the Yak and Yeti until they became silhouetted when they stepped out into the bright sunshine together.

Whatever was to come, Dave knew the Earth would continue to shake. Eager mountains would rise and fall like waves across time. Footsteps, buried by snow and washed away by rain and wind, would remain theirs. Melting ice would uncover what was left behind.

He was mothered by mountains.

AFTERWORD

The 2015 RMI Expedition was Dave's last Everest climb as of 2020; he continues to guide on Rainier, Denali, Vinson Massif, and Kiliminjaro. He eventually traveled back to the Khumbu in the fall of 2018 to guide an Everest Base Camp trek as a fundraiser to benefit the Juniper Fund. He would never see Miss Elizabeth Hawley again.

Elizabeth retired from her work on the Himalayan Database in early 2016 at the age of ninety-two and was succeeded by her longtime assistant Billi Bierling. She suffered a stroke in January of 2018 at the age of ninety-four; she died a week later in Kathmandu. Her pine coffin was carried in the back of a sky-blue pick-up truck, adorned with silk scarves and strings of bright marigolds, to Swayambu where she was ceremoniously cremated on a traditional Buddhist open-air funeral pyre. Wrapped in white sheets, she was laid gently on top of stacked logs and covered with orange, gold, red, and white scarves. Her Nepalese pallbearers piled straw and bouquets of flowers brought by her many mourners atop the scarves and encircled her body with marigolds, spelling her name with them on the ground below her feet. The pyre was doused with fuel contained in old soda bottles and then ignited by her nephew, Michael Hawley Leonard, as Buddhist monks sounded longhorns, rang bells, crashed cymbals, and intoned prayers. Black smoke billowed into the sky.

A month later, Lama Geshe died, on February 22, 2018, at the age of eighty-seven. "Rocks come down, mountains change, and people finish their lives," Dave wrote in elegy. "That doesn't mean the game is finished. There isn't any shortage of Everest left to climb at the head of the valley. There will still be great folks to send you off to your mountain with a blessing and perhaps even a knock on the head to settle your stomach butterflies and stiffen your vertebrae. And afterward, in Kathmandu, good folks will still document your achievements and endeavors. But that is all for a new era."

Chhering Dorjee has not returned to Everest since the quake. He accepted a guiding position with Yamnuska Mountain Adventures in 2015 and now lives in Seattle, Washington, with his wife Yanzee and their two daughters, Cheyyang and Emma. Chhering's niece, Tshering Doka, born two months after her father (Chhering's brother) Pemba's death, has grown up in Buena Vista, Colorado, with her mother and her stepfather, an American climber. The two families spend as much time together as possible.

After guiding expeditions for eighteen years, JJ graduated from criminal justice training in February of 2017. His police badge was pinned on him on March 1, 2017, in Ocean Shores, Washington. He has not returned to Everest.

HP, Larry, Hans, Hao, Robbie, and Peter all took different routes back around the globe from Kathmandu to their home cities after surviving the earthquake. Due to the disaster, HP was rerouted through New Delhi where he spent time with his in-laws in India. "You will not go climbing again," his mother-in-law decreed. "Over my dead body!"

Following two consecutive years of major disasters in 2014 and 2015, Everest returned to "business as usual" in 2016, according to mountaineering journalist Alan Arnette. Arnette noted, however, that there were 40 percent fewer trekkers to the Khumbu in 2016, negatively impacting Nepal's fragile economy. At Everest Base Camp, climbers worried about the noticeably warmer temperatures, with a river of meltwater running through Base Camp in early April when it was typically still frozen solid. In spite of increasing glacial instability, the 2016 season progressed relatively uneventfully and without a natural disaster; six hundred climbers summited Everest.

In 2018, an unusually wide eleven-day weather window allowed for a record number of eight hundred summits. In stark contrast, a remarkably narrow weather window in 2019 was caused by a wobbly jet stream conspiring with a tropical cyclone named Fani. The tight time frame for summiting, combined with a record number of climbers—many

desperately inexperienced—caused bottlenecking near the top and resulted in a deadly season that claimed the lives of 21 climbers. Due to
escalating global warming and glacier melt, 2019 also generated head-
lines for the exposure of dead bodies along the route that had remained
buried by snow and ice for years. In spite of the chaos of the season, Hao
Wu summited Everest on May 23, 2019.

ACKNOWLEDGMENTS

If it were not for my husband, Oban Lambie, this book would not have been written. When I first tried to talk myself out of it, he said, in his characteristically common-sense style, "If you don't do this, it's only because you're too insecure, too Catholic, and too self-loathing." He was only half kidding. I thank him for knowing me well enough to say that, as well as for his unwavering belief, generous and patient support, trusted encouragement, and his smart, insightful edits. I could not have done it without him.

When Dave Hahn paid one of his visits to my classroom of sixth, seventh, and eighth grade students at Taos Middle School on March 7, 2000, he left us with a copy of *Ghosts of Everest* (a chronicle of the 1999 Mallory and Irvine Research Expedition) in which he inscribed, "For a class of kids who are true class! Thanks for keeping track of us." I thank him for allowing me to pursue this project and for giving us all the privilege of keeping track of him through his pitch-perfect blog posts and stunning photographs that testify to his extraordinary life, well lived, in the mountains. (I also thank Kristin and Ross Ulibarri for first inviting Dave to visit our class. I wrote this book with that group of remarkable students in mind.)

At first, I had hoped Dave would write this book since it was a story that I felt needed telling, but over a breakfast of huevos rancheros at the Taos Diner, he made it clear to me he had no intentions of doing so. He was reverent about the tragedy inherent in the 2015 Everest season and was determined not to profit from anyone's loss. Plus, he explained, he would rather be climbing. It is an honor to tell any piece of his story and I am grateful for every minute he gave me. I will not forget the sight of him recalling his first, harrowing summit of Everest while patiently plucking grains of rice out of the crevices of my iPhone with tweezers, after I had accidentally dropped the phone in the toilet mid-interview and had then made an ill-advised attempt to salvage it by placing it in a bag of rice.

Dave is well loved and esteemed in the climbing community, and almost everyone he helped me contact for my research graciously obliged. I am deeply appreciative of the 2015 RMI Everest Expedition co-guides and clients who contributed their time and memories. Sherpa sirdar Chhering Dorjee Sherpa served as a particularly accessible resource, generously sharing his rich and compelling personal story. It was my pleasure to talk with him and with guide Jeffrey James Justman, as well as with clients Erin Machinchik, Robbie Massie, Hemanshu Parwani, Bonny Rogers, Peter Rogers, Larry Seaton, and Hao Wu. I thank Nomita Parwani, too, for sharing her invaluable perspective. I was honored to conduct one of the final interviews of the irreverent and legendary Elizabeth Hawley through the efforts of her intrepid assistant, Billi Bierling, who has succeeded Hawley at the Himalayan Database. The loss of Elizabeth Hawley and the loss of Lama Geshe were felt keenly in the Everest community, and I would like to extend my sympathy. I would also like to express my profound condolences to the loved ones of the victims of the 2015 quake.

I am indebted to Stephen Hull, my (unrelated) namesake and the editor of the nonprofit UNM Press, for his belief in this book. His faith in it and the thoughtful guidance I've received from him and the wonderful team at UNM Press (with a special shout-out to Alexandra Hoff for her eagle-eyed and perceptive copyediting) have steered this book to publication. I thank Stephen for his astute and invaluable notes, his steady hand, and for giving this book the opportunity to exist in its perfect home.

I am grateful to RMI for allowing me to use their blogs, as well as for the research treasure trove provided by the Eddie Bauer/First Ascent dispatches and videos (also published by *National Geographic*) from their elegant 2009 "Return to Everest Expedition." I thank *Outside Magazine* for their wealth of in-depth Everest reporting, particularly by Grayson Schaffer. My appreciation goes to Alan Arnette and Adrianna Blake for serving as expert readers, Dorie Hagler for taking my photo questions, and David Benavides for sharing his Hyder House memories. I thank authors David Wright, Timothy Weed, Dave Hannigan, Will Mackin, and book advocates Catherine Drayton, Katie Freeman, and Ellen Schatz for their invaluable professional advice.

This book grew largely out of my time spent at the Southampton Writer's Conference. I am forever grateful for the conference's luminous, world-class faculty and for the inspiration of the writer friends I have made in that oceanside, summertime writing haven. I thank Taos treasure Summer Wood for honoring the craft of writing in her workshops. The 2019 UNM Writing Conference was critical in helping me navigate the publishing process. Concentrating on this project would not have been possible for me without the committed educators at Albuquerque Academy and Anansi Charter School. I also thank Phyllis Turner for the inspiration, my inimitable Taos book club, my beloved 302ers, and my loyal OFC crew.

Over the course of this project, my family and I were shook by serious health challenges. I am especially grateful for doctors Robert LaPrade, Jennifer Bishop, Jennifer Chan, Katrina Mitchell, John Ferretti, Ursa Brown-Glaberman, and Brian O'Hea. They are my heroes.

I completed this book because of an army of love. I'd like to acknowledge my husband, Oban; my parents, Barbara and John Hull; my sisters, Elena and Christina Hull; my talented family-in-law; and the extraordinary, devoted friends who have lighted my way—it is a profound gift to be fortified, and uplifted by such creative, generous friends. I am forever grateful for their belief, valued feedback, relentless encouragement, shared contacts and resources, and "boots-on-the-ground" support. I thank my sun and my moon, Jack and Liam.

BIBLIOGRAPHY

Epigraph

Abbey, Edward. *Desert Solitaire*. University of Arizona Press, 1988.

Chapter 1

Chang, Kenneth. "Ancient Collision Made Nepal Earthquake Inevitable." *New York Times*, 2015, www.nytimes.com/2015/04/26/science
/ancient-collision-made-nepal-earthquake-inevitable-epochs-later
.html.

Hahn, Dave, et al. Expedition Dispatches Everest Southside with Dave
Hahn. *RMI Expeditions Blog*, Mar.–May 2015, www.rmiguides.com
/blog/expedition/everest_3_21_2015/desc.

Hull, Jennifer. Personal interview of Chhering Dorjee Sherpa.
Apr. 2016.

———. Personal interview of Hao Wu. May 2017.

———. Personal interview of Hemanshu Parwani. Aug. 2017.

———. Personal interview of JJ Justman. May 2016.

———. Personal interview of Larry Seaton. Apr. 2016.

———. Personal interview of Peter Rogers. July 2016.

———. Personal interview of Robbie Massie. Apr. 2016.

———. Personal interviews of Dave Hahn. 2018.

"Survival Stories from Mount Everest." *Men's Journal*, 2015, https://
www.mensjournal.com/travel/survival-stories-mount-everest.

Chapter 2

Akelson, Michael. "Life in the Mountains: Former UB Swimmer
Dave Hahn Discusses Legendary Mountain Guiding Career." *The
Spectrum*, 4 May 2017, www.ubspectrum.com/article/2017/05/life
-in-the-mountains.

Bierling, Billi. "Chronicling High-Peak History with Elizabeth Hawley." *Outdoor Research*, 5 Aug. 2013, www.outdoorresearch.com /blog/article/chronicling-high-peak-history-with-elizabeth-hawley.

Hahn, Dave, and Rebecca Ruddell. "The Day the Mountain Shook." *At Buffalo*, 2015, www.buffalo.edu/atbuffalo/article-page-fall-2015 .host.html/content/shared/www/atbuffalo/articles/Fall-2015 /features/day-the-mountain-shook.detail.html.

Hahn, Dave, et al. Expedition Dispatches Everest Southside with Dave Hahn. *RMI Expeditions Blog*, 2015, www.rmiguides.com/blog /expedition/everest_3_21_2015/desc.

Hansen, Eric. "The High Priestess of Posterity." *Outside Online*, 9 Mar. 2011, www.outsideonline.com/1825881/high-priestess-posterity.

Hill, Craig. "IMG Guide Dave Hahn Sets Record with 10th Everest Summit." *The Tacoma News Tribune*, 28 May 2008, www.mountain guides.com/pop_news_newstribune_08_05b.shtml.

Hull, Jennifer. Personal interviews of Dave Hahn. 2018.

Hull, Jennifer, and Billi Bierling. Personal interview of Elizabeth Hawley. Mar. 2017.

McDonald, Bernadette. *I'll Call You in Kathmandu: The Elizabeth Hawley Story*. The Mountaineers Books, 2005.

Nestler, Stefan. "Miss Hawley: 'I'm Just a Chronicler.'" *DW*, 5 Apr. 2016, blogs.dw.com/adventuresports/miss-hawley-im-just-a -chronicler.

Otto, Allison, director. *Keeper of the Mountains*. XTreme Video, 2013, www.x-tremevideo.com/films/keeper-of-the-mountains.

Simonson, Eric, et al. "Ghosts of Everest." *Outside Online*, 1 Oct. 1999, www.outsideonline.com/1909046/ghosts-everest.

Chapter 3

Blauweiss, Stephen, and Lynn Wood, producers/directors. *Lost Rondout: A Story of Urban Renewal*. Lost Roundout Project, 2016, www .lostrondoutproject.com.

Don McLean. "Bye Miss American Pie." *American Pie*, United Artist
Records, 1971.

Hawley, Elizabeth. "Ascents." *Himalayan Database*, Expedition Ar-
chives, 2014, www.himalayandatabase.com/2014%20Season%20
Lists/2014%20Spring%20A2.html.

Hull, Jennifer. Personal interviews of Dave Hahn. 2018.

Krakauer, Jon. *Into Thin Air*. Anchor Books, 1997.

"Local Death Record." *Kingston Daily Freeman*, 14 Jan. 1972, pp. 4–4,
www.newspapers.com/newspage/86278273.

Schupp, Edward M. "Interview Dave Hahn." *Facebook*, 2008, www
.facebook.com/pg/Wormtrax.

Chapter 4

Borenstein, Seth. "Nepal Earthquake Experts There a Week
Ago to Plan for Earthquake." *U.S. News & World Report*,
25 Apr. 2015, www.usnews.com/news/world/articles/2015
/04/25/experts-gathered-in-nepal-a-week-ago-to-ready
-for-earthquake.

Guyott, Lisa. "Reaching for the Top of the World." University of
St. Thomas, 22 Apr. 2015,https://news.stthomas.edu/reaching-top
-world/.

———. "St. Thomas Magazine Interview Transcript." Unpublished,
2015.

Hahn, Dave, et al. Expedition Dispatches Everest Southside with Dave
Hahn. *RMI Expeditions*, Mar.–May 2015, www.rmiguides.com
/blog/expedition/everest_3_21_2015/desc.

Hull, Jennifer. Personal interview of Bonny Rogers. June 2016.

———. Personal interview of Erin Machinchik. Apr. 2016.

———. "Personal interview of Robbie Massie. Apr. 2016.

———. "Personal interviews of Dave Hahn. 2018.

Kleinekoenen, Von Ulrike. "Okrifteler Erlebte Das Beben Von Nepal
Am Mount Everest." *Frankfurter Neue Presse*, 8 May 2015, www.fnp

.de/lokales/main-taunus/okrifteler-erlebte-beben-nepal-mount
-everest-10719010.html.

Roberts, Rich. "A Crowd Gathers at the Top of the World: International Peace Climb Gets 20 People to Summit of Mt. Everest Over Four Days." *Los Angeles Times*, 13 June 1990, www.latimes.com
/archives/la-xpm-1990-06-13-sp-293-story.html.

Chapter 5

Abbey, Edward. *Desert Solitaire*. University of Arizona Press, 1988.

Akelson, Michael. "Life in the Mountains: Former UB Swimmer Dave Hahn Discusses Legendary Mountain Guiding Career." *The Spectrum*, 4 May 2017, www.ubspectrum.com/article/2017/05/life
-in-the-mountains.

Berg, Aimee. "Dave Hahn Is Always Climbing Higher." *Live Happy Magazine*, 10 Feb. 2015, www.livehappy.com/self/resilience/dave
-hahn-always-climbing-higher.

"Denali Prep Course." Mountain Madness, www.mountainmadness
.com/adventures/schools/north-america/denali-prep.

Dunn, George, and Dave Hahn. "Intro: Seattle to Zurich." *Mountain Zone.com*, 1998, www.mountainzone.com/climbing/alps.

Hahn, Dave, et al. Expedition Dispatches Everest Southside with Dave Hahn. *RMI Expeditions Blog*, Mar.–May 2015, www.rmiguides.com
/blog/expedition/everest_3_21_2015/desc.

Hill, Craig. "IMG Guide Dave Hahn Sets Record with 10th Everest Summit." *The Tacoma News Tribune*, 28 May 2008, www.mountain
guides.com/pop_news_newstribune_08_05b.shtml.

Hull, Jennifer. Personal interview of JJ Justman. May 2016.

———. Personal interview of David Benavides. 17 Jan. 2018.

———. Personal interviews of Dave Hahn. 2018.

Schupp, Edward M. "Interview Dave Hahn." *Facebook*, 2008, www
.facebook.com/pg/Wormtrax/posts.

Chapter 6

Arnette, Alan. "How Much Does It Cost to Climb Mount Everest?" *The Blog on alanarnette.com*, 1 Dec. 2019, www.alanarnette.com /blog/2019/12/01/how-much-does-it-cost-to-climb-mount-everest -2020-edition.

Barronian, Abbie. "So You Want to Climb Everest? A Record-Setting Guide Tells You How." *Adventure Journal*, 6 Jan. 2017, www.adventure-journal.com/2017/01/want-climb-everest-record -setting-guide-tells.

"Earthquakes." National Seismological Centre, Government of Nepal Department of Mines and Geology, 2019, seismonepal.gov.np /earthquakes.

Green, Stewart. "The Geology of Mount Everest." *Liveabout*, updated 18 May 2018, www.liveabout.com/geology-of-mount-everest -755308.

Hahn, Dave, et al. Expedition Dispatches Everest Southside with Dave Hahn. *RMI Expeditions Blog*, Mar.–May 2015, www.rmiguides.com /blog/expedition/everest_3_21_2015/desc.

———. "Climbers Arrive in Sherpa Capital Namche." *RMI Expedi- tions Blog*, 30 Mar. 2009, www.rmiguides.com/blog/2009/03/30 /climbers_arrive_in_sherpa_capital_namche1.

Hawley, Elizabeth. "Ascents." *Himalayan Database*, Expedition Ar- chives, 2014, www.himalayandatabase.com/2014%20Season%20 Lists/2014%20Spring%20A2.html.

Huey, Raymond, et al. "Effects of Age and Gender of Success and Death of Mountaineers on Mount Everest." *Biology Letters*, vol. 3, no. 5, 2007, doi.org/10.1098/rsbl.2007.0317.

Hull, Jennifer. Personal interview of Bonny Rogers. June 2016.

———. "Personal Interview of Chhering Dorjee Sherpa. Apr. 2016.

———. Personal interview of Erin Machinchik. Apr. 2016.

———. Personal interview of Hao Wu. May 2017.

————. Personal interview of Hemanshu Parwani. Aug. 2017.

————. Personal interview of JJ Justman. May 2016.

————. Personal interview of Larry Seaton. Apr. 2016.

————. Personal interview of Peter Rogers. July 2016.

————. Personal interview of Robbie Massie. Apr. 2016.

————. Personal interviews of Dave Hahn. 2018.

Huntington, Anna. "A Debilitating Disease That Is Often Unknown." *New York Times*, 9 Oct. 2008, www.nytimes.com/2008/10/10/sports /othersports/10celiac.html.

Jenkins, Mark. "Climbing Finished for Season on Everest After Deadly Avalanche?" *National Geographic*, 22 Apr. 2014, www.national geographic.com/news/2014/4/140420-mount-everest-climbing -mountain-avalanche-sherpa-nepal.

Kleinekoenen, Von Ulrike. "Okrifteler Erlebte Das Beben Von Nepal Am Mount Everest." *Frankfurter Neue Presse*, 8 May 2015, www.fnp .de/lokales/main-taunus/okrifteler-erlebte-beben-nepal-mount -everest-10719010.html.

Megroz, Gregor. "Are You Too Sensitive?" *Outside Online*, 15 June 2011, www.outsideonline.com/1885916/are-you-too-sensitive.

Pino, Raul. "Hiking in Nepal: On the Way to Namche Bazaar! (Day 2)." *I Live to Travel*, ilivetotravel.me/nepal-hiking-trekking-namche -sagarmatha.

Sandeford, Mike, et al. "The Science Behind Nepal Earthquakes." *Earth and Sky*, 12 May 2015, earthsky.org/earth/the-science-behind -the-nepal-earthquake.

"Why Climb with RMI?" RMI Expeditions, www.rmiguides.com /about-us/why-climb-with-rmi.

Yune, Howard. "Avalanche Aborts Napa Man's Everest Dream." *Napa Valley Register*, 17 May 2015, napavalleyregister.com/news/local /avalanche-aborts-napa-man-s-everest-dream/article_9b36cc9c -17b4-510a-a9fb-00121f38b81a.html.

————. "Napa Climber Survives Avalanche at Mount Everest Base Camp." *Napa Valley Register*, 29 Apr. 2015, napavalleyregister.com /news/local/napa-climber-survives-avalanche-at-mount-everest -base-camp/article_cdff9d56-36e9-56d4-ae41-0eca33641cd1 .html.

Chapter 7

Berg, Aimee. "Dave Hahn Is Always Climbing Higher." *Live Happy Magazine*, 10 Feb. 2015, www.livehappy.com/self/resilience/dave -hahn-always-climbing-higher.

Dennison, Richard, director. *The Fatal Game*. Making Movies, 2013, vimeo.com/ondemand/thefatalgame.

Doggett, Scott. "To Save or Be Saved." *Los Angeles Times*, 27 Jan. 2004. www.latimes.com/archives/la-xpm-2004-jan-27-os-voidside27 -story.html.

Douglas, Ed. "No One Can Keep Her Down." *Independent*, www .independent.co.uk/life-style/no-one-can-keep-her-down-1587305 .html.

Flatow, Ira. "Mount Everest Still Holds Mysteries For Scientists." *NPR Talk of the Nation*, 16 Mar. 2012, www.npr.org /2012/03/16/148753432/mount-everest-still-holds-mysteries -for-scientists.

Hahn, Dave. "Dave Hahn Reflects on His Tenth Everest Summit." *GreatOutdoors.com*, 12 June 2008, www.greatoutdoors.com /published/dave-hahn-reflects-on-his-tenth-everest-summit.

Hull, Jennifer. Personal interviews of Dave Hahn. 2018.

McDonald, Bernadette. *Keeper of the Mountains: The Elizabeth Hawley Story*. Rocky Mountain Books, 2012.

Simonson, Eric. "Asia, Tibet, Everest Ascents and Tragedy." *American Alpine Journal*, 1995, publications.americanalpineclub.org/articles /12199530100/Asia-Tibet-Everest-Ascents-and-Tragedy.

Chapter 8

Arnette, Alan. "Everest 2013: Tributes to the Sherpas." *The Blog on alan-arnette.com*, 11 Apr. 2013, www.alanarnette.com/blog/2013/04/11 /everest-2013-tributes-to-the-sherpas.

Brown, Chip. "Sorrow on the Mountain." *National Geographic*, Nov. 2014, www.nationalgeographic.com/magazine/2014/11/mount -everest-avalanche-tragedy-sherpas.

Foreman, Bruce. "The Sherpa Cheat Sheet: 9 Things You Were Embarrassed to Ask." *CNN*, 12 July 2017, www.cnn.com/travel/article /sherpa-facts/index.html.

Hahn, Dave. "RMI Team Continues Trek to Everest—Namche to Deboche." *RMI Expeditions Blog*, 2 Apr. 2009, www.rmiguides .com/blog/2009/04/02/rmi_team_continues_trek_to_everest _namche_to_deboche.

Hull, Jennifer. Personal interview of Bonny Rogers. June 2016.

———. Personal interview of Chhering Dorjee Sherpa. Apr. 2016.

———. Personal interview of Larry Seaton. Apr. 2016.

———. "Personal interviews of Dave Hahn. 2018.

Klatzel, Frances. *Gaiety of Spirit: The Sherpas of Everest*. Rocky Mountain Books, 2010.

Loomis, Molly. "A Year After Everest Disaster, This Sherpa Isn't Going Back." *National Geographic*, 10 Apr. 2015, www.national geographic.com/news/2015/04/150410-Everest-climbing-sherpas -mountaineering-Nepal-Himalayas-guides.

"Sherpa and the Culture of Nepal." *RMI Expeditions Blog*, 17 Apr. 2009, www.rmiguides.com/blog/2009/04/17/sherpa_and_the _culture_of_nepal.

Chapter 9

Arnette, Alan. "Blessings from Lama Geshe." *The Blog on alanarnette. com*, 5 Apr. 2011, www.alanarnette.com/blog/2011/04/05/blessings -from-lama-geshi.

Brown, Chip. "Sherpas: The Invisible Men of Everest." *National Geographic*, 26 Apr. 2014, www.nationalgeographic.com/news /special-features/2014/04/140426-sherpa-culture-everest-disaster.

Callaghan, Anne. "Climate Change Is Melting Everest." *Outside Online*, 12 Apr. 2016, www.outsideonline.com/2067651/climate -change-melting-everest.

Hahn, Dave, et al. Expedition Dispatches Everest Southside with Dave Hahn. *RMI Expeditions Blog*, Mar.–May 2015, www.rmiguides.com /blog/expedition/everest_3_21_2015/desc.

———. "Acclimatizing at Deboche." *RMI Expeditions Blog*, 3 Apr. 2009, www.rmiguides.com/blog/2009/04/03/acclimatizing_at _deboche.

———. "RMI Team Continues Trek to Everest—Namche to Debo-che." *RMI Expeditions Blog*, 2 Apr. 2009, www.rmiguides.com /blog/2009/04/02/rmi_team_continues_trek_to_everest_namche _to_deboche.

Hahn, Dave. "Remembering Lama Geshe, Blesser of Everest Climbers." *Outside Online*, 22 Feb. 2018, www.outsideonline.com /2282326/lama-geshe.

Hull, Jennifer. Personal interview of Chhering Dorjee Sherpa. Apr. 2016.

———. Personal interviews of Dave Hahn. 2018.

"Miyolangsangma, the Goddess of Inexhaustible Giving." *Tsem Rin-poche*, 13 June 2019, www.tsemrinpoche.com/tsem-tulku-rinpoche /buddhas-dharma/miyolangsangma-the-goddess-of-inexhaustible -giving.html.

"The Nuns—Deboche Project." Deboche Project, www.debocheproject .org/the-nuns.

Chapter 10

Hahn, Dave, et al. Expedition Dispatches Everest Southside with Dave Hahn. *RMI Expeditions Blog*, Mar.–May 2015, www.rmiguides.com /blog/expedition/everest_3_21_2015/desc.

Hahn, Dave. "Lama Geshe Gives His Blessings." *RMI Expeditions Blog*, 4 Apr. 2009, https://www.rmiguides.com/blog/2009/04/04 /lama_geyshe_gives_blessing

———. "Remembering Lama Geshe, Blesser of Everest Climbers." *Outside Online*, 22 Feb. 2018, www.outsideonline.com/2282326 /lama-geshe.

Hull, Jennifer. Personal interview of Hemanshu Parwani. Aug. 2017.

———. Personal interview of Robbie Massie. Apr. 2016.

———. Personal interviews of Dave Hahn. 2018.

Lageson, Dave. "What Is the Yellow Band on Everest?" *YouTube*, uploaded by MSU Outreach, 29 Mar. 2012, www.youtube.com /watch?v=0ZH7WFQtdQg.

Chapter 11

Arnot, Melissa. "Above Pheriche Dangers of Altitude Begin." *RMI Expeditions Blog*, 5 Apr. 2009, www.rmiguides.com/blog/2009 /04/05/above_pheriche_dangers_of_altitude_begin.

"Everest Wrap up: Two Teams for Two Faces of a Lonely Mountain." ExplorersWeb, 11 Sept. 2006, www.explorersweb.com/news.php?id =15017.

Hahn, Dave, et al. Expedition Dispatches Everest Southside with Dave Hahn. *RMI Expeditions Blog*, Mar.–May 2015, www.rmiguides.com /blog/expedition/everest_3_21_2015/desc.

Hahn, Dave. "RMI Team Moves Up the Khumbu Valley." *RMI Expeditions Blog*, 5 Apr. 2009, www.rmiguides.com/blog/2009/04/05 /rmi_team_moves_up_the_khumbu_valley.

Himalayan Rescue Association Nepal, himalayanrescue.org.np.

Hull, Jennifer. Personal interview of Erin Machinchik. Apr. 2016.

———. Personal interview of Larry Seaton. Apr. 2016.

———. Personal interview of Peter Rogers. July 2016.

———. Personal interviews of Dave Hahn. 2018.

"Khumbu Cough." Basecamp MD, www.basecampmd.com/expguide
/khumbucough.shtml.

Chapter 12

Griggs, Mary Beth. "Massive Earthquake Shakes Nepal; Avalanches on
Everest." *Popular Science*, 27 Apr. 2015, www.popsci.com
/massive-earthquake-shakes-nepal-causes-avalanches-everest.

Hagerman, Eric. "He Ain't Your Sherpa." *Outside Online*, 1 Apr. 2001,
www.outsideonline.com/1928686/he-aint-your-sherpa.

Hahn, Dave, et al. Expedition Dispatches Everest Southside with Dave
Hahn. *RMI Expeditions Blog*, Mar.–May 2015, www.rmiguides.com
/blog/expedition/everest_3_21_2015/desc.

Hahn, Dave. "Everest Expedition Arrives in Lobuche." *RMI Expeditions Blog*, 6 Apr. 2009, www.rmiguides.com/blog/2009/04/06
/everest_expedition_arrives_in_lobuche.

"The History of Ev-K2-CNR." Ev-K2-CNR, 2008, www.evk2cnr.org
/cms/en/evk2cnr_committee/story.

Hull, Jennifer. "Personal Interview of JJ Justman." May 2016.

———. "Personal Interview of Larry Seaton." Apr. 2016.

———. "Personal Interview of Peter Rogers." July 2016.

———. "Personal Interviews of Dave Hahn." 2018.

"Late Babu Chiri Sherpa." Spirit Travel, Oct. 2014, www.spirittravel.se
/wp-content/uploads/2014/10/late_babu_chiri_sherpa.jpg.

Morical, Mark. "A Grim Day on Everest;." *Bend Bulletin*, 15 June 2014,
www.bendbulletin.com/localstate/a-grim-day-on-everest/article
_cc0e694f-1c3b-5c61-9f2c-86f93e46b7b5.html.

Chapter 13

Hahn, Dave, et al. Expedition Dispatches Everest Southside with Dave Hahn." *RMI Expeditions Blog*, Mar.–May 2015, www.rmiguides.com /blog/expedition/everest_3_21_2015/desc.

Hahn, Dave. "Carry High, Sleep Low—Everest Ascent Strategy." *RMI Expeditions Blog*, 13 Apr. 2009, www.rmiguides.com/blog/2009 /04/13/carry_high_sleep_low_everest_ascent_strategy.

————. "Dispatch 20: Dave Hahn on the Tragic Death of Ang Phinjo Sherpa." *GreatOutdoors.com*, 21 Apr. 2006, www.greatoutdoors. com/published/dispatch-20-dave-hahn-on-the-tragic-death-of-ang -phinjo-sherpa.

————. "RMI Team Arrives at Everest Basecamp." *RMI Expeditions Blog*, 9 Apr. 2009, www.rmiguides.com/blog/2009/04/09/rmi _team_arrives_at_everest_basecamp.

————. "Training for the Khumbu Icefall." *RMI Expeditions Blog*, 11 Apr. 2009, www.rmiguides.com/blog/2009/04/11/training_for _the_khumbu_icefall.

————. "Visteurs & Hahn, Lifelong Friends, First to Test Icefall Route." *RMI Expeditions Blog*, 14 Apr. 2009, www.rmiguides.com /blog/2009/04/14/viesturs_hahn_lifelong_friends_first_to_test _icefall_route.

Hull, Jennifer. Personal interview of Bonny Rogers. June 2016.

————. Personal interview of Chhering Dorjee Sherpa. Apr. 2016.

————. Personal interview of Erin Machinchik. Apr. 2016.

————. Personal interviews of Dave Hahn. 2018.

Wetzler, Brad. "Base Camp Confidential." *Outside Online*, 1 Apr. 2001, www.outsideonline.com/1912281/base-camp-confidential.

Chapter 14

Hahn, Dave, et al. Expedition Dispatches Everest Southside with Dave Hahn. *RMI Expeditions Blog*, Mar.–May 2015, www.rmiguides.com /blog/expedition/everest_3_21_2015/desc.

———. "Night in Gorak Shep, Basecamp Tomorrow." *RMI Expeditions Blog*, 8 Apr. 2009, www.rmiguides.com/blog/2009/04/08 /night_in_gorak_shep_basecamp_tomorrow.

Hull, Jennifer. Personal interview of Bonny Rogers. June 2016.

———. Personal interview of Erin Machinchik. Apr. 2016.

———. Personal interview of Peter Rogers. July 2016.

———. Personal interviews of Dave Hahn. 2018.

Koerselman, Jayme. "Climbing Mount Rainier with Dave Hahn." *Our Life Walkabout*, Mar. 2009, www.ourlifewalkabout.com/2009/03 /climbing-mount-rainier-with-dave-hahn.

Solomon, Christopher. "True Tales of the World's Best Job." *Outside Online*, 30 Apr. 2015, www.outsideonline.com/1969906/secret-life -guides.

Chapter 15

Brown, Chip. "Sherpas: The Invisible Men of Everest." *National Geographic*, 26 Apr. 2014, www.nationalgeographic.com/news /special-features/2014/04/140426-sherpa-culture-everest-disaster.

Hahn, Dave. "Climbers Receive Puja Blessing." *RMI Expeditions Blog*, 12 Apr. 2009, www.rmiguides.com/blog/2009/04/12/climbers _receive_puja_blessing.

Hahn, Dave, et al. Expedition Dispatches Everest Southside with Dave Hahn. *RMI Expeditions Blog*, Mar.–May 2015, www.rmiguides.com /blog/expedition/everest_3_21_2015/desc.

Hull, Jennifer. Personal interview of Chhering Dorjee Sherpa. Apr. 2016.

————. Personal interview of JJ Justman. May 2016.

————. Personal interviews of Dave Hahn. 2018.

Jenkins, Mark. "Climbing Finished for Season on Everest After Deadly Avalanche?" *National Geographic*, 22 Apr. 2014, www.national geographic.com/news/2014/4/140420-mount-everest-climbing -mountain-avalanche-sherpa-nepal.

————. "Mapping the Killer Path of the Everest Avalanche." *National Geographic*, 23 Apr. 2014, www.nationalgeographic.com /news/2014/4/140421-everest-avalanche-sherpas-nepal-climbing -expedition.

————. "The Aftermath of Everest's Deadly Avalanche." *National Geographic*, 20 Apr. 2014, www.nationalgeographic.com/news /2014/4/140419-everest-avalanche-sherpas-climbing-aftermath.

Schaffer, Grayson. "Everest's Darkest Year." *Outside Online*, 8 July 2014, www.outsideonline.com/1924596/everests-darkest-year.

Chapter 16

Arnette, Alan, and Dave Hahn. "The State of Everest: A Conversation with Dave Hahn." *The Blog on alanarnette.com*, 14 Nov. 2016, www.alanarnette.com/blog/2016/11/14/the-state-of-everest-a -conversation-with-dave-hahn.

Brown, Chip. "Sherpas: The Invisible Men of Everest." *National Geographic*, 26 Apr. 2014, www.nationalgeographic.com/news /special-features/2014/04/140426-sherpa-culture-everest-disaster.

Callaghan, Anne. "Climate Change Is Melting Everest." *Outside Online*, 12 Apr. 2016, www.outsideonline.com/2067651/climate -change-melting-everest.

Hahn, Dave, et al. Expedition Dispatches Everest Southside with Dave Hahn. *RMI Expeditions Blog*, Mar.–May 2015, www.rmiguides.com /blog/expedition/everest_3_21_2015/desc.

Hahn, Dave. "Good Preparation at Basecamp Critical for Success on

Everest." *RMI Expeditions Blog*, 16 Apr. 2009, www.rmiguides.com
/blog/2009/04/16/good_preparation_at_basecamp_critical_for
_success_on_everest.

———. "Training for the Khumbu Icefall." *RMI Expeditions Blog*,
11 Apr. 2009, www.rmiguides.com/blog/2009/04/11/training_for
_the_khumbu_icefall.

Hull, Jennifer. Personal interview of Chhering Dorjee Sherpa. Apr.
2016.

———. Personal interview of JJ Justman. May 2016.

———. Personal interviews of Dave Hahn. 2018.

Loomis, Molly. "What Is the SPCC and Why Does It Control the
Route Through the Icefall?" *Outside Online*, 22 Apr. 2015, www
.outsideonline.com/1969601/what-spcc-and-why-does-it-control
-route-through-icefall.

Ogles, Jonah. "Everest Deaths: How Many Sherpas Have Been Killed?"
Outside Online, 18 Apr. 2014, www.outsideonline.com/1922431
/everest-deaths-how-many-sherpas-have-been-killed.

Schenck, Ben. "Half a Percent to the Moon." *MtnMeister*, 28 Oct. 2014,
mtnmeister.com/meister/dave-hahn.

Silverman, Jacob. "Is Global Warming Destroying Mount Everest?"
How Stuff Works, 13 July 2007, science.howstuffworks.com
/environmental/green-science/everest-global-warming.htm.

Chapter 17

Breslow, Peter. "The Beast Born of Snow: What It Feels Like in the
Jaws of an Avalanche." *NPR*, 3 July 2016, www.npr.org/2016/07
/03/484199296/the-beast-born-of-snow-what-it-feels-like-in-the
-jaws-of-an-avalanche.

Hahn, Dave, et al. Expedition Dispatches Everest Southside with Dave
Hahn. *RMI Expeditions Blog*, Mar.–May 2015, www.rmiguides.com
/blog/expedition/everest_3_21_2015/desc.

Hull, Jennifer. Personal interview of Hao Wu. May 2017.

———. Personal interview of JJ Justman. May 2016.

———. Personal interview of Peter Rogers. July 2016.

———. Personal interview of Robbie Massie. Apr. 2016.

———. Personal interviews of Dave Hahn. 2018.

Tremper, Bruce. *Staying Alive in Avalanche Terrain*. 3rd ed., The Mountaineers Books, 2018.

Trianni, Francesca. "What It Feels Like to Be Caught in an Avalanche—and Live." *Time*, 13 Feb. 2014, science.time.com/2014/02/13/how-to-survive-an-avalanche.

Wilkinson, Freddie. "Meet the Sherpa Bringing Wi-Fi to Everest." *National Geographic*, 22 May 2019, www.nationalgeographic.com/adventure/2019/05/mount-everest-link-internet-wifi.

Chapter 18

Arnette, Alan. "Everest 2015: Season Summary—Summits Don't Matter." *The Blog on alanarnette.com*, 6 May 2015, www.alanarnette.com/blog/2015/05/06/everest-2015-season-summary-summits-dont-matter-2.

Hahn, Dave, et al. Expedition Dispatches Everest Southside with Dave Hahn. *RMI Expeditions Blog*, Mar.–May 2015, www.rmiguides.com/blog/expedition/everest_3_21_2015/desc.

Hahn, Dave. "Anatomy of an Everest Summit Bid." *MountainZone.com*, July 2002, www.mountainzone.com/2002/story/hahn/html/hahn_071102.html.

———. "Supplemental O2 Necessary for Most Above Camp III." *RMI Expeditions Blog*, 29 Apr. 2009, www.rmiguides.com/blog/2009/04/29/supplemental_02_necessary_for_most_above_camp_iii.

———. "Teams Making Progress on Everest." *RMI Expeditions Blog*,

14 May 2009, www.rmiguides.com/blog/2009/05/14/teams
_making_progress_on_everest.

Hull, Jennifer. Personal interview of Chhering Dorjee Sherpa.
Apr. 2016.

———. Personal interview of JJ Justman. May 2016.

———. Personal interviews of Dave Hahn. 2018.

Jenkins, Mark. "Climbing Finished for Season on Everest After Deadly
Avalanche?" *National Geographic*, 22 Apr. 2014, www.national
geographic.com/news/2014/4/140420-mount-everest-climbing
-mountain-avalanche-sherpa-nepal.

———. "Surge in Everest Climbers Year After Mountain's Worst Tragedy." *National Geographic*, 8 Apr. 2015, www.nationalgeographic.
com/news/2015/04/150408-everest-climbing-sherpas-mountain
eering-nepal-himalaya-guides.

Martin, Jeff. "Dave Hahn and Melissa Arnot Return from Record Everest Climb." *PRWeb*, 21 Aug. 2019, www.prweb.com/releases/2012/5
/prweb9560002.htm.

Morical, Mark. "A Grim Day on Everest." *Bend Bulletin*, 15 June 2014,
www.bendbulletin.com/localstate/a-grim-day-on-everest/article
_cc0e694f-1c3b-5c61-9f2c-86f93e46b7b5.html.

Chapter 19

Flatow, Ira. "Mount Everest Still Holds Mysteries for Scientists."
NPR Talk of the Nation, 16 Mar. 2012, www.npr.org/2012/03/16
/148753432/mount-everest-still-holds-mysteries-for-scientists.

Hahn, Dave, et al. Expedition Dispatches Everest Southside with Dave
Hahn. *RMI Expeditions Blog*, Mar.–May 2015, www.rmiguides.com
/blog/expedition/everest_3_21_2015/desc.

Hahn, Dave. "Visteurs and Whittaker Make Camp on the Western
Cwm." *RMI Expeditions Blog*, 18 Apr. 2009, www.rmiguides.com

/blog/2009/04/18/viesturs_and_whittaker_make_camp_on_the
_western_cwm.

Hull, Jennifer. Personal interview of Larry Seaton. Apr. 2016.

———. Personal interviews of Dave Hahn. 2018.

Simonson, Eric, et al. "Ghosts of Everest." *Outside Online*, 1 Oct. 1999,
www.outsideonline.com/1909046/ghosts-everest.

"The Way to the Summit." *NOVA Online*, Nov. 2000, www.pbs.org
/wgbh/nova/everest/climb/waytosummitsou.html.

Chapter 20

Hahn, Dave, et al. Expedition Dispatches Everest Southside with Dave
Hahn. *RMI Expeditions Blog*, Mar.–May 2015, www.rmiguides.com
/blog/expedition/everest_3_21_2015/desc.

Hahn, Dave. "Close Call with Avalanche at Camp I." *RMI Expeditions
Blog*, 15 Apr. 2009, www.rmiguides.com/blog/2009/04/15/close
_call_with_avalanche_at_camp_i.

———. "Dave Hahn Preps for Climb to Camp I." *RMI Expeditions
Blog*, 29 Apr. 2009, www.rmiguides.com/blog/2009/04/20/dave
_hahn_preps_for_climb_to_camp_i.

———. "RMI Teams Have Diverging Agendas." *RMI Expeditions
Blog*, 19 Apr. 2009, www.rmiguides.com/blog/2009/04/19/rmi
_teams_have_diverging_agendas.

———. "Visteurs and Whittaker Make Camp on the Western
Cwm." *RMI Expeditions Blog*, 18 Apr. 2009, www.rmiguides.com
/blog/2009/04/18/viesturs_and_whittaker_make_camp_on_the
_western_cwm.

Hull, Jennifer. Personal interview of Peter Rogers. July 2016.

———. Personal interview of Robbie Massie. Apr. 2016.

———. Personal interviews of Dave Hahn. 2018.

"The Way to the Summit." *NOVA Online*, Nov. 2000, www.pbs.org
/wgbh/nova/everest/climb/waytosummitsou.html.

Chapter 21

Arnette, Alan. "Mt. Everest Southeast Ridge." *The Blog on alanarnette. com*, May 2011, www.alanarnette.com/everest/everestsouthroutes.php.

Hahn, Dave, et al. Expedition Dispatches Everest Southside with Dave Hahn. *RMI Expeditions Blog*, Mar.–May 2015, www.rmiguides.com /blog/expedition/everest_3_21_2015/desc.

Hahn, Dave. "Dave Hahn's Team Reaches Camp 2." *RMI Expeditions Blog*, 24 Apr. 2009, www.rmiguides.com/blog/2009/04/24/dave _hahns_team_reaches_camp_2.

———. "Noisy, Windy Night at Camp 2." *RMI Expeditions Blog*, 26 Apr. 2009, www.rmiguides.com/blog/2009/04/26/noisy_windy _night_at_camp_2.

———. "RMI Teams Have Diverging Agendas." *RMI Expeditions Blog*, 19 Apr. 2009, www.rmiguides.com/blog/2009/04/19/rmi _teams_have_diverging_agendas.

———. "Team Hahn Test Themselves Past ABC." *RMI Expeditions Blog*, 25 Apr. 2009, www.rmiguides.com/blog/2009/04/25/team _hahn_test_themselves_past_abc.

Hull, Jennifer. Personal interview of Chhering Dorjee Sherpa. Apr. 2016.

———. Personal interview of Hemanshu Parwani. Aug. 2017.

———. Personal interview of JJ Justman. May 2016.

———. Personal interviews of Dave Hahn. 2018.

Pokhrel, Rajan. "Climbers in Camp Rotation See Trash 'Here and There' on Everest." *The Himalayan Times*, 21 Apr. 2017, thehimalay antimes.com/nepal/trash-is-everywhere-on-everest-say-climbers -in-camp-rotation.

Sherpa, Kancha. "Bend Climbing Guide Helped Rescue Effort on Everest When Sherpas Killed." *Oregon Live*, 15 June 2014, www .oregonlive.com/pacific-northwest-news/2014/06/bend_climbing _guide_helped_res.html.

Chapter 22

Barry, Ellen. "Earthquake Devastates Nepal, Killing More than 1,900."
New York Times, 26 Apr. 2015, www.nytimes.com/2015/04/26/world
/asia/nepal-earthquake-katmandu.html.

Bierling, Billi. "Chronicling High-Peak History with Elizabeth Hawley." *Outdoor Research*, 5 Aug. 2013, www.outdoorresearch.com
/blog/article/chronicling-high-peak-history-with-elizabeth-hawley.

Buckley, Chris, and Nida Najar. "A Scene of Destruction After Ice
Thunders Into Everest Base Camp." *New York Times*, 27 Apr. 2015,
www.nytimes.com/2015/04/28/world/asia/mount-everest-nepal
-earthquake.html.

Frankel, Todd, et al. "When Mount Everest Shook: A Minute of Horror, Hours of Panic." *Washington Post*, 2 May 2015, www.wash
ingtonpost.com/world/a-minute-of-horror-then-hours-of-panic
-on-the-path-to-mount-everest/2015/05/02/8088b96a-ef61-11e4
-8050-839e9234b303_story.html.

Hull, Jennifer, and Billi Bierling. Personal interview of Elizabeth Hawley. Mar. 2017.

Hull, Jennifer. Personal interview of Billi Bierling. Apr. 2017.

———. Personal interview of Larry Seaton. Apr. 2016.

———. Personal interviews of Dave Hahn. 2018.

Nestler, Stefan. "Miss Hawley: 'I'm Just a Chronicler.'" *DW*, 5 Apr.
2016, blogs.dw.com/adventuresports/miss-hawley-im-just-a
-chronicler.

Ozeki, Ruth. *A Tale for the Time Being: A Novel*. Penguin Books, 2013.

Schaffer, Grayson. "The Everest Earthquake." *Outside Online*, 25 Apr.
2015, www.outsideonline.com/1972636/everest-earthquake.

Yune, Howard. "Avalanche Aborts Napa Man's Everest Dream." *Napa
Valley Register*, 17 May 2015, napavalleyregister.com/news/local
/avalanche-aborts-napa-man-s-everest-dream/article_9b36cc9c
-17b4–510a-a9fb-00121f38b81a.html.

———. "Napa Climber Survives Avalanche at Mount Everest Base Camp." *Napa Valley Register*, 29 Apr. 2015, napavalleyregister.com /news/local/napa-climber-survives-avalanche-at-mount-everest -base-camp/article_cdff9d56-36e9-56d4-ae41-0eca33641cd1.html.

Chapter 23

Feagans, Brittany. "Plano Man Evacuated after Earthquake Avalanche." *Plano Star Courier*, 5 May 2015, starlocalmedia.com/planocourier /news/plano-man-evacuated-after-everest-avalanche/article_e189e a7c-f37b-11e4-8ec5-1f0aba5d9e40.html.

Hull, Jennifer. Personal interview of Nomita Parwani. Oct. 2017.

Montgomery, Kelly. "Quick Facts: What You Need to Know about the Nepal Earthquake." *Mercy Corps*, 14 Mar. 2016, www.mercycorps. org/articles/nepal/quick-facts-what-you-need-know-about-nepal -earthquake.

"Nepal Quake 700 Times the Power of Hiroshima Bomb Says Expert." *Euronews*, 5 May 2015, www.euronews.com/2015/05/05/nepal -quake-700-times-the-power-of-hiroshima-bomb-says-expert.

Schaffer, Grayson. "The Everest Earthquake." *Outside Online*, 25 Apr. 2015, www.outsideonline.com/1972636/everest-earthquake.

Sharma, Gopal, and Ross Adkin. "Nepal Seeks Help, Death Toll Seen Rising after Devastating Quake." *Reuters*, 25 Apr. 2015, www.reuters .com/article/us-quake-nepal-collapse/nepal-seeks-help-death-toll -seen-rising-after-devastating-quake-idUSKBN0NG07B20150425.

Simonson, Eric, et al. "IMG's 2015 Mt. Everest Expedition Coverage." International Mountain Guides, 2015, www.mountainguides.com /everest-south15.shtml.

Spector, Dina. "Climbers Are Tweeting about Being Trapped on Mount Everest after Earthquake-Triggered Avalanche Kills 18." *Business Insider*, 27 Apr. 2015, www.businessinsider.com.au /mount-everest-climbers-tweet-status-2015-4.

Chapter 24

Arnette, Alan. "Everest 2015: North Closed, South Res — A Full Recap." *The Blog on alanarnette.com*, 29 Apr. 2015, www.alanarnette.com /blog/2015/04/29/everest-2015-north-closed-south-res-a-full-recap.

Bradham, Sarah. "Avalanche on Everest." *Mazama Annual 2015*, June 2015, pp. 3–5. issuu.com/mazamas/docs/mazamaannual_2015 _color.

Borenstein, Seth. "Nepal Earthquake: Experts There a Week Ago to Plan for Earthquake." *U.S. News & World Report*, 25 Apr. 2015, www.usnews.com/news/world/articles/2015/04/25/experts -gathered-in-nepal-a-week-ago-to-ready-for-earthquake.

Cadwalladr, Carole. "Nepal Earthquake: British Doctor Saved 23 Lives after Everest Avalanche." *The Guardian*, 9 May 2015, www .theguardian.com/world/2015/may/09/nepal-earthquake-british -doctor-everest-avalanche-rachel-tullet.

Hahn, Dave, et al. Expedition Dispatches Everest Southside with Dave Hahn. *RMI Expeditions Blog*, Mar.–May 2015, www.rmiguides.com /blog/expedition/everest_3_21_2015/desc.

Hamill, Mike. "Read an Everest Guide's Diary of Chaos Amid Quake, Avalanche." *National Geographic*, 28 Apr. 2015, www.national geographic.com/news/2015/04/150428-everest-earthquake-base -camp-nepal-himalaya-climbing-sherpa.

Hull, Jennifer. Personal interview of Chhering Dorjee Sherpa. Apr. 2016.

———. Personal interview of Hao Wu. May 2017.

———. Personal interview of Hemanshu Parwani. Aug. 2017.

———. Personal interview of JJ Justman. May 2016.

———. Personal interview of Robbie Massie. Apr. 2016.

———. Personal interviews of Dave Hahn. 2018.

Loomis, Molly. "Inside the ER at Mt. Everest." *Smithsonian Magazine*,

31 May 2011, www.smithsonianmag.com/travel/inside-the-er-at-mt
-everest-180237745.

Montgomery, Kelly. "Quick Facts: What You Need to Know about the
Nepal Earthquake." *Mercy Corps*, 14 Mar. 2016, www.mercycorps
.org/articles/nepal/quick-facts-what-you-need-know-about-nepal
-earthquake.

Narula, Svati Kirsten. "I Survived the Deadliest Day in Everest's History, and I'm Still Surviving It." *Kent Online*, 25 Sept. 2015, www
.kentonline.co.uk/weald/news/kent-doctor-saves-25-lives-37041.

Schaffer, Grayson. "The Aftermath on Everest." *Outside Online*, 26 Apr.
2015, www.outsideonline.com/1972696/aftermath-everest.

———. "The Everest Earthquake." *Outside Online*, 25 Apr. 2015,
www.outsideonline.com/1972636/everest-earthquake.

Sherpa, Kancha. "Bend Climbing Guide Helped Rescue Effort
on Everest When Sherpas Killed." *Oregon Live*, 15 June 2014, www
.oregonlive.com/pacific-northwest-news/2014/06/bend_climbing
_guide_helped_res.html.

Tullet, Rachel, and Megan Walmsley. "Season End Summary." *Everest
ER*, 2015.

Wilkinson, Freddie. "Everest Base Camp a 'War Zone' After Earthquake Triggers Avalanches." *National Geographic*, 25 Apr. 2015,
www.nationalgeographic.com/news/2015/04/150425-everest-earth
quake-basecamp-nepal-himalaya-climbing-sherpa.

———. "Helicopters Rescue Climbers Trapped on Everest After
Quake." *National Geographic*, 27 Apr. 2015, www.national
geographic.com/news/2015/04/150427-everest-earthquake-base
-camp-nepal-himalaya-climbing-sherpa.

Young, Anna. "Kent Doctor Rachel Tullet, from Cranbrook, Saved
Lives after Nepal Earthquake Triggered Everest Avalanche." *Kent
Online*, 16 May 2015, www.kentonline.co.uk/weald/news/kent
-doctor-saves-25-lives-37041.

Chapter 25

Akelson, Michael. "Life in the Mountains: Former UB Swimmer Dave Hahn Discusses Legendary Mountain Guiding Career." *The Spectrum*, 4 May 2017, www.ubspectrum.com/article/2017/05/life-in-the-mountains.

Arnette, Alan. "Everest 2013: Can I Be Rescued on Everest?" *The Blog on alanarnette.com*, 15 May 2013, www.alanarnette.com/blog/2013/03/15/everest-2013-can-i-be-rescued-on-everest.

Browdie, Brian. "Why Helicopters Haven't Evacuated Everyone from Mount Everest Yet." *Quartz*, 26 Apr. 2015, qz.com/391598/why-helicopters-havent-evacuated-everyone-from-mount-everest-yet.

Callaghan, Anna, and Grayson Schaffer. "The Impact Beyond Everest." *Outside Online*, 27 Apr. 2015, www.outsideonline.com/1973381/impact-beyond-everest.

Hahn, Dave, et al. Expedition Dispatches Everest Southside with Dave Hahn. *RMI Expeditions Blog*, Mar.–May 2015, www.rmiguides.com/blog/expedition/everest_3_21_2015/desc.

Hahn, Dave. "Chopper Gumbo and the Midlife Crisis." *MountainZone.com*, Sept. 2002, www.mountainzone.com/2002/story/hahn/html/hahn_090302.html.

Hull, Jennifer. "Personal interview of Chhering Dorjee Sherpa. Apr. 2016.

———. Personal interview of JJ Justman. May 2016.

———. Personal interview of Robbie Massie." Apr. 2016.

———. Personal interviews of Dave Hahn. 2018.

"Indian Army Pulls Out 22 Bodies after Everest Avalanche." *India Today*, 28 Apr. 2015, www.indiatoday.in/nepal-earthquake-2015/story/everest-base-camp-nepal-earthquake-avalanche-indian-army-250332-2015-04-26.

Mussen, Deirdre. "Queenstown Pilot Jason Laing Rescues Trapped

Climbers from Mt Everest." *Stuff*, 29 Apr. 2015, www.stuff.co.nz
/world/asia/68105618.

Parker, Laura. "Will Everest's Climbing Cirucs Slow Down After
Disasters?" *National Geographic*, 13 May 2015, www.national
geographic.com/news/2015/05/150513-everest-climbing-nepal
-earthquake-avalanche-sherpas.

Paur, Jason. "Worry Birds." *Outside Online*, 4 Jan. 2003, www.outside
online.com/1821426/worry-birds.

Pursell, Robert. "The Craziest Mountain Rescue Stories." *Men's Journal*, June 2015, www.mensjournal.com/adventure/craziest
-mountain-rescue-stories#zw9oHYtVIsb67qKT.97.

Sherpa, Kancha. "Bend Climbing Guide Helped Rescue Effort on
Everest When Sherpas Killed." *Oregon Live*, 15 June 2014, www
.oregonlive.com/pacific-northwest-news/2014/06/bend_climbing
_guide_helped_res.html.

Simonson, Eric, et al. "IMG's 2015 Mt. Everest Expedition Coverage."
International Mountain Guides, 2015, www.mountainguides.com
/everest-south15.shtml.

Tullet, Rachel, and Megan Walmsley. "Season End Summary." *Everest
ER*, 2015.

Wilkinson, Freddie. "Helicopters Rescue Climbers Trapped on Everest
After Quake." *National Geographic*, 27 Apr. 2015, www.national
geographic.com/news/2015/04/150427-everest-earthquake-base
-camp-nepal-himalaya-climbing-sherpa.

———. "Survivors and Dead Evacuated from Everest Base Camp."
National Geographic, 26 Apr. 2015, www.nationalgeographic.com
/news/2015/04/150426-everest-earthquake-basecamp-nepal-hima
laya-climbing-sherpas.

Zurowski, Cory. "Robbie Massie Was Determined to Climb Everest,
but the Mountain Said No." *City Pages*, 28 Oct. 2015, www.citypages
.com/news/robbie-massie-was-determined-to-climb-everest-but
-the-mountain-said-no-7785297.

Chapter 26

Aisch, Gregor, et al. "Maps of the Damage from the Nepal Earthquakes." *New York Times*, 4 Apr. 2015, www.nytimes.com/interactive/2015/04/25/world/asia/nepal-earthquake-maps.html.

Hahn, Dave, et al. Expedition Dispatches Everest Southside with Dave Hahn. *RMI Expeditions Blog*, Mar.–May 2015, www.rmiguides.com/blog/expedition/everest_3_21_2015/desc.

Hull, Jennifer. Personal interview of Chhering Dorjee Sherpa. Apr. 2016.

———. Personal interview of Hao Wu. May 2017.

———. Personal interview of Hemanshu Parwani. Aug. 2017.

———. Personal interview of JJ Justman. May 2016.

———. Personal interview of Larry Seaton. Apr. 2016.

———. Personal interview of Peter Rogers. July 2016.

———. Personal interview of Robbie Massie. Apr. 2016.

———. Personal interviews of Dave Hahn. 2018.

Kleinekoenen, Von Ulrike. "Okrifteler Erlebte Das Beben Von Nepal Am Mount Everest." *Frankfurter Neue Presse*, 8 May 2015, www.fnp.de/lokales/main-taunus/okrifteler-erlebte-beben-nepal-mount-everest-10719010.html.

Sherpa, Kancha. "Bend Climbing Guide Helped Rescue Effort on Everest When Sherpas Killed." *Oregon Live*, 15 June 2014, www.oregonlive.com/pacific-northwest-news/2014/06/bend_climbing_guide_helped_res.html.

Simonson, Eric, et al. "IMG's 2015 Mt. Everest Expedition Coverage." International Mountain Guides, 2015, www.mountainguides.com/everest-south15.shtml.

Spencer, Richard, and Will Wintercross. "Hilary and Tenzing's Sons Describe Surviving the Everest Avalanche." *The Telegraph*, 1 May 2015, www.telegraph.co.uk/news/worldnews/asia/nepal/11574840/Hillary-and-Tenzings-sons-describe-surviving-the-Everest-avalanche.html.

Wilkinson, Freddie. "Everest Base Camp a 'War Zone' After Earthquake Triggers Avalanches." *National Geographic*, 25 Apr. 2015,
www.nationalgeographic.com/news/2015/04/150425-everest-earth
quake-basecamp-nepal-himalaya-climbing-sherpa.

Yune, Howard. "Avalanche Aborts Napa Man's Everest Dream." *Napa
Valley Register*, 17 May 2015, napavalleyregister.com/news/local
/avalanche-aborts-napa-man-s-everest-dream/article_9b36cc9c
-17b4-510a-a9fb-00121f38b81a.html.

———. "Napa Climber Survives Avalanche at Mount Everest Base
Camp." *Napa Valley Register*, 29 Apr. 2015, napavalleyregister.com
/news/local/napa-climber-survives-avalanche-at-mount-everest
-base-camp/article_cdff9d56-36e9-56d4-ae41-0eca33641cd1.html.

Zurowski, Cory. "Robbie Massie Was Determined to Climb Everest,
but the Mountain Said No." *City Pages*, 28 Oct. 2015, www.citypages.
com/news/robbie-massie-was-determined-to-climb-everest-but
-the-mountain-said-no-7785297.

Chapter 27

Akelson, Michael. "Life in the Mountains: Former UB Swimmer
Dave Hahn Discusses Legendary Mountain Guiding Career." *The
Spectrum*, 4 May 2017, www.ubspectrum.com/article/2017/05/life
-in-the-mountains.

Arnette, Alan, and Dave Hahn. "The State of Everest: A Conversation
with Dave Hahn." *The Blog on alanarnette.com*, 14 Nov. 2016, www
.alanarnette.com/blog/2016/11/14/the-state-of-everest-a-convers
ation-with-dave-hahn.

Hahn, Dave, et al. Expedition Dispatches Everest Southside with Dave
Hahn. *RMI Expeditions Blog*, Mar.–May 2015, www.rmiguides.com
/blog/expedition/everest_3_21_2015/desc.

Hahn, Dave. "Bombs Before Breakfast." *MountainZone.com*, 1999,
www.mountainzone.com/climbing/2000/hahn/column2.

Hull, Jennifer. Personal interviews of Dave Hahn. 2018.

Krakauer, Jon. *Into Thin Air*. Anchor Books, 1997.

Rudell, Rebecca, and Dave Hahn. "The Day the Mountain Shook." *At Buffalo*, 2018, www.buffalo.edu/atbuffalo/article-page-fall-2015.host .html/content/shared/www/atbuffalo/articles/Fall-2015/features /day-the-mountain-shook.detail.html.

Afterword

Arnette, Alan. "Everest by the Numbers: 2019 Edition." *The Blog on alanarnette.com*, 2019, http://www.alanarnette.com/blog/2017/12/17 /everest-by-the-numbers-2018-edition.

Bhandari, Rayneesh, and Kai Schultz. "Elizabeth Hawley, Who Chronicled Everest Treks, Dies at 94." *New York Times*, 26 Jan. 2018, www.nytimes.com/2018/01/26/obituaries/elizabeth-hawley -who-chronicled-everest-treks-dies-at-94.html.

Bruscan, Angelo. "Styner to Retire as Police Chief This Month." *The North Coast News*, 1 Mar. 2017, www.northcoastnews.com/news /styner-to-retire-as-police-chief-this-month.

"Elizabeth Hawley: 'Chronicler of the Himalayas' Dies at 94." *BBC*, 26 Jan. 2018, www.bbc.com/news/world-asia-42830955.

Hahn, Dave. "Remembering Lama Geshe, Blesser of Everest Climbers." *Outside Online*, 22 Feb. 2018, www.outsideonline. com/2282326/lama-geshe.

Hull, Jennifer. Personal Interview of Billi Bierling. Apr. 2017.

———. Personal interview of Chhering Dorjee Sherpa. Apr. 2016.

———. Personal interview of Hemanshu Parwani. Aug. 2017.

———. Personal interviews of Dave Hahn. 2018.

Sherpa, Thukten. "Albidha ! Albidha !! Albidah !!!. Ms. Elizabeth Hawley." *YouTube*, uploaded by thukten sherpa, 31 Jan. 2018, www.youtube.com/watch?v=XctQEyDPbck.